ROUGH-WATER MAN

ELWYN

BLAKE'S

COLORADO

RIVER

EXPEDI-

TIONS

Richard E.

Westwood

foreword by

Bruce Babbitt

University
of Nevada
Press *Reno,*
Las Vegas,
London

ROUGH-WATER MAN

The paper used in this book meets the minimum
requirements of American National Standard for
Information Sciences—Permanence of Paper for
Printed Library Materials, ANSI Z39.48-1984. Binding
materials were chosen for strength and durability.

Library of Congress Cataloging-in-Publication Data
Westwood, Dick, 1921–
Rough-water man : Elwyn Blake's Colorado River
expeditions / Richard E. Westwood ; with foreword by
Bruce Babbitt.
p. cm.
Includes bibliographical references and index.
ISBN 0-87417-188-1 (cloth : acid-free paper)
1. Colorado River Watershed (Colo.-Mexico)—Description and travel. 2. Blake, Henry Elwyn, d. 1980.
3. River engineering-Colorado River Watershed
(Colo.-Mexico)—History. 4. Colorado River Watershed (Colo.-Mexico)—Surveys. 5. Boatmen—Colorado River Watershed (Colo.-Mexico)—Biography.
6. United States—Exploring expeditions. 7. Canyons-
Colorado River Watershed (Colo.-Mexico) I. Title.
F788.W47   1992
917.91'30452—dc20   92-1233
                                                       CIP

D
917.91'30924
WES

University of Nevada Press, Reno, Nevada 89557 USA
Copyright © 1992 University of Nevada Press
Designed by Mary Mendell
Printed in the United States of America
9 8 7 6 5 4 3 2 1

Contents

Maps

Foreword

As recently as 1922 the Colorado River ran free and wild from the peaks of the Wind River Range in Wyoming and the heights of the Colorado Rockies all the way to the salt water in the Sea of Cortés. In that year the river received a death sentence in the form of the Colorado River Compact signed by the seven basin states and the United States.

Having divided the waters on paper, the political leaders sent the writ of execution to the Bureau of Reclamation, commanding it to kill the river with a series of dams, lakes, levies, channels, and canals. Before construction could begin, however, the surveyors and hydrologists had to locate the best dam sites. Remarkably, even as late as the 1920s there was little accurate survey data for the still inaccessible canyons of the Colorado and its tributaries.

This book is about Henry Elwyn Blake, an adventuresome young westerner who found his way, quite by chance, into the three expeditions organized by the United States Geological Survey to fill in those blank spots on the topographic maps and to locate the places where hard rock and narrow canyons would support large dams. These surveys, which have gone largely unnoticed in the literature of the river, were something of a historical divide, separating a wilderness past from a new and complex development future.

Along the San Juan and the Colorado, Blake saw and noted much evidence of past failures by individual settlers to come to terms with the land and to make it productive. Occasionally the river parties would encounter a homesteader still struggling to produce a green patch in the wilderness, but what they usually discovered were ruined cabins, and abandoned homesteads, and rusting debris from abandoned gold diggings. The land still belonged to Navajos and Paiutes. Bert Loper, the legendary miner and boatman, led the boat crews by day on the San Juan and entertained them by night with accounts of the prospectors and beaver trappers of an earlier time.

If Blake was drawn to the enchantment of the canyons and their past, he still had hard and dangerous work to perform to help bring a new future to the river, a future of flood control, hydroelectric power, and reclamation that would guarantee success for the next generation of homesteaders and farmers in the West. Accurate topographic maps required running a continuous line down the river from one point to the next, charting direction and changes in elevation. If the line was broken the data became useless. In a time without aerial photographs and modern instruments, the mapmaker had to set up his plane table and shoot a line to the rodman at a point on the bank downriver; the mapmaker would then pack up and move down to a point below the rodman and shoot a line back up to the stadia rod; finally, he would wait for the rodman to move downstream, and they would repeat the process over and over as the party moved downriver.

At night in camp the party feasted off the bounty of the land — mountain sheep, deer, and geese, supplemented with trout and chubb, now an endangered species, which swarmed thick through the rivers. On more than one occasion in Cataract Canyon the boatmen lit up the night by setting fire to the vast flows of driftwood in the river.

The third and last expedition led by Colonel Claude Birdseye, chief topographer of the United States Geological Survey, set off from Lees Ferry in 1923 and marked something of a departure from the more informal expeditions on the San Juan and in Cataract Canyon. The Colorado River Compact had just been signed and Congress would soon be debating the authorization of a high dam. The engineers, scientists, and politicians were still debating whether the dam should be in the upper basin at Glen Canyon or in one of the gorges below the Grand Canyon.

The Birdseye Expedition did not lack interesting participants. In addition to Birdseye, the Geological Survey sent Clyde La Rue, its chief hydrologist. Lewis Freeman, a flamboyant journalist and river adventurer, was invited to help with publicity. At the last minute the Geological Survey decided against inviting Bert Loper as head boatman and instead chose Emery Kolb. The Southern California

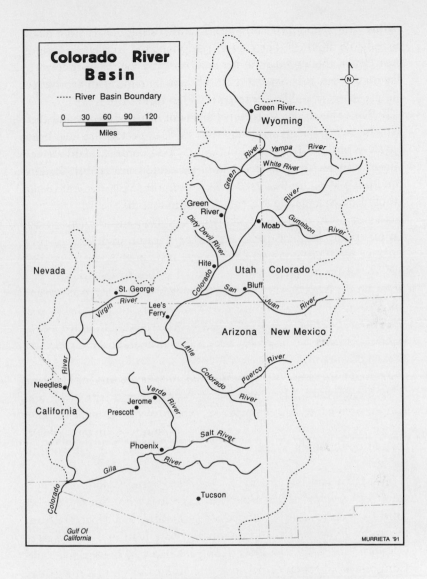

Colorado River Basin

----- River Basin Boundary

0 30 60 90 120
Miles

Green River
Wyoming

Yampa River
White River
Green River
River
Green River
Moab
Gunnison River
Dirty Devil River
Nevada
Hite
Utah Colorado
Colorado
Bluff
San
St. George
Juan River
Virgin River
Lee's Ferry
Arizona New Mexico
Little
Colorado
Puerco River
River
Needles
River
Verde River
Jerome
California
Prescott
Salt River
Phoenix
Gila
River
Colorado
Tucson
Gulf Of California
MURRIETA '91

Edison Company and the Utah Power and Light Company were in the background, actively helping with preparations.

With so many strong personalities and divergent interests the Birdseye party had more than its share of quarrels. At Hermit Creek Emery Kolb quit the expedition in a fit of anger over intrusions by other photographers, including those from the Fred Harvey Company, which had sent photographers down the Hermit Trail to film the passage through the rapids. Before the day was over, however, Kolb was back in the expedition, thanks largely to emotional pleas by his wife, Blanche, and his daughter Edith. The Birdseye men finally patched up their differences, left the spectators, and headed downriver; the rest is reclamation history.

Ironically and happily, after decades of contention and some very close calls at Marble Canyon and Bridge Canyon, not a single dam has ever been built on the river stretch traversed by the Birdseye expedition. Grand Canyon National Park is still a testimonial to the limits of the dam-building impulse. And I suspect that Henry Elwyn Blake, a river man at heart, would be proud to know that this last expedition yielded nothing more than additional scientific knowledge about one of the great wild places of the West.

BRUCE BABBITT

Acknowledgments

This book could not have been written without the generous help of many people. My cousin Alice Blake Burrell got me started in the summer of 1986 when she brought me a box of diaries, an autobiography, and other papers of my uncle, Elwyn Blake. Thanks go to her and other family members, Charlotte Blake Schafer, Prescott Blake, Stanley Blake, Virginia Blake Schafer, Kathryn Blake Edwards, and Martin Blake for permission to use these papers. Many scholars and experts gave me invaluable assistance. William Mullane, special collections librarian at Northern Arizona University, guided me through the Emery Kolb Collection and pointed the way to other research facilities. Floyd A. O'Neil, director of the American West Center at the University of Utah, and Gregory C. Thompson, assistant director for Special Collections, Marriott Library, University of Utah, read the manuscript and gave me every encouragement and much valuable advice. Dr. Gary Topping, curator of manuscripts, Utah State Historical Society, made available the microfilms of the River Bed Case, *The United States v. Utah*, in which most of the old river runners testified, and gave me copies of papers from his personal files. Debbie Rowan, field records librarian at the Denver Federal Center Geological Survey Archives, and her fine staff helped with archival maps, photographs, and field records. William P. Frank, assistant curator of western manuscripts at The Huntington Library, guided me through the Marston Collection, a gold mine of Colorado River history.

Special thanks go to Dr. William Phillips, professor of history, Arizona State University, who not only read and commented on the manuscript line by line, but included me in a party he organized for his fourth float trip through Grand Canyon. Others who read the manuscript and gave me valuable input in their areas of expertise were: geologist Wayne D. Ranney, archaeologist Don Keller, history professor Dr. William Lyon of Northern Arizona University, Roy Webb of the University of Utah Marriott Library—an author in his own right—and Dr. Melvin N. Westwood of Oregon State University. Lee Farquhar, formerly of the University of Colorado, edited various versions of the manuscript. My wife Jean, without whose help this book would never have been written, went over every version, found grammatical errors, other boo-boos, and gave invaluable criticism and input. My daughter, Beth Davies, helped with the research in Utah. Bill Gookin, past director of the Arizona State Water Department, generously dug his plane table and alidade out of storage to show me how they worked. Cartographers Joel H. Ahles and Penny Murietta did a great job of producing the maps for this book. George (Red) Gates assisted by recopying photos at the U.S. Geological Archives in Denver.

I am especially grateful to the river guides who made my trips so enjoyable and meaningful. Don Keller led our party down the San Juan. His excellent crew included Wayne Ranney, Leslie Hutchinson, Ann Walka, Nancy Erger, and Dan Dagget. Curt (Whale) Hansen and Don Sullivan got our party as far into Grand Canyon as a rock in the middle of Hance Rapid. From there we split up and five of us were the guests of some amiable Texans on the raft of Ray Pope and his helper David Kashinski. On the Green River through Ladore, Whirlpool, and Split Mountain, Kerry M. Jones led us with the able assistance of boatmen Peter Schmidt and Steve Boccagno. Through Desolation and Gray canyons Peter Schmidt was in charge, and boatmen were Robert (Flash) Cheney and Jake Tratiak.

I owe a special debt of thanks to the two anonymous critical readers for the University of Nevada Press for their valued criticism of fact and form on the first version of the manuscript sent to them. Their comments led me to further research and other needed revisions. I have tried to make all the corrections suggested by these knowledgeable people, but any mistakes are mine alone. And last but not least I want to thank the friendly editorial staff at the University of Nevada Press for their help, especially in-house editor Cynthia Wood and out-of-house editor Peggy Lee for their excellent and persistent editing.

Prologue

This is a true story about the men of the U.S. Geological Survey who in 1921–1923 mapped the last deep canyons of the Colorado River system and surveyed possible dam sites. They charted the gorges of the main stem of the Colorado River and its two principal tributaries, San Juan River in southeastern Utah and the Green River below Green River, Wyoming.

Their journeys differed from other Colorado River trips before and after because the team had to land every few hundred yards for an instrument reading while keeping their last survey point in sight. It did not matter that vertical cliffs or rapids sometimes made this almost impossible. The work was carried on in spite of whatever dangers lay ahead.

This is also the story of Henry Elwyn Blake, Jr., the only man to take part in the mapping of all three rivers. In doing so he developed from a novice boatman into an expert rapids runner, acquiring a life-long love of the river. Elwyn may not have realized it at the time, but these expeditions were instrumental in the development of the West as we know it today. The resulting dams also ruined forever some of the country's pristine river canyons.

The Colorado Plateau is knifed by the Colorado River and its two main tributaries, the Green and San Juan rivers. The river's drainage basin covers 242,000 square miles and was the last part of the West to be explored.

By the early part of this century the Bureau of Reclamation had big plans for the Colorado River. Proposals for irrigation projects, flood control, water storage, and power production created a need for accurate surveys of the entire Colorado River system. In 1909, the U.S. Geological Survey began making such surveys. In 1921 it set out to complete the job by surveying the deep, unsurveyed canyons, thereby hooking together previously mapped sections.

The Bureau of Reclamation could not go ahead with any major projects until the geology of the canyons was recorded, the surveys completed, and the best dam sites located and mapped. Only boatmen could take the geologists and engineers where they needed to go and much of the work could only be done by boat.

Elwyn Blake did not know much about the Colorado River Basin when the expeditions began. He knew a lot more about it when the survey trips were over—the section of the Green between the Wyoming-Utah border and Green River, Utah; the San Juan Canyon below Bluff, Utah; and the long section of the Colorado from its confluence with the San Juan to Needles, California.

Before 1869 much of the Colorado Plateau was marked "unknown" on government maps. Major John Wesley Powell, a one-armed Civil War veteran, began to change this with his famous exploration of the Colorado River that year. Contrary to popular belief, Powell did not survey the river, but he did make maps, explore, and make geologic and other observations.[1]

Other parties, mostly trappers, miners, or adventurers, later traveled the rivers. Only a few of them made it all the way through Grand Canyon. Robert Brewster Stanton and party did so in 1890.[2] Next trapper George Flavell ran the canyon in 1896 with Ramón Montéz, a Mexican from near Los Angeles. Nathaniel (Than) Galloway, another trapper, followed closely behind Flavell in the fall of 1896. Prospector Elias (Hum) Woolley and two companions went through in 1903. In 1907 Charles Silver Russell and Edwin R. Monett ran it on a prospecting trip. In 1909 Julius Stone accompanied Than Galloway, the first man to go through twice.[3] Finally, in 1911–1912, brothers Ellsworth (Ed) and Emery Kolb made the first motion pictures inside the canyons while on a trip from Green River, Wyoming, to Needles, California.[4] Before 1923, when the U.S. Geological Survey party surveyed the Grand Canyon portion of the Colorado, only twenty-seven men had boated completely through it.

Major Powell is remembered best as the daring explorer who led the first boating expedition through the Grand Canyon. Of far greater importance were his later surveys of the West and his far-sighted proposals for sensible use of water in the arid regions.[5]

The Mormons are sometimes given credit for initiating irrigation in the West. They were in fact the first whites to divert water from the streams on a large scale, learning this technique from Mexicans in New Mexico and Indians in Arizona. Powell was impressed with the Mormon system of irrigation, and in 1870 he obtained $10,000 from Congress for a study of it and a geographical and geological survey of the Colorado Plateau.[6]

The government was encouraging settlement of the West, and in 1862 Congress passed the Homestead Act. Under its provisions, any person over the age of twenty-one could claim 160 acres of federal land by paying a filing fee. After living on the land and working it for five years, the settler would own it. Powell saw that in most parts of the West there was not enough rainfall to raise crops except by irrigation. In the first twenty years of the program only thirty-five percent of those in the West survived long enough to gain ownership due largely to the scarcity of water.[7]

Powell believed that water use should be restricted to actual settlers on family-sized farms. He correctly prophesied that "all waters of the arid lands will eventually be taken from their natural channels, and they can be utilized only to the extent to which they are thus removed, and water rights must of necessity be severed from the natural channels."[8]

Powell eventually concluded that only the federal government could handle the large mainstream projects. He believed that in order to make the best use of public lands in the arid region, detailed geologic studies should be made of the river canyons. He also thought the lands should be classified before any large-scale projects were begun. Others thought differently. Promoters, land grabbers, and politicians pressed for the immediate commencement of their pet projects to harness the rivers, while Major Powell continued to fight for fair and orderly development of the western waterways.

Powell's work contributed in a large way to passage of the Newlands (Reclamation) Act in 1902. This law created the Reclamation Service (later changed to Bureau) under the Department of the Interior. It came just before Major Powell's death and was a fitting tribute to his lifelong efforts to bring order to western development.

The law called for the government to build a series of dams in seventeen western states to provide irrigation for arable desert lands. The irrigation projects were to be paid for with funds acquired from the sale of public lands in these seventeen states and from the sale of water. In later years this was amended to include the sale of power generated at the dams. The law was of special significance to people in the Colorado River Basin states of California, Arizona, Utah, New Mexico, Nevada, and Wyoming. Irrigation in these states was a necessity for agricultural development, upon which people in that area then believed their future depended.[9]

In 1896 the California Development Company had been formed to take water from the Colorado and divert it by canal to the Imperial Valley, where it supplied irrigation water to settlers. By 1902 14,000 people had 120,000 acres under cultivation.

In 1905 the Colorado flooded over its banks at the headgate—which was located at an old overflow channel called the Alamo River—leaving its existing channel. It made new channels, flooded farms in the Imperial Valley, and began filling the Salton Sink in Southern California, eventually creating the Salton Sea. The flooding bankrupted the California Development Company. Southern Pacific Railroad bought the defunct company at a receiver's auction and, after several failed attempts, succeeded in sealing off the river from the valley. Later the railroad sold its water interests to the Imperial Irrigation District for three million dollars. Many people regarded the river as a "natural menace" rather than a natural resource. Demands began mounting for flood-control dams on the Colorado, and this concern was added to the need for dams to provide irrigation water.

In 1910 the Colorado left its bed at the old Bee River channel and began filling Volcano Lake. If the lake overflowed, the Imperial Valley would again be threatened. Congress appropriated a million dollars to try to stem the flow. When floods washed out the government dam, Imperial farmers built a dike at Volcano Lake, forcing the waters back toward the gulf.

In 1915 the river was so low that *all* its water was diverted into the Imperial Canal. In 1916 a winter flood broke over the levees and four feet of muddy, putrid water swirled down the main street of Yuma, Arizona, wreaking havoc and "melting" adobe buildings. People felt that something had to be done.

The first reclamation projects were scattered among the western states, but because of California's greater political muscle, the Reclamation Service concentrated its efforts on the development of the Colorado and the problems of the Imperial Valley.

The possibilities for power production brought the utility companies into the search for river dam sites. At the turn of the century only five percent of the industrial machinery in the country was run by electricity, but by 1914 thirty percent was run by electricity and

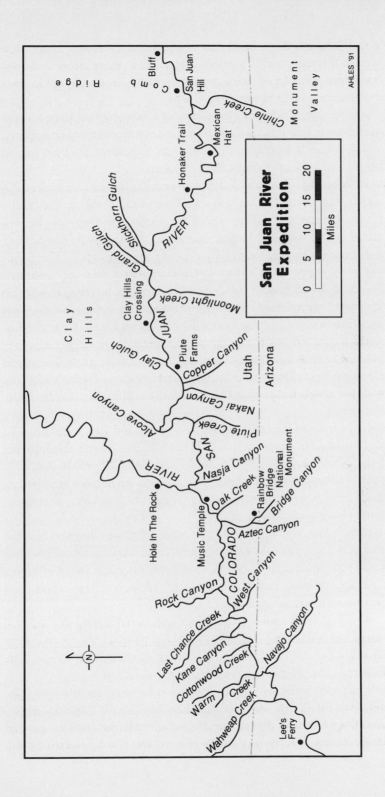

San Juan River Expedition

Miles

0 5 10 15 20

AHLES '91

Comb Ridge

Bluff

Comb Ridge

San Juan Hill

Mexican Creek

Chinle Creek

Monument Valley

Honaker Trail

Mexican Hat

RIVER

Slickhorn Gulch

Grand Gulch

Clay Hills Crossing

JUAN

Moonlight Creek

Clay Hills

Clay Gulch

Piute Farms

Copper Canyon

Nakai Canyon

Utah

Arizona

Alcove Canyon

Piute Creek

SAN

RIVER

Nasja Canyon

Hole In The Rock

Music Temple

Oak Creek

Rainbow Bridge National Monument

Bridge Canyon

COLORADO

Aztec Canyon

West Canyon

Rock Canyon

Last Chance Creek

Kane Canyon

Cottonwood Creek

Warm Creek

Wahweap Creek

Navajo Canyon

Lee's Ferry

N

xix

Prologue

by 1929 seventy percent.[10] The Colorado River was one of the last big, undeveloped power and water sources in the West.

In 1916 E. C. La Rue published his *Water Supply Paper No. 395: Colorado River and Its Utilization*. He reported all the existing and proposed irrigation projects using Colorado River water.[11] The upper basin states became alarmed, fearing some of their share might be lost to California through the "prior use" concept of water law that meant the first user had first right to use of the water.[12]

Controversies arose because the laws pertaining to water rights differed in most states and "would be a patchwork of improvisations, compromises, state law and federal law, interstate agreements and agreements between states and the federal government, riparian rights, appropriation rights, preferential uses, [and] the Wyoming doctrine of tying water rights to land titles."[13]

Southern California was hungry for water and electricity to support its growing population, but it needed the support of the other basin states to obtain federal financing for large Colorado River dam construction. The other states fought development until their own water rights, which they needed for future expansion, were settled. It became clear that the states would have to agree upon a compact before full development of the river could take place.

In 1921 President Warren Harding named Secretary of Commerce Herbert Hoover to head a Colorado River Commission to try to forge an agreement. In 1922 members of the commission signed the Colorado River Compact at Santa Fe, New Mexico, dividing the river into two basins. The dividing line was near the mouth of the Paria River at Lee's Ferry, Arizona, a short way south of the Utah-Arizona boundary. Each basin would receive 7.5 million acre-feet of water. An acre-foot is equivalent to an acre of water one foot deep or 325,851 gallons. The compact guaranteed the upper basin states of Utah, Wyoming, Colorado, and New Mexico full use of their half of the Colorado River water. California would still have to deal with Nevada and Arizona before going ahead with its plans for the lower basin.[14]

By the spring of 1921 government or private agencies had mapped all the stretches of the Colorado River system accessible by land. The Reclamation Service and some power companies had located and surveyed some tentative dam sites. The proposed dams would be used for water storage, irrigation, flood control, and generation of electric power. No major dams had been built because of political wrangling over water rights. A master plan was needed for the orderly development of power and irrigation resources along the river system. Each earlier canyon voyage and survey had added something to the general fund of information. Still, accurate survey data upon which to base a master plan was not complete.

In 1921 Southern California Edison Company and Utah Power and Light Company began to aid the government by financing some of the topographic surveys and supplying a few crew members.

The last major survey work in the Colorado River Basin, the subject of this book, took the surveyors into deep wilderness river gorges and side canyons accessible only by boat. Besides running all sorts of dangerous rapids, the crew had to scramble over boulder-strewn tali and scale high cliffs. They had to land their boats in the most difficult places to take instrument readings.

This is the story of the men who did the work and surveyed San Juan Canyon and Cataract Canyon in 1921, the upper Green in 1922, and the Grand Canyon in 1923. It is also the personal story of how young Elwyn Blake, the author's uncle, became enamored with the river, returning to it whenever he could for the rest of his life.

Elwyn kept diaries of his river trips. His journals of the San Juan and Green trips were lost in a fire, but he reconstructed them in "As I Remember," his unpublished autobiography. His Grand Canyon diaries were in Washington being copied and escaped the fire. The author has also used the diaries and field notes of other party members and many other sources of Colorado River history to supplement Elwyn's records. Together they make a fascinating story.

At the time of these surveys the purposes they would serve — the building of dams for irrigation, flood control and power production — were viewed as great benefits to the West and the entire country. Other aspects, including environmental concerns, came much later.

PART ONE
SAN JUAN RIVER EXPEDITION

CHAPTER 1

Preparation and Start

On a sunny July day in 1921 H. Elwyn Blake, Jr., twenty-four, left the back room of the *San Juan Record*, the weekly newspaper at Monticello, Utah, where he worked as a part-time printer. A cool breeze off the Abajo Mountains to the west ruffled his sandy brown hair as he walked toward the drugstore on Main Street. He was sucking the side of his hand to ease a fresh burn from the infernal linotype machine. At the drugstore he took a seat at the counter and was sipping a root beer when some dusty men walked in and sat down at a side table.

Turning to look at them, he saw a big fellow in faded bib overalls who seemed familiar, someone he had worked with before the war. Five years had passed, though, so he was not quite sure. The group sat down and ordered ice cream, then one of them cranked up the phonograph and put on a record. As music filled the room, the man in the overalls laid down his spoon and listened quietly. Then Elwyn was sure. The only person he had ever known who would stop eating to listen to good music was Bert Loper.

Elwyn grinned as he walked over and said, "Bert, how are you?"

The man looked up, thrust out his hand and exclaimed, "You old desert rat. I thought I should know you. Come sit down." [1]

Bert Loper was almost fifty-two years old, a miner by trade. He had spent much of his life in rough country and as a result was strong in body and somewhat crusty in temperament. In the 1890s he had tried placer mining on the San Juan River and had his first boating experience there. [2]

Elwyn had met Loper while working for a placer outfit at North Wash in the Henry Mountains in south-central Utah. It had been

Elwyn's first job after graduating from high school at Green River, Utah. He had been assigned to work on a ditch being blasted to the placer site. Bert Loper was the powderman-foreman of the ditch project. He suffered headaches when handling dynamite, so he sat in the shade while directing Elwyn on how to do it. Loper was the same age as Elwyn's father. Both were born in 1869, the year that Major John Wesley Powell first explored the Grand Canyon. Still, Loper and Elwyn had taken to each other from the start. Loper liked Elwyn because he was a good worker and because he would stand up to him in an argument. Elwyn enjoyed Loper's tales of the mining camps. Later they worked together as part of a survey crew on the San Rafael Desert and again in the Robbers Roost area. Elwyn even camped at Lost Spring for a while with Loper and his wife Rachel.

That was all before Elwyn went to Europe to fight in World War I. Now he was back home in Monticello but not satisfied with his humdrum life. In the drugstore, as the two friends talked of old times, Loper suddenly asked, "Do you want a job?"

"If it's outdoors I sure do," Elwyn replied. "I'm fed up with inside work."

"It's outside, all right," Loper said. He explained that he and his companions were heading for the San Juan River at Bluff, Utah, to survey that river's canyons down to the Colorado. He said, "A couple of applications are in ahead of yours, but the boss will listen to me. Your survey work on the desert would help."

Loper introduced Elwyn to Kelly Trimble, topographical engineer for the United States Geological Survey, who was in charge of the crew that would map and explore the San Juan River Canyon. With him was Robert Allen from Los Angeles, California, the survey recorder.

Kelly Trimble had hired Bert Loper as head boatman for the expedition because of his boating experience and knowledge of the San Juan River. Loper was serving as rodman on the first leg of the work. He was to pick up an elevation at Moab and run the line to a point on the San Juan River several miles below the town of Bluff, Utah.[3] Trimble, Allen, and Loper had stopped in Monticello.[4]

Elwyn landed the job as rodman. A few days later, on July 17, 1921, he began the trip perched on the back of a truck headed south toward Bluff.[5] The truck carried two boats, equipment, supplies, and crew members of the expedition. Elwyn spent the time visiting with Loper and getting acquainted with the others. He would not sleep under a roof for the next five months.

The expedition was a joint effort of the United States Geological Survey and the Southern California Edison Company. Robert N. Allen, the recorder, was a civil engineer representing the power company. The Edison Company had ordered the boats made in San Pedro, California, and had shipped them by rail to Green River, Utah. Trimble had purchased food staples and other supplies in Salt Lake City, had shipped them by rail to Green River, and had hired a truck to haul them and the boats on to Bluff.[6]

Heber Christensen, a tall, bilingual Mormon from Moab who had grown up on the Navajo Indian reservation at Tuba City, Arizona, had signed on as cook. He was thirty-eight and had spent some time on the San Juan River during the oil boom.[7] His knowledge of the Navajo language would come in handy before the trip was over.

Hugh D. Miser, from Arkansas and Washington, D.C., a geologist for the United States Geological Survey, joined the party at Monticello. He was overweight but would lose some pounds before the trip was over. He would be a cohesive force in the party during the expedition.

Hugh Hyde, a lanky twenty-one-year-old Mormon descendant of one of the early settlers of Bluff, joined them there as rodman. This completed the party of seven.

On Monday, July 18, 1921, the party arrived at the launch site four miles below Bluff, the present site of Sand Island picnic area where float trips are now launched. The truck was unloaded by about 10:00 A.M. They slid the boats down a steep place in the bank and eased them into the shallow water. Miser noted, "4412 elevation of terrace on side of San Juan just north of launching locality."

Loper looked the duffel over and found much more than the boats could safely carry. He proceeded to sort out extra clothes, suitcases, and other unnecessary things. This upset some crew members, but Trimble backed Loper, relying on his boating experience and knowledge of the river. Even then the two small boats could carry barely enough supplies to last until the party would reach Goodridge (now Mexican Hat).

Trimble sent the surplus provisions by truck to Goodridge for storage until needed. The excess baggage was loaded on the truck addressed to various homes.

Elwyn Blake wrote in his autobiography:

We had two sixteen-foot skiffs, about sixteen inches deep, with probably a four foot beam. The boats would be used mainly

Trimble party on the San Juan River. Left to right: Robert Allen, Hugh Hyde, Elwyn Blake, Bert Loper, and Kelly Trimble; Hugh D. Miser and Heber Christensen not shown. (Courtesy of Marston Collection, The Huntington Library, San Marino, California)

for transportation of supplies and equipment, but occasionally both men and equipment had to be transported. On these occasions the boats sat very low in the water.[8]

They had the boats loaded by lunchtime. Christensen, the cook, was supposed to help Loper move camp with the boats. The two pushed off at 12:45 P.M., Loper in one boat and Christensen in the other. Before they had gone far, sand waves began to take form ahead of them. Loper, in the lead boat, kept his craft headed straight into them.

Sand waves were something new to Christensen. The waves grew higher and higher, then began to comb with their roaring back-curl. This was too much for him. He panicked and quit rowing. When Loper looked back to see how Christensen was doing, he was disgusted to see the boat wallowing out of control. He rowed to it, tied the painter to the seat of his own boat, and towed Christensen to shore. He vowed then never to let Christensen row a boat again.

Unlike most rivers, sand waves occur frequently in the San Juan. They only form in swiftly moving streams when the silt load is heavy and contains just the right combination of suspended clay and sand particles. When the gradient of the riverbed flattens a little, sand particles settle along the bottom forming ripples that grow into dunes. These sand dunes are called anti-dunes, and they grow higher and higher causing corresponding waves on the surface of the stream. In time the anti-dunes build too high and are washed out, only to build again. The waves break upstream before them and roar before flattening out. This is known as combing. Miser tells us:

> The usual length of sand waves, crest to crest, on the deeper sections of the river is 15 to 20 feet, and the height, trough to crest, is about 3 feet. However, waves of at least 6 feet were observed. The sand waves are not continuous, but follow a rhythmic movement. Their appearance, as seen on the lower San Juan, is as follows: At one moment the stream is running smoothly for a distance of perhaps several hundred yards. Then suddenly a number of waves, usually from 6 to 10, appear. They reach full size in a few seconds, flow for perhaps two or three minutes, then suddenly disappear. Often, perhaps half a minute before disappearing, the crests of the waves go through a combing movement, accompanied by a roaring sound.[9]

After the encounter with sand waves, Loper took Christensen into his own boat. He rowed one boat and led the other for the three or four miles they had left to go. At the mouth of Comb Wash they started to make camp but quickly moved to another spot when they discovered the area was home to millions of black ants. Loper and Christensen would be together for most of this trip, but after the incident with the sand waves there would be no real comradeship between them. With Loper, if one did not do his job, he just did not matter.

From the launch site Elwyn and the survey team traveled on foot carrying the survey along the right side of the river while Miser explored and made geologic notes. At Mile Three they saw steps in the cliff carved long before by the "Anasazi."[10] Loper had seen these steps at an earlier time and described them to Elwyn as "too steep for me to climb."

At Butler Wash they saw a small cliff dwelling, and just below that they came to a grand tapestry of petroglyphs in the desert varnish (a dark stain composed of manganese) of the cliff face.[11] One panel had the figures of several desert bighorn sheep, the largest one much lighter in color and perhaps more recent than the others.

A bigger panel depicted large, square-shouldered, necklace-clad

Sand waves, cresting at a height of up to six feet, posed a danger to the open boats. (H. D. Miser 583, U.S. Geological Survey)

figures standing among what seemed to be lesser beings. The larger figures appeared to be wearing stacks of halos over their heads. They also looked like they might be blowing smoke rings off to the side. Elwyn wondered what story the ancient writings might tell if he could only decipher their meaning. Don Baars and Gene Stevenson, in their *San Juan Canyons: A River Runner's Guide*, say, "The large, square-shouldered figures are believed to be 'Kachinas,' or gods, who are given rank by the stripes over their heads and may be seen to be giving speeches by the 'sound waves' marked beside their heads." [12] Don Keller, an archaeologist who has worked in this area, says that "Kachina panel" is a misnomer since the petroglyphs here predate the Hopi Kachina cult by centuries. They can be thought of as proto-Kachinas.

A couple of miles farther on the surveyors came to a widening benchland where they discovered a large cliff dwelling tucked up under an overhang of the orange cliff. Anglos have named it "River House" or "Plumed Serpent" for the pictographs on the rock face there. Again Elwyn wondered about the life of the ancient ones who built it.

Farther down on the same benchland they came to the foot of San Juan Hill. Mormon pioneers had carved a dugway up the rocky side of Comb Ridge in March 1880 on their way to settle the town of Bluff.[13] It had taken them several days to blast the mile-long wagon road up the steep sandstone ledges. Aside from Hole-in-the-Rock on the Colorado River, San Juan Hill was the steepest crossing of that pioneer journey. By this time their horses were worn out from the wintry trip on insufficient feed. To make it up the dugway, the pioneers hooked seven span of horses to one wagon, whipping them all the way. If some of the horses were down on their knees, fighting to get up, those on their feet could still pull upward.[14]

This author hiked up that old dugway in 1987. Near the top is an inscription carved on a rock face by those hardy pioneers. It reads "WE THANK THEE OH GOD."

On the benchland near the foot of San Juan Hill stood the partial walls of a red sandstone building. These were the only remains of a pioneer trading post built there in 1886 by William Hyde and Amasa Barton, Hugh Hyde's grandfather and uncle. It had been abandoned in 1887 after Barton was killed by a Navajo during an argument over some pawned jewelry.[15]

From the spine of Comb Ridge one can see the Mule Ear Diatreme located a mile south of the river. Miser photographed this distinctive geologic landmark. The San Juan River meanders through eroded orange and buff sandstone hills in this area, and the shores of several islands are lined with green cottonwoods and willows, a pleasing contrast to the surrounding bluffs.

About six that evening the surveyors reached camp just above the mouth of Comb Wash on the right side. They were hungry and ready for supper. Christensen had set up the camp stove and had the meal nearly ready. The smell of fresh coffee further whetted their appetites. They all washed up in the river while he finished cooking.

After supper the men sat around talking. Christensen began telling stories, a practice he would continue throughout the trip. Elwyn said he entertained them the entire time and never told the same story twice. When one of the men complimented him on the meal, he answered, "The secret of being a good cook is to first get your customers good and hungry."

Kelly Trimble explained the purpose of the trip—to map the river and look for possible reservoir sites and power possibilities. He said they would also have to survey all side canyons, together with contours up to the 3,900-foot elevation, in order to determine the storage basin of a proposed dam in Glen Canyon.[16] Until they reached the 3,900-foot elevation of the river four miles below Honaker Trail, however, they would be concerned only with mapping the traverse of the river. Miser would record geological data along the way.

For a long time after going to bed Elwyn lay gazing at the sky. The stars seemed almost close enough to touch. How lucky he was to have landed this position. Working at the newspaper had been just a job. He preferred being out of doors. Lately he had spent three days a week at the newspaper office and the rest of the week grubbing brush on his homestead northeast of town. That had kept him in good physical condition.

He could hear the splash and ripple of the fast-moving river. With a fall of nearly eight feet to the mile, the wave action created a soft roar that could be heard a hundred or more yards away. How different it was from the docile Green River beside which he had spent his teenage years. At the town of Green River, Utah, the slow-moving stream made little gurgles and splashes one could only hear close to shore.

Thinking of Green River brought back memories of another river trip. In the spring of 1909 the Blake family had arrived in Utah from Denver and settled in Elgin, a small village across the stream from the town of Green River.

Elwyn's father, H. E. Blake, along with others, wanted to establish a freight and tourist route by boat between the railroad at Green River and the town of Moab on the Grand (now Colorado) River. That spring H. E. built a twenty-four-foot boat equipped with a fourteen-horsepower engine, naming it the *Ida B.* for his wife.

He made several trips on the river with the *Ida B.* before deciding to build another boat, one with less draft. The second boat was longer and narrower and used the engine from the *Ida B.* He called it the *Utah*.

Needing capital for the proposed venture, he invited some outside businessmen and officials from Moab to take a sight-seeing boat ride down the Green River to the Grand, then upstream to Moab.[17] If the venture worked out, the Denver and Rio Grande Railroad agreed to give two acres of land next to the railroad bridge for a landing area.

Thirteen-year-old Elwyn watched longingly as the crew loaded freight onto the *Utah*. When his father turned and asked, "Son, would you like to go along?" Elwyn replied, "Wow! Would I ever." He had loved the river for fishing, for swimming, and for short boat trips. To get a long trip on it was a dream come true.[18]

On the trip to Moab the *Utah* carried 2,000 pounds of freight besides the passengers. It was an exciting journey for Elwyn. They visited squatters on the bottoms along the Green River and paused to view Indian ruins and scenic places of interest. He saw his father shoot a large buck from the moving boat, and he himself shot a bobcat, the first game he had killed that was larger than a rabbit.

A few miles above the confluence of the Grand and the Green, the bearings burned out on the boat's engine. He watched with amazement as his father made molds from riverbank clay and recast the bearings, getting the engine back in running order.

Moab is set in a narrow valley that protects it from the wind, and it has one of the earliest growing seasons in Utah. H. E. bargained for 1,000 pounds of peaches to take back to Green River. According to Elwyn, the fruit was so large that when his father laid out nine peaches on a yardstick, the last one hung over the end.

His dad made a few more trips on the river that fall, but hopes for a commercial route fizzled, so he turned to farming. There was no wagon bridge across the Green River, only the railroad bridge and a ferry, so Elwyn's father built a rowboat for crossing the river. Elwyn used it to go to Green River and to fish, hunt ducks, and just have fun.

In February of 1917 his father took a job with the *Grand Valley Times* in Moab. There, under the tutelage of his father and Loren (Bish) Taylor, Elwyn began learning the linotype trade.

Within a few months the Blakes moved on to Monticello where H. E. became editor of the *San Juan Record*. Elwyn filed on a homestead near Monticello.

In 1918 Elwyn joined the army and served in France and Germany. Returning from overseas, he bought a team and some farm equipment, making good money for a while at custom plowing and hauling wood. When the heavy snows of winter set in he returned to operate the linotype at the *San Juan Record*.

The following summer he bought some cows and a crop of wheat already planted on a farm east of town. That did not work out because, although the wheat looked good, it turned out to be full of smut. Furthermore, the seller had said the field contained eighty acres, but it measured only sixty-five. In the wrangling and lawsuit that followed he lost his investment plus another $100. So he went back to the newspaper job, which was how he happened to be in town when the surveyors came through.

Lulled by the music of the river and his memories of the past, Elwyn drifted off to sleep beside the San Juan.

CHAPTER 2

Comb Wash to Mexican Hat

The next morning, July 19, the party broke camp and the survey team went to work with their miniature plane table, alidade, and stadia rods. The plane table is used by topographic engineers for mapping in the field. The alidade is an optical sighting instrument that sits freely on the leveled plane-table surface. When unfolded, the stadia rod is a tall board with vertical graduations on it. By using the sighting capabilities of the alidade, the engineer is able to make readings from the stadia rod, which is held at key points some distance away. From the readings he calculates distances and elevation changes and plots these directly on the map paper mounted on the flat surface of the plane table.

For the first half day Elwyn, with the survey team, worked down the right bank. Elwyn and Hyde carried their stadia rods to designated key points for the engineer, Kelly Trimble, to take readings. Robert Allen, the recorder, would write down the information and make the calculations that Trimble would then transfer back onto the plane table as a two-dimensional map with elevation contour lines.

After loading both boats with camp gear and equipment, Loper took Christensen on the first boat and drifted down the river to the head of the upper canyon. There he tied the boat on the right side and hiked back up the rocky shore to the other boat, which he used to take Miser across the river for geology work up Chinle Creek.

Just below the mouth of Chinle Creek the river enters the head of the upper San Juan Canyon. The crew came back together there for lunch, hunting out a shady spot to escape the midsummer heat.

The San Juan River, named for St. John in 1686 by Fray Alonso de Posadas, starts out in the San Juan Mountains of southern Colorado, flows into the northwest corner of New Mexico, flows back into Colorado, then enters southeastern Utah and flows west through a series of deep canyons to join the Colorado River near the Utah-Arizona line. The portion in Utah passes through an arid section of the Colorado Plateau where most of the ten inches of average annual rainfall comes in sudden thunderstorms that erode the countryside and wash the soil away down the canyon. Both the military and railroad surveys of the mid-1800s avoided the lower San Juan.

The San Juan had cut through a major geologic uplift called the Monument Upwarp to create its canyons, which extend sixty-three miles from the mouth of Chinle Creek to the Colorado as the crow flies. But the river is so winding that it is 133 miles by stream. The canyons are as much as half a mile deep, interrupted only in a few short stretches where the river flows through open country. Side canyons spill their periodic flows into the San Juan, some at river level and some from falls over the canyon rim. Lake Powell now backs up through the lower portions of the lower canyons all the way to Grand Gulch, near the deepest part of the main canyon.

After lunch the survey team left the orange and buff sandstone bluffs behind and worked into the canyon. Here the geologic uplift exposes new rock formations—stacked terraces of hard gray limestone with slopes of softer shales between the layers. The limestone appears pink near the top of the cliffs, shading to gray at river level. The pink color is a coating of fine silt and mud washed down from ferrous-bearing red-rock layers above and behind the limestone. In some places the gray and pink colors alternate.

Inside the canyon, about a mile below the mouth of Chinle Creek, they came to a potential dam site located in 1914 by the Reclamation Service. Miser examined the site, recording the rock formations and other geologic data. A dam 264 feet high at that place would submerge the town of Bluff.

While the surveyors worked their way downstream, Loper and Christensen looked for a suitable place to make the next camp. Loper kept pace with the surveyors so he could ferry party members across the river when necessary.

In charting the river Trimble decided to have one rodman work down each side where possible, so he sent Elwyn to the left bank. On the way across Elwyn watched how Loper plied the oars, wondering idly how it would be to row a boat again. But his own work kept him too busy to think much about that.

At some difficult places the rodman would stay in place until those with the plane table passed on by and took a reading back to his rod. This kind of station was referred to as a turning point. It enabled them to establish the location and elevation of a new point farther on.

Besides making geologic notes and sketches, Miser took many photographs, as did Robert Allen. When Loper or Christensen were not busy with their own work, they sometimes accompanied Miser on his photographic or geological hikes.

On the night of July 19 the party camped about three and a half miles inside the canyon on the right bank near a perched meander. The cliffs near camp were composed of gray limestone, which began about thirty feet above the water's surface. The river had cut a narrow canyon in the limestone and in places it was only fifty feet wide. Miser thought this place would make an excellent dam site since a potential site needed to be in a narrow place with high walls, have suitable rock strata, and be accessible.

Next morning the survey team went right to work leaving the loading and moving to Loper and Christensen. The team made good progress. Late in the day they reached a place called the Narrows where the canyon walls rose almost vertically for 150 feet above the water on both sides of the stream. There was a spring on the right side but no place to camp near it, so Loper boated the surveyors to a sandbar on the left side.

That evening and again the next morning Loper tried without success to find a way to get past the Narrows on foot, afraid that if he took one boat through it would be impossible for him to walk back for the other one.

By next morning the river had risen a few inches and the red, pungent floodwaters carried an abundance of driftwood. When the river made another rise, Trimble decided they should stay in that camp one more day. Christensen and Miser climbed over a cliff on the left side of the Narrows searching for a way to bypass the box canyon on foot. They descended to the stream by way of a crack in the cliff and a talus slope, but still found no way to follow along the shore.

Later that day the river began dropping, so the party decided to venture on. They still had not figured out how to get both boats through the Narrows and keep the survey intact. Loper wrote: "It was here that we had to break in another boatman. My choice was reduced to one man, and Elwyn delivered the goods in fine shape."

The only place where a stadia rod could be seen from both upstream and downstream was behind a big boulder that could only be reached by boat. If a boat failed to land there, the survey line would be broken.

"Which of you men can handle a boat?" Loper asked. He was looking directly at Elwyn, but Elwyn said nothing. It had been a long time since he had used oars, and then it had been on slow water unlike the fast-moving San Juan.

"I can handle one," Hugh Hyde stated. "Up at Bluff I would take one oar and a Navajo the other and we would cross the river."

Loper paid no attention to Hyde. He said, "Elwyn, you used to row a boat at Green River, didn't you?"

"I rowed some, below the dam at Green River," Elwyn replied.

Loper pointed to the big boulder just inside the Narrows, and asked Elwyn if he thought he could make a landing there. "I can sure try," was Elwyn's reply.

Miser and Hyde rode with Elwyn while the other three stayed behind to come with Loper. Trimble would have to take a reading on the stadia rod before going on through and landing below on the opposite shore.

As the current caught the boat, Elwyn bent to the oars, rowing against the current to retard progress. When just above the big rock, he thrust the prow of the boat toward it as if to ram it. As it passed the big rock he pulled mightily on the oars and slid into a small eddy behind it. His career as a U.S.G.S. boatman started at that moment.

Miser leapt to the small sandspit and held the boat, while Hyde held the rod for Trimble to take his reading. Then Loper took the other boat and passengers through the Narrows to where the instrument could be set up again. It was a long shot, but Hyde's rod position could be seen from below, something they had not been sure was possible.[1]

They ate lunch just below the Narrows where the river entered Soda Basin. From there Loper again took up the handling of both boats. Soon after lunch the upper canyon was behind them. They stopped at one point to investigate an Indian sweathouse, which is used by Native Americans for a spiritual cleansing ceremony. Rocks are heated until red hot in a fire outside the sweathouse, then transferred to a pit inside. The Indian male takes off his clothes, crawls inside, and closes the door flap. He pours water on the hot rocks causing the small room to fill with steam. As sweat pours from his body, he chants a prayer asking that his spirit be attuned to all nature and the universe. The ceremony is supposed to cleanse both body and mind.

They made camp that night on the left side a mile and a quarter below Soda Springs. Since the river water was too muddy to drink, they dug a well in the gravel bar. Cool, almost-clear water seeped into it allowing them to fill their water bags and have water for cooking. This was an operation they would repeat often for the rest of the survey.

After supper they all climbed to the top of the high cliff behind camp. From there they could see Mexican Hat Rock and many of the great red monoliths of Monument Valley. Elwyn thought it was awesome but did not want to appear naïve, so he did not say anything until some of the older men spoke of the grand view.

The next day they moved rapidly downstream in more open country and reached Mexican Hat Trading Post about noon. This village (as Miser called it) got its name from a nearby red butte capped by a wide, circular rock. The formation looked like a large Mexican sombrero. The party estimated Mexican Hat rock to be about twenty feet in diameter and five feet thick at the brim.

At that time Mexican Hat Trading Post was located about two miles above the present-day bridge and was operated by John L. Oliver. It was twenty-five miles from Bluff and half a mile west of the river. Only a couple of other families lived there. Oliver's stock of merchandise was meager.

In the afternoon they ran down another three and a half miles and camped just above the mouth of Gypsum Creek opposite the present location of the Mexican Hat town site. The sand waves were running high, and after supper Elwyn and Hyde went swimming, riding the swells of a series of sand waves, frolicking like a pair of river otters.

Loper had expected trouble at Gypsum Creek because a bad rapid there had given him plenty of trouble twenty-seven years earlier. But the rapid had been mostly scoured away by later floods.

Rapids are formed when rocks and other debris are washed from tributary streams producing an alluvial construction that chokes the main stream. According to Stegner:

> There is a rough physical law to the effect that the carrying power of water increases as the sixth power of its velocity, which is to say that a stream moving two miles an hour will carry particles sixty-four times as large as the same stream moving one

mile an hour, and that one moving ten miles an hour will carry particles a million times as great.[2]

This means that steep tributaries, when in flood, can transport huge boulders, smaller rocks, and large quantities of other erosional debris into the river much faster than they can be moved downstream. The resulting constriction backs up the main stream until the water spills over the edge producing rapids. When floods in the main stream are greater or more frequent than those in the tributary, the constrictions tend to be eroded away and the rapid may lessen or disappear. More frequent large floods in the tributary can cause the rapid to worsen.[3]

Loper had spent two and a half years prospecting for gold in San Juan Canyon beginning in 1893. At that time he had made a trip with Bill and John Clark on a lumber raft from Chinle Creek to Slickhorn Gulch.[4] Many places along the river brought back memories of those earlier experiences. He liked to tell those tales to Elwyn and the rest of the party.

On the morning of July 23 they reached the bridge near Goodridge where the road to Monument Valley crossed the river. They made camp against a cliff on the right bank. The cliff reflected such intense heat that they put up a shade. They spent the rest of the day cleaning, shaving, and writing letters before going to Spencer's Trading Post near the Goodridge Bridge.

The town of Mexican Hat today covers both the site of Oliver's Trading Post and Spencer's Trading Post. In 1879 Emery Langdon Goodridge from Ohio worked his way by boat from Animas, Colorado, down the San Juan to its confluence with the Colorado, and then on down to Lee's Ferry. He reported sighting oil seeps coming out of the loose boulders above the mouth of Slickhorn Gulch and flaked gold glistening in the gravel beds in several places along the San Juan. In 1882 he returned to carve his name on a sandstone cliff near the present town of Mexican Hat. He filed his first oil claim near a low wooden bridge spanning the river near Mexican Hat. The bridge and its successors (the flooding San Juan was hard on bridges) became known as the Goodridge Bridge.

Goodridge's report of gold in San Juan Canyon set off a gold rush there with several thousand placer miners searching for the elusive metal. When little gold was found, the rush subsided almost as fast as it had begun. The village that grew up to support the oil and mining interests was still called Goodridge when Kelly Trimble's survey crew reached the area in 1921.[5]

After lunch on July 23, most of the crew went to the trading post where the trucker had stored their supplies.[6] Looking back across the river to the south they could see an interesting erosional formation that looked like red chevrons against a gray background. Today it is referred to as the Navajo Rug or Raplee Monocline.

They moved the supplies over to a cellar at Oliver's Trading Post where they would keep better. Allen and Miser bought Navajo rugs, and they asked Billie Nevills, who lived near the store, to mail the rugs out for them.

That evening a Navajo visited their camp and had supper with them. After supper Elwyn and some of the others went back up to the Nevills's home to spend the evening. Billie Nevills was well known in Elwyn's hometown of Monticello. Billie's son Norman, who later gained renown as a rough-water boatman and guide, was then just a little boy.

The trip was delayed while Trimble waited for Taylor Norton, a packer from Colorado he intended hiring to pack supplies into the canyon by burro train. Norton had sent word that he would be along in a couple of days.

During the delay Miser roamed the countryside taking photographs of strange rock formations and visiting old oil well sites. He located Goodridge Well No. Four. Other drillers had used oil from this well as fuel for their own drilling operations.

One day Elwyn and Loper hiked a couple of miles downriver to the old Mendenhall cabin located at the first gooseneck.[7] In the early 1890s Walter E., F. W., and F. R. Mendenhall, father and sons, had located a mine there. They built a stone cabin on the saddle between loops of the canyon. The old cabin with its sagging roof is frequently visited by present-day river runners.

Loper said the Mendenhalls had found gold at places among rock fragments, but the pay streaks were mostly below the present water level. He said that in 1894 and 1895 Walter Mendenhall, working the claim only during low water, mined $4,000 worth of gold at water's edge.

Loper had known and worked with the Mendenhalls. He said he mined twenty ounces of gold at the Mendenhall claim the year after Mendenhall and others quit mining by using copper plates and quicksilver. He told Elwyn that in February 1895 he had seen the largest sand waves of his life just a mile or so above the Mendenhall cabin.

An ice jam at the head of the canyon had shut off the flow of water so completely that he could walk across the river without getting his feet wet. He was in the riverbed panning for gold when he heard the dam break. He said he moved his placer outfit twice, but the water rose so fast the flood still carried part of it away. After the ice went through he walked about a mile upstream, where he estimated the waves were ten feet high. He said the roar of the combing waves could be heard a mile or two away. That was the last work Loper had done in San Juan Canyon until the present trip. After that he had walked to Bluff and taken a job for the next two years making brick for the Mormon settlers.

CHAPTER 3

Mexican Hat to Clay
Hills Crossing

In 1921 few trails penetrated the area and there were no roads to the river below Mexican Hat. It was more than 150 miles to the nearest railroad, and Bluff was the nearest post office. The villages of Goodridge and Mexican Hat, with their combined population of half a dozen people, were the only white settlements near the canyon.[1]

When the packer had still not shown up by the morning of July 27, Trimble decided to wait no longer. He left word for Norton to meet them at Honaker Trail, the next place where the river could be reached by land.

They started down the river at midday. Elwyn took the left side using one boat while the other surveyors took the right. Miser and Christensen rode with Loper in the other boat.

The party camped a mile and a half below the Mendenhall Loop on the right side. They were careful to put their beds well up from the river, because a rise in the water level could be expected at any time. Before going across to camp, Elwyn had placed his stadia rod atop an eight-foot-high boulder to keep it safe from the rising water.

Next morning they found the river on another rampage. Elwyn had rolled out his bed higher than anyone else, saying that the river was not going to make him move that night. About daylight someone passed the head of his bed dragging his bed to higher ground. Soon another bed was shifted out of the way of the rising river. Six beds were moved while he smugly looked on.

Christensen had moved the cooking utensils up to high ground and started breakfast before Elwyn got up. Before going to breakfast Elwyn raked up a high sandbank around the side of his bed since the water was coming pretty close. He wanted to make good his brag

Camp below Mendenhall Loop, where a flood drove the party high above the river. (H. D. Miser 576, U.S. Geological Survey)

that the river would not make *him* move. But while they were eating Elwyn glanced toward his bed just as a small wave slopped over his sand dike. He ran to the rescue, but not before the bed was soaked.

After breakfast Loper rowed Elwyn across the river to the turning point where he had last held rod for Trimble. They got there just in time; the water was lapping at the stadia rod and it would soon have floated away in the still-rising tide. Trimble's turning point was lost under the flood. The river rose another six feet in three hours, so they did not break camp until afternoon.

Elwyn and Loper took the boats as far as the Tabernacle, a gooseneck-surrounded point of land shaped like the Mormon Tabernacle in Salt Lake City. Loper wrote:

> It was me that named it the Tabernacle in 1894 but it seems as though the name had went out o[f] use in the last 27 years it being that long since I had been away from that part of the river so I told the boss and he re-christened it and so put it on the map as that— [2]

Loper let Elwyn off on the left side of the Tabernacle, then rowed one boat and towed the other one to the right side. Elwyn carried his rod along the river for a short distance, but his way was soon blocked by vertical cliffs. Loper had to recross the river with both boats to pick him up again. He approached the ledge where Elwyn was waiting and shouted for him to jump.

Holding his rod and water bag in one hand, Elwyn jumped into the second boat landing on a roll of bedding. The boat rocked back and forth violently, but took on little water. Loper then threw the painter to Elwyn.

By the time he got settled and had control, both boats were floating toward some rocks protruding out of the water near the left shore. They had a hard pull to clear the rocks. They then continued downstream and ran several riffles safely before stopping at the head of the Second Narrows.

Where they landed the river was so turbulent they had to pull the boats out of the water to keep them from being beaten to pieces against the rocks. Loper and Elwyn spent the remainder of the afternoon playing rummy while waiting for the rest of the men, who were working along the talus on the right side.

On the morning of July 29 they tried to find a way through the Second Narrows on foot, but by 10:45 A.M. decided this was impossible. Trimble carried his line high up the side of the canyon so he could see the river beyond the bend below. Meanwhile Loper and Christensen got the boats loaded.

It was again necessary to work Elwyn as boatman. The sand waves were running high. In dividing the load, Loper again assigned Miser and Hyde to Elwyn's boat. He figured that these men would not get overly excited in a pinch.

Elwyn was to take the boat down to where Trimble could get a sight from above. The three started down the river about 11:30. Elwyn headed the boat toward the left bank to avoid the swift water against the near cliff, but soon decided to cross to the right to avoid the then swifter water along the left bank. As they reached the middle, high but short sand waves began to form. They got higher and higher — as much as six or seven feet high according to Miser. Elwyn hit the waves endwise, as was proper to prevent an upset, but a big one half filled the boat with water. Hyde grabbed a can and began bailing while Miser took off his hat and bailed with it. They hit two more waves that poured water into the boat.

As the waves began to subside, Elwyn headed for the left shore to bail out the rest of the water. He pulled so heavily at the oars that an oarlock broke. Quickly testing the depth with an oar, he found that the water was only waist deep, so Hyde jumped out and grabbed the nose of the boat. The other two followed, and they quickly towed the waterlogged boat to shore.[3]

Fortunately their position could be seen by Trimble from his perch upstream on the side of the canyon. Elwyn held the rod so Trimble could make a reading and establish his turning point.

Then the group that had remained behind with Trimble made the run with Loper in the other boat. As the boat approached, Elwyn shouted directions to Loper so he could land safely. They made camp at that place on the left bank. Miser shook as much water as possible out of his compass, camera, telescope, aneroid, and notebook.[4] He then left them in the hot sun to finish drying. Elwyn soon had his oarlock repaired.

This was their last camp in the Goosenecks. As they passed through the canyon a half mile below this camp, they saw boulders as big as eighteen feet square both in the river and on the talus slopes. Lighter gray areas on the cliffs indicated that rocks had fallen from there recently. Four and a half miles below camp they noted a strong gasoline-like odor. They located some small streams of petroleum and gas coming from the sand at the edge of river. Christensen saturated a chip with the petroleum and set it on fire.[5]

Loper and Elwyn ran the boats downriver to the foot of Honaker Trail where they unloaded them and pitched camp. The river was rough in some spots, but they had no mishaps. Clouds had covered the sky the entire day and a light rain began to fall at 4:00 P.M. As usual, they dug a well in the sand beside the river where the water could seep in and provide drinking water. Everyone carried water bags, an essential in the 100-degree-plus heat.

The Honaker Trail was completed in 1904 by gold prospectors who intended using pack animals on it, but the only horse ever to attempt the descent fell off a particularly steep, narrow stretch known as "The Horn." Its bleached bones could still be seen at the base of the cliff. The canyon wall rose only 1,235 feet above the river, but the trail was so crooked it was about two-and-a-half-miles long.[6]

In his journal Bert Loper told about an early experience at Honaker Trail. He said that in 1894 he and George Edmondson were working for Augustus Honaker, who had a placer claim at the foot of the cliff.

At that time there was no trail into the canyon, just a crevice in the sixty-foot ledge at the place where the trail now comes over. That was the only place they could get down and then only with ropes.

On their first trip into the canyon Loper and George Edmondson carried four horse loads of provisions down to the big ledge. By tying a rope to a rock and letting it hang over the ledge, they managed to get up and down. George went below and Loper let each load down for him to untie. They finished just about dark. But they had a problem.

Honaker would not go down the rope since he was deathly afraid of heights. It was growing late and all their gear, including their beds, was at the foot of the ledge. In desperation the two young men jumped on their boss, tied him hand and foot, and lowered him by rope to the campsite.

Loper said the trail was named for Honaker since it went down to the old Honaker camp. He said Honaker never saw the trail because it had been built by others after Honaker quit the canyon.[7]

July 31 was Loper's fifty-second birthday, but he said it was just another day. The packer, Norton, was not at Honaker Trail, even though Trimble had left word for him to meet them there. So after breakfast Loper and Miser walked from camp at the foot of Honaker Trail back to Mexican Hat, a distance of nine miles overland. They picked up the mail at John Oliver's store and bought sugar, salt, and baking powder at Spencer's Trading Post. Miser also bargained for forty-four pounds of beef at a cost of ten cents a pound. They hired Wesley Oliver, John Oliver's twenty-year-old son, to haul their supplies by team and wagon to the head of Honaker Trail.

Elwyn met them at the head of the trail and helped Loper carry the side of beef down the steep, rocky trail. It was quite a struggle. Afterward they wished they had thought to cut it in two. Nonetheless, the beef was welcome to the crew.

To keep the meat from spoiling they hung it out to cool during the night and at daybreak wrapped it in a tarpaulin inside a bedroll. For men doing heavy work it would last only a few days.

During the night the splash of rising water woke up Loper, who shook some of the others awake to help move the camp to higher ground. A heavy storm upstream had swollen the river again making it a torrent of mud. Just below camp they observed the largest sand waves they had yet seen.

Next morning they could see shark-like fins moving in the muddy water. These turned out to be humpbacked chubs cruising near the surface where there was more oxygen and less mud. No one was averse to eating suckers, so each man improvised a club and went after the fish. Forgetting that they needed only two or three for food, they soon had a pile of about 300 pounds of fish. They threw most of them back into the river. They had waded after the fish in their B.V.D.s and were never able to get the red-mud color out of them.[8]

On the morning of August 2 Allen, Loper, and Elwyn again hiked to Mexican Hat to take and get mail and pick up a few more supplies. On the second day there was still no word from Norton, so they gave up on him and hired Wesley Oliver as their packer for the rest of the trip.

On August 4 they were again on their way downriver. They passed several canyons where flooding had pushed boulder fans out into the stream causing rapids.

They passed the Nephi claim on a bar that had been worked by Dulin and Grant Elliot in 1894. It was reported that they had taken out $3,000 in thirty days, the greatest production of any bar along the San Juan.[9]

About four miles below Honaker Trail they reached the 3,900-foot elevation of the river, below which they would have to survey side canyons up to that level. They came to no appreciable side canyons that day, however, and camped on the right side near Mile 54.5, having traveled about ten miles with a ten-foot-to-the-mile fall in the river.

The enchantment of the landscape was not lost on these men. The whitest cotton-puff clouds anyone can imagine are those overhead in the bluest of blue skies when floating through San Juan Canyon in midsummer. The ever-changing, colorful rock formations are enough to lure an artist and stir a poet's pen. Years later, on a June night at dusk, from a tamarisk and willow-fringed bar, I watched bats cruising the air waves for their meal of insects. As the evening wore on, listening to the music of the fast-moving river, a full moon flooded its light across the canyon wall opposite. Changing ever so subtly, the light and shadow cast a magic spell over the entire landscape, the enchantment and mood of the scene never to be forgotten.

On August 5 Loper ferried Elwyn across to his usual position on the left side of the river. About a half mile below camp those walking along the right talus saw a desert bighorn sheep across the river from them. Christensen started downstream on the run for the boat with the gun in it, while the sheep started upstream. Elwyn, who was upstream from the main group, was unable to head off the sheep, so it got away. Christensen did not know this until after he had run three miles downstream and back up one mile, where Miser met him and told him what had happened.

A little later Loper had to ferry the main group across the river because their way was blocked. In crossing they ran into some sand waves. One of the bedrolls was thrown out of the boat, but they recovered it in an instant. Farther on Loper stopped to pick up the second boat where Elwyn had tied it up.

At the head of a small rapid Loper and Trimble got into one boat and Hyde and Allen got into the other one. Miser described the rapid they were about to enter as "long and rough." Their arrangement for running this rapid was rather unwieldy. Loper rowed the first boat while Trimble held the rope to the second one, towing it behind them. Loper headed the boats out from the bank to near midstream, but before getting far an oarlock broke. The boats went through the rapid at a fast rate, tossed this way and that in the waves. The trailing boat struck a boulder and began to leak badly, and by the time they reached a landing place below the rapid, it was swamped. The force of the impact had split the boat for its entire length along one side. Allen said, "Splitting [the] boat was funny. I was in the boat that cracked open. As we approached the shore I was throwing stuff ashore. I had the plane table."

They unloaded the beds and provisions, bailed out the water, and repaired the boat, discovering that the ribs of the boat, which were supposed to be held together with dowels, had only been held together with light finishing nails. The boat builders had forgotten the dowels on one side. They checked the other boat and found it properly constructed.

This landing was at the mouth of John's Canyon, named for John Adams who ran cattle there about 1918.[10] After repairing the boat and eating lunch, they went swimming in a clear pool formed by a waterfall at the canyon's mouth.

The next day at Mile 63.5 Loper came to the head of a rough rapid formed by a boulder bar that extended most of the way across the river. Miser and Christensen were walking downstream from the boats, so Loper called to them and they came back and helped him portage the loads around the rapid. After Loper ran each boat through, they helped him reload. The place is now called Government Rapid, perhaps in memory of that day.

About a mile upstream from the mouth of Slickhorn Gulch the

Bert Loper shooting a small rapid above Slickhorn Gulch. (H. D. Miser 588, U.S. Geological Survey)

crew began to find oil seeps leaking into the river from the Hermosa Group rocks. It reeked of hydrogen sulfide. Soon they reached the mouth of Slickhorn Gulch and made camp, where they awaited the arrival of Wesley Oliver and fresh supplies. In 1894 this had been the camp of Bill and John Clark and Al Rogers, who placered out a small bar just above the mouth of the canyon.

According to Ann Zwinger, Slickhorn Gulch was named after a distinctive herd of longhorns that ran in the canyon.[11] Zwinger, in her book, *Wind in the Rock*, wrote:

> Slickhorn rises in an ascending series of limestone ledges for almost a mile, nearly every tread cradling a serene spring-fed pool reflecting the sinuous curves of the canyon walls and their subtle colors.

Early river runner E. L. Goodridge first discovered the oil seeps above Slickhorn in 1879, although he filed his first claim upriver at Mexican Hat in 1882. Later, about 1920, he returned and attempted to put down a well at Slickhorn. Goodridge trucked a drill engine all the way from Gallup, New Mexico, some 175 miles. Then he hauled it by wagon across the mesa from Mexican Hat to Slickhorn Gulch. His crew was easing it down the trail near the drill site when it rolled over the edge and was smashed on the rocks below. It still lay there rusting when the survey party came through.[12]

An old oil well site is located at the base of the cliff and a more recent one on a shelf seventy-five feet higher up. The wagon road leading down to the old site looks more like a mountain goat's trail than a road.

In the late afternoon Miser and Allen went exploring. At a bend of the river just above the mouth of Slickhorn, underneath a narrow cliff on the right bank, Miser found a perfectly intact prehistoric pot. It had a capacity of about three quarts. They also found a burnt corncob and a bed of charcoal several inches thick.

On Sunday, August 7, they took the day off, lounging around camp, cleaning, shaving, and reading. The packtrain came in about 3:00 P.M. with supplies and mail.

Slickhorn was the first side canyon of any consequence that had to be surveyed to the 3,900-foot level. Unlike the main canyon, willows, shrubs, and small plants grew along the small stream in its bottom. Today boaters regularly hike up Slickhorn to dive and swim in a deep, clear pool at the base of one of the limestone ledges.

Slickhorn Canyon had a fall of 150 feet in the last half mile. Boulders had tumbled from the cliffs on both sides, and many of them had been washed by floods into the river forming a narrow rapid. On August 8 Loper ran both boats through it.

Following their established procedure, Elwyn worked the left side of the river where possible, while Hyde, Trimble, and Allen worked the right side. Trimble would point to a position on a ledge or other spot where he needed a reading, and it was up to the rodman to figure out how to get there. Sometimes he went up a crevice in the ledge and at other times he had to take a roundabout route. The two rodmen wore out plenty of shoe leather scrambling over the sharp rocks.

The party worked about four miles downstream and reached the mouth of Grand Gulch by noon. They saw many signs of bighorn sheep along the way. A little rain fell that day, helping to keep the heat to a bearable level.

At Grand Gulch Trimble had to carry his line well up the canyon to reach the 3,900-foot contour. The floor of the canyon was strewn with huge boulders, some as big as boxcars, worn smooth on the edges from being tumbled in flash floods. There were clear pools at the base of hard ledges similar to those found in Slickhorn. A few years ago this author saw cottonwood logs there, but few trees, although there was plenty of shrubbery and desert plants. Mormon

"Hole-in-the-Rock" pioneers gave Grand Gulch its name when they skirted its upper reaches, where there were extensive cliff dwellings, in 1880 on their way to settle Bluff.

Loper got a surprise when he came to Grand Gulch. In 1894 on a trip from Honaker's Camp, he had come to an impassable rapid at the mouth of Grand Gulch. He and his companions had been forced to portage their sixteen-foot boat around the immense boulders that clogged the stream. Loper said they had a pennyweight and a half button of gold with them, but very little grub. At a place just below Copper Canyon they traded the gold to a placer mining outfit for ten pounds of flour and returned back up the river.

In 1921 a fifty-foot waterfall out of Grand Gulch was still there, but the big rocks that had clogged the river had disappeared. The rapid was so gentle they took the boats through with no trouble at all. The rapid at Grand Gulch and the rest of the San Juan River below it are now buried beneath the still waters of Lake Powell (when it reaches its maximum height of 3,700 feet). Silt has completely covered the rapid and the waterfall now appears to be less than twenty feet high. In fact, this silt deposition reaches upriver to the very foot of Slickhorn Rapid.

After the survey party finished charting Grand Gulch they made their way downriver a couple of miles and made camp on the right. Next morning the river was still quite low. On a high sandbar below last night's camp they saw many tracks of desert bighorn sheep. The river widened somewhat below Grand Gulch where the hard limestone strata tilted down into the riverbed, replaced by shales and sandstones. The wide channel made the water so shallow that the men sometimes had to wade and nose the boats around to find water deep enough to get through.

Following known trails to the river, Wesley Oliver would come in about twice a month with his string of pack mules bringing fresh supplies. Trimble estimated the pack-in cost to be about a dollar a pound, so there were no luxuries. Flour, bacon, and dried fruit were staples. Coffee did not weigh much, but sugar and canned milk for it were usually in short supply. Any wild game or fish that could be taken made a welcome supplement to their diet.

As they traveled down the river, they saw many bighorn sheep tracks and all the men were on the lookout for them. One day they became aware of a band of bighorn sheep ahead of them on the left side, and eventually the sheep became rimmed and made a break back up the river. Hugh Hyde had brought along a thirty-thirty carbine in case they saw any wild game. Someone saw a sheep running high on a ledge going upstream while the boats were drifting through some low swells. The gun was in the boat in which Christensen was riding.

Christensen was known to be a good shot, but no one thought he could hit a running animal from a rolling boat in midstream. He took careful aim and fired. The sheep took a somersault and rolled downhill for a short way, its neck broken, testifying to Christensen's skill with a rifle.

The boat was near the opposite side of the river, so Loper rowed across to get to the sheep, which was lodged on a steep hillside. Elwyn, already on the left side, went with Christensen and Loper to inspect the kill, a three-year-old ram. While they were dressing out the animal, Elwyn accidentally loosened a large, pointed rock that rolled down and struck Loper's foot and broke his little toe. It did not seem to bother Loper much at the time, but it would later. They loaded the meat into the boat and continued their work.

Around 6:00 P.M. they ran out of the canyon into open country and camped about a mile above Clay Hills Crossing on the right bank. For supper they had desert bighorn sheep steaks. Loper stated:

> I believe that I can claim without fear of contradiction that that was the very best meat anyone ever ate and to prove the fact the 7 of us ate all the loin and about half of one hind quarter, but I will admit that we were in good training for just that very feat.[13]

For hungry men fresh meat is always a welcome change from a diet of bacon and beans.

CHAPTER 4

Clay Hills Crossing to
Piute Canyon

Clay Hills Crossing was a historic ford on the San Juan, taking its name from the clay-rich Chinle formation located at the base of Red House Cliffs to the west. This colorful formation includes the tawny Navajo at the skyline, down through red Kayenta and Wingate sandstones; purple Chinle, dark-red Moenkopi, De Chelly sandstone, and Organ Rock shale, with red Cedar Mesa sandstone at the base.[1] The ford was an easy way for Navajos to reach the Hole-in-the-Rock road when traveling to trade with the Mormons west of the Colorado. "Anglo" Americans' first extensive use of the ford was by miners in the gold rush of 1892–1893.

At Clay Hills Crossing the survey team had a wide area to work to reach the 3,900-foot level. One can appreciate the extent of their work by observing the present-day shoreline of Lake Powell from Clay Hills Crossing to Piute Farms, then extending it on back to another 200 feet of elevation.

With the heat soaring to over 100 degrees nearly every day, the men needed lots of good drinking water. The shallow wells they dug did not always give an ample flow, so everybody was pleased when Elwyn found some tanks of clear water near camp.[2]

On August 10 the surveyors began several days' work in the area. With no camp to move, Loper spent the first day loafing and resting. By evening he was getting itchy feet, so he proposed that he and Miser take a hike the next day into what was known as cow-tank country. Loper had been to the tanks from the opposite direction, but was not familiar with the intervening territory, so he did not know the exact distance from camp to the tanks.

Miser, a little fleshy at the beginning of the trip, had lost about thirty pounds and was becoming tough and strong. He was interested in the history and geology of that area, so he accepted Loper's plan.

Loper told him they could take a side trip on the way back and go over Clay Hills Pass where the Mormon pioneers had come off the high mesa on their way to settle Bluff, making road as they went. Miser and Loper got an early start, their destination for the first day being Red House, a small rock cabin near a pair of reservoirs. Red House had been built as a line cabin for cowboys.

The terrain sloped upward to the north, placing the blazing sun at their backs all day. They started out with about one and a half gallons of water, but by midmorning the water was all gone. Miser was still a little heavy and the heat was harder on him than Loper. Loper later told Elwyn that, although he became very thirsty, his thoughts were not always on his own dry mouth. He said he worried more about how the heat and lack of water were affecting Miser. Despite his thirst, Miser sketched geological features along the way.

They passed a series of red points jutting out from the main ledge, and Loper thought that the Red House would be behind each one of them. By sundown both men were in a bad way. Their lips were cracked, their tongues stuck to the roofs of their mouths, and their saliva had turned to cotton. Eventually Miser began to doubt Loper's sense of location. He decided to go down a dry canyon that ran parallel to their course, knowing it would eventually lead to the river. At this, Loper got concerned and made a dash up the next ridge and looked over it. Sure enough, there was one of the ponds. He hurried back and caught up with Miser, convincing him that water was just over the ridge.

They found two ponds that had filled from a recent rain. The red mud had not completely settled in the ponds, and hundreds of tadpoles inhabited them, but the water tasted good just the same. Loper told Miser he should take just six swallows of water and no more, so he lay down on his belly and took the prescribed six swallows. In about twenty minutes Loper told him it was safe to take six more swallows, which he did. Loper followed the same rule.

They had to sleep out that night, with no bed and only a sack of cold biscuits for supper. Although it had been blistering hot through the day it got uncomfortably cool during the night. They slept just outside the tumbled-down rock house, and all night long Loper could hear Miser go to the edge of the water, take six swallows, and then lie back down.

Between the hard ground and the chill air, it was difficult to get any sleep, but the night finally came to an end. They had more biscuits for breakfast and started on their return journey. Miser still wanted to hike up the old Mormon road to where it came off the top of the mesa, and in doing so they got a good idea of the hardships the pioneers had gone through on their trek to colonize Bluff.[3]

Mormon pioneers had built the road over Clay Hills Pass in 1880 when they traveled from Hole-in-the-Rock to the site of Bluff, but they only used the road for about a year before abandoning it. While Loper and Miser were up on the high mesa, they had a spectacular view of Monument Valley to the south and east. They could also look across the rough country to the west in the direction of the Colorado River.

Starting with full canteens at Red House, they found no more water until arriving at camp, which took them about ten hours. So they got very thirsty again, but not as dry as the day before because there was some cloud cover and a sprinkle of rain fell at midday.

The survey team had spent the two days advancing their work. Elwyn was glad to have Loper back in camp and to hear about the trip. Loper told him, "I thought of you often. My sore toe seemed to get bigger and sorer as we went along. I never realized just what good a little toe was until I made this trip."

While surveying a wide flatland, Trimble sent Hyde to hold his stadia rod on top of a low knoll. In a little while he looked through the instrument to take a reading.

"Well, I'll be doggoned," he said to Allen. "The heat must have gotten to Hugh. Take a look."

Hyde stood bare naked in the hot sun holding the stadia rod. Trimble took the reading and then signaled for him to come in. But Hyde just stood there for awhile before he put on his clothes and joined the others.

Hyde explained his actions thus:

> I felt something on my stomach. Opening my shirt I saw a big centipede on my belly. I had heard that if a fellow touched a centipede while it is on his flesh, it would sting him, and the flesh would rot to the bone, so I carefully took off my shirt, then my pants and shoes. After a while the centipede crawled off.[4]

When the party broke camp on August 13 they found the riverbed wide and shallow and once again had trouble finding water deep enough to float the boats. Elwyn took one boat, ran it down a short distance, and tied up on the left side, where he continued his work with the rod. Loper took Christensen and Miser as passengers in the other boat. They grounded so often that Loper soon asked his passengers to get out and help him. In a few places they had to lift and carry one end of the boat and then the other until they reached deeper water. They only went about two and a half miles before making camp by a willow thicket on the left bank.

As they worked on down to Piute Farms, they found the river channel spread out to 3,300 feet wide. According to Loper, this place had been a big cottonwood bottom twenty-seven years before that covered a flat area about a mile long and up to a half-mile wide. He said Paiute Indians had used it to grow corn and squash until the huge floods of 1911 had washed away the bottomland and left only wide sandbars. The Paiutes never returned.

While camped at the lower end of Piute Farms, the party encountered clouds of mosquitoes. They tried everything they could think of to repel the ravenous insects. Elwyn thought that Miser would smother when he pulled his tarp up over his head and covered up completely. Miser said that the mosquitoes must have hatched out under the canvas, for they were still with him all night long.

At this camp, while the survey team was busy carrying the line up to the 3,900-foot level, Loper took Miser down the river several miles in a boat to do some geology work. They went almost to the mouth of Copper Canyon and camped overnight.[5] The river was shallow in many places, so they had to wade and pull or push the boat. It began to rain shortly after they made camp.

After camping overnight in the rain, they started towing the boat back upstream. The rocky shore, willow thickets, and rising river made towing difficult and it took over a day and a half to reach base camp.

No rain had fallen at the base camp, but it was hot and humid. The mosquitoes were still bad, so they built fires of cow chips to make a smudge. This worked pretty well until the wind kicked up and blew sand into their eyes, bedding, and everything else in general. But it got rid of the mosquitoes.

By August 19 they were running short of grub, but they still had a week's work at this place before they could leave. Wesley Oliver came in with his pack string just in time.

During the sixteen days they worked the open country around Piute Farms there were several floods in the river. One day they heard the roar of onrushing water and gathered to watch its approach. They saw a big wall of water advancing with little tongues licking out ahead. This flood covered the whole 3,300-foot width of the river with seven feet of water, and huge sand waves roared in their combing. The flood undermined the bank where the boats were moored, and large chunks of earth fell into the boats. One boat sank, and Loper needed some quick help to save it. They estimated that the flood would have been as much as thirty-five-feet deep in the upper canyon. They lost two oars and one oarlock, but through good foresight they had spares. From that time on they dragged the boats up on dry land whenever they were camped by a sandbank.

On August 23 Miser took a field trip into Monument Valley. He noted:

> Left camp 6:40 A.M. Arrived Organ Rock 11 a.m. ahead of approaching storm from SW. Took pictures of Organ Rock. Rock is 275 feet high and rises that distance above base of Chinle. The lowest beds of the Chinle forming the rock are brown fine-grained earthy sandstones, and brown sandy shales in nearly equal proportions. Area of Chinle here is 1,000 to 1,200 feet long.[6]

Miser would come back from these field trips and describe what he had seen to the others. At such times Elwyn wished he could see these wonders of nature close up, though he was seeing plenty of fantastically colorful rock formations anyway.

It rained hard during the night of August 25 and the river rose about two feet. They had planned to move camp downstream but could not because of the flooding river. So the survey team spent the day working downstream from their present camp.

The next day the river was passable and they broke camp. Because of the high water, Loper called on Elwyn to man the second boat. The sand waves were running high, so Elwyn's boat took a little water, but he made the trip safely. Loper said, "He sure has the stuff for the making of a real boatman." They moved down about three and a half miles and made camp that night.

The next afternoon Wesley Oliver brought T. G. Jardine, Trimble's boss in the topographic division of the U.S. Geological Survey, and Harry Schenk, a civil engineer from the Edison Company, to the river. The survey party was camped on the right bank, so Loper took a boat across and brought the visitors to camp. They brought in mail and a small quantity of provisions. Elwyn was impressed with the "big shots" who were responsible for this expedition and counted himself quite lucky to be part of it all. Early the next morning, August 28, Jardine, Schenk, and Oliver left for Bluff.

In the forenoon of August 29, Loper, Miser, and Christensen moved camp down near the mouth of Copper Canyon. Rocks up to nine-feet long lay in the boulder fan there, the most common size being two feet in length. A boulder fan results when floods from a side canyon push and tumble rocks to its mouth. As the flood escapes the confines of the canyon, its waters spread out in a fan shape; as the current diminishes, the rocks slow down in their tumbling and come to rest while the floodwater spills into the river over the widened area.

By August 31 Elwyn and the survey team were still busy carrying the 3,900-foot contour up Copper Canyon and other nearby ravines. Miser resumed his geologic work and explored Williams Bar, where he found the remains of old mining equipment. He also found ruins of a stone building and shallow gravel pits over a wide area. On his first visit he saw an upright boiler on the riverbank, but on his second trip he found that it had fallen into the river due to erosion of the bank.

Elwyn's father was a mining man whenever he could get away from his newspaper or other work, so Elwyn was interested in the old mine relics. He enjoyed the stories Loper told about the San Juan gold rush.

By September 2 their provisions were almost exhausted. For breakfast they had coffee, cream of wheat mush, and corn bread, and for lunch they each got two biscuits. They were glad when Wesley Oliver arrived that afternoon with mail and enough provisions for the next two weeks. They celebrated by having a big dinner. On full stomachs, they continued their work.

The pack string with fresh supplies was due to come in at the old Spencer Camp, a distance of fifteen miles from Piute Farms. Along the way down the river to Spencer Camp they passed several old diggings where some prospector was going to make his fortune but never did. Many of the old, crude means of working were still there rusting and rotting away. They also came to many canyons that had to be surveyed to the 3,900-foot level.

Allen was stung on the toe by a scorpion one night, but suffered no lasting effects. At another camp Elwyn sat down on an open pocket-knife, causing Trimble to chuckle as he doctored the wound with iodine. Elwyn said these two incidents and Loper's broken toe were the only accidents suffered by the men for the entire trip.

The farther downstream they advanced, the farther they had to work up the side canyons to reach the 3,900-foot contour. In the forenoon of September 8 they moved downstream to Zahn's Camp on the left bank at Gable Bar. Miners had worked Gable Bar in 1892, site of the largest gold mine operation on the San Juan in the 1890s. In 1902 the Zahn Brothers took it over and worked it off and on until about 1915. The camp was known as Zahn's Camp but the Zahn brothers called it Camp Angeleno.[7]

Miser found a sign on a rock at Gable Bar which read,

Hector N. Zahn   1902
U 1903
Los Angeles, California S 1915
A

Miser hiked up Nokai Canyon beyond Trimble's 3,900-foot contour and, about six miles southeast of the mouth of the Nokai Canyon, found this inscription on a rock:

CAMPO ANGELENO.
THIS CAMP WAS REACHED BY THE 5 ZAHN BROS. OF
LOS ANGELES, CAL. SEPT. 15, '15.
IN A FRANKLIN AUTOMOBILE. THE FIRST CAR HERE.

On September 12 Loper and Christensen moved camp downstream to a place on the right bank opposite Spencer's Camp, named for Charles H. Spencer who had tried to extract gold from crushed Wingate Sandstone.[8] He had branched off the Zahn Brothers' road and, with Indian labor, carved a trail up over a high shoulder of Piute Mesa and down to the river. Spencer named the place "Camp Ibex" because, he claimed, only a mountain goat would attempt to reach the place.

Two days later they moved camp across to the left bank and waited for the pack string to come in. There they found a gasoline engine, plus a roller, and a crusher with which Spencer had attempted to recover the fine gold that he could find by assay but could not recover by panning. While waiting there, Miser had a close call.

In the afternoon he and the others went into the river for a swim. The others went into the deep water next to the left bank ahead of him. He followed and swam for a short distance in the swift current, attempting to reach a sandbar on the right. The swift current next to the sandbar prevented him from making much headway. After he had spent most of his strength trying to reach the bar, he turned and headed downstream with the main current, aiming diagonally for the rocky left bank. He soon found himself under water and struggling to get back to the surface. An undercurrent may have taken him down when he passed through a whirlpool.

Making it back to the surface, he swam and floated as best he could, trying to stay on top of the water. As he neared the left bank he was able to touch bottom at some places. He caught hold of a large boulder projecting into the river and hung on until he could regain some strength. Then he got out pretty well exhausted. He figured he floated and swam 1,000 to 1,200 feet.[9]

Elwyn commented on the same incident:

I was swimming along the shore when I saw Mr. Miser on his back, his face just barely above the surface. He seemed to be struggling, his cheeks puffed out. I did not know that he could not swim, so merely watched as the current swept him against the gravelly bank.

As Miser felt the shore rocks he turned over and held on to one of the larger ones, not trying to climb out. It was then I realized I had nearly witnessed a tragedy, for the muddy San Juan hides its victims beneath its murky surface. Had Miser gone completely under, I could not have traced the course of his drifting body.[10]

Wesley Oliver arrived early the next afternoon with provisions and mail. Both items were a big thing with these men, since they hungered not only for food, but also for news of their families and outside events. Elwyn's family kept him up on what was going on in Monticello, while Elwyn wrote them about the river trip. Each man read his mail eagerly, then finished writing letters to be taken out.

Next day everyone went back to work. Miser spotted two high-walled cliff dwellings in alcoves downriver from Spencer Camp on the right side.

On September 16 the party worked downstream into the Great Bend, which at eight and a half miles was the longest loop in San Juan Canyon. The distance across the neck was only half a mile. The Colorado was a mere five miles in a direct line from the west end of

Pack animals at Spencer's Camp. Wesley Oliver brought in supplies and mail about twice a month over wilderness trails, since there were no roads below Mexican Hat. Note the shoe last in the right foreground, which the surveyors used frequently to resole their shoes. (Courtesy of Prescott Blake)

the loop, but to reach it by way of the San Juan River would take a journey of thirty-four miles.

In the first part of the Great Bend, a line of grass and bushes grew along the base of the Wingate formation about fifty feet above the river where water seeped from a seam in the rock. Farther on, sandstone cliffs came down to the water's edge. At one place a small spring issued from the base of a lavender sandstone layer and flowed over a steep cliff. They made camp on the right bank, midway through the Great Bend.

Next day, as the party passed on downriver, the water became so low the men had to pull the boats over the shallow places. They now found the wading unpleasant because the water had become uncomfortably cold. At one place they had to take the boats fifty feet to deep water by lifting and carrying one end and then the other.

On this day the water was so clear they could drink it without waiting for the sediment to settle. They camped on the left bank near the end of the Great Bend where the river gorge began to widen.

A sandstorm came up by 11:00 A.M. The gusting wind was shaking the plane table and getting sand into everyone's eyes, so they unloaded the boats and did no more work that day. The roar of the wind over the high cliffs sounded like a distant waterfall or wind in a forest. When the dust settled they could see Navajo Mountain. Much surveying was needed there, so they stayed for several days.

At 5:30 A.M. on September 19 the temperature was fifty-five degrees, the lowest reading to that point in the trip. While the surveyors were at work on the twenty-first, Loper, Miser, and Christensen went to look over the rapids below the mouth of Piute Creek. Loper had been complaining of lumbago for a few days but was still able to walk around. The temperature that morning was forty-seven degrees.

The fall of Piute Creek Canyon for the last nine miles above its mouth was eighty feet per mile, causing it to spew great quantities of debris during floods. The debris fan at the mouth of Piute Creek formed an outer circle of about 1,200 feet, with a radius of 500 feet. The debris was composed mostly of pebbles and boulders up to six feet in the longest dimension.

Hundreds of boulders extended into and across the river forming a rapid. The Chinle, Wingate, Toldito, and Navajo were the most abundantly exposed rocks in Piute Canyon, and all of the bars within a mile below its mouth were formed of pebbles and cobbles from Piute Canyon.[11]

On the morning of September 22, while Elwyn and the survey team worked, Miser took a hike up Piute Canyon. About eight miles above the river he saw two horses near a cluster of cottonwoods about a mile to the south. Looking through his field glass, he spotted an Indian woman. Wanting to get information about Piute Creek and the trail crossing it to the west, he walked to the vicinity of the horses.

Near the trees he found a small hogan and close by a garden with pumpkins in one patch and melons in another. A shallow ditch from the nearby stream provided irrigation for the gardens. But he found no sign of the Indian woman. He yelled "Hello" several times but got no response. After he had walked and stood for some fifteen or twenty minutes in the vicinity, he saw the woman riding upstream toward him on a gray pony. As she approached he spoke and tried to talk to her.

They understood a few signs that each made, but the only common words were "Bluff City." The woman was very friendly, apparently trying to find out where he came from and where he was going. He tried to explain to her that he was on the river boats. Miser made her understand that he wanted a watermelon. He paid her fifty cents for it. Then she picked out two small melons, which they shared.[12]

The party had often been low on food before the pack string arrived, and while they were camped at Piute Creek it happened again. Wesley Oliver was four days overdue with the new supplies. They surveyed up to the 3,900-foot level, then loitered in camp waiting for him.

While they were waiting, the Indian woman whom Miser had met in Piute Canyon a few days before and her twelve-year-old grandson rode into camp on a burro. Both Hyde and Christensen spoke Navajo and were able to converse with her. By this time they were almost completely out of food and worried that they might have to abandon the survey.

They knew that a cache of food was supposed to be waiting for them at the junction of the Colorado and the San Juan. But even if they made a run for it to keep from starving they would not be able to make it back up the San Juan to continue the survey.

Christensen talked to the woman and bargained with her to butcher a sheep for them. She agreed, but said it would take her two days to have it butchered and bring the meat back. She agreed to bring them a burro-load of melons in the meantime.

As they lolled in the shade of a boulder, Christensen pointed to a large rock near the eastern side of the wash. "There's a dead man buried at the base of the rock with the Indian writing," he said.

The men doubted that he knew what he was talking about, so Christensen took a shovel and started to dig. Presently he unearthed what he called a medicine pot, then another and another, all arranged in a semicircle. Behind them was the skeleton of a man. Christensen then covered the remains back up and wiped out the signs of his digging. He said that the Indians frowned on desecration of their graves. When the Indian woman arrived with the melons, they were relieved that she did not notice where Christensen had dug. She went back up the canyon for the mutton, which she would deliver the next day.

When the Navajo woman and her husband arrived in camp with the dressed mutton, Trimble paid her four dollars. Now they would not starve.

As they sat around the campfire that evening they heard a pistol shot from up the canyon. They shouted an answer, and soon Wesley Oliver came riding in on a jaded horse. He said he was hungry. When asked where his pack mules were, he said, "The trail has slipped out of Nokai Canyon, so I could not get the packs up the mesa. I had

Hugh Hyde chats with Navajo woman at Piute Canyon. He and Heber Christensen spoke Navajo fluently and so were able to bargain for melons and mutton when the crew ran short of food. (Courtesy of Marston Collection, The Huntington Library, San Marino, California)

to leave them, but managed to get my horse past the slide." He said there was no chance of repairing the trail with only a shovel to work with. In attempting to get one of the pack mules across the slide the mule had floundered on the rocks and injured its leg, so he had left the packs and provisions at Nokai Canyon while he came on to camp with the mail.[13]

It was many miles to the mouth of Nokai Canyon, and they had to have supplies before going on with the survey. Trimble asked Loper what they should do. Loper told him to have Oliver pack the supplies back overland to the old Spencer Camp and that he would take a boat back and get the grub.

On the early morning of September 25, Miser joined Loper for the trip upstream. They stripped down to their underwear, which they rolled above their knees, and began wading upstream towing the boat behind. The seventeen-mile trip would be a strenuous one.

The two made about eleven miles the first day. They rowed across the river a few times, but most of the time they waded. The water was uncomfortably cool, and in places they encountered quicksand, sometimes as much as waist deep. By night they were bone weary and happy to make camp.

The following day while wading near the riverbank, Miser stepped on a greasewood thorn. He said it felt like the sharp fin of a catfish. The pain was severe at first but soon eased up. They waded the river both days with trousers, shoes, and socks off, their bare legs exposed for about six inches above the knees. That leg area got severely sunburned the first day, and on the second day their hurting legs got burned even more.

By 1:00 P.M. on the second day they reached their old camp by the big boulder on the left bank of the river, about a half mile below Spencer Camp. Wesley Oliver arrived with the pack string fifteen minutes later. He left again at 4:00 P.M.

The first thing Miser and Loper did after unloading the packs was fix something to eat. They were bone tired, so they stayed in camp and took it easy for the rest of the day and slept there that night. They were on their way early the next morning.

Miser's toe was still tender, and both men had sunburned legs sore enough to make them limp when they first started walking. Fortunately Loper's lumbago had not been made much worse by the day and a half grind in towing the boat upstream. His union suit had a big gash on the right side, though, causing a severe sunburn where the skin was exposed.

They left Spencer Camp at 7:30 A.M. and after five hours of wading and rowing reached the mouth of Piute Creek. It had taken fourteen hours to make the trip upstream.

When they arrived in camp they found Christensen laid up with a pain in the small of his back. The pain had struck him about noon the day before. Hugh Hyde prepared dinner. To augment their supplies, Trimble had bought another mutton and more melons from the Navajo woman.

The rapid at the mouth of Piute Creek had a fall of eight feet. While Loper and Miser were away the others had moved all the camp equipment below the rapid. They unloaded the new provisions at the head of the rapid and carried them down to camp. Then Loper nosed each boat over the head of the rapid and ran the rest of it.

CHAPTER 5

Piute Canyon to the Colorado

On September 28 the party broke camp at the foot of Piute Rapid hoping to reach the Colorado by the end of the month. During the day they encountered several rapids, and Elwyn's passengers, Hyde and Miser, helped nose the boat over them when necessary.

As the party passed through the narrow, high-walled canyon, they leapfrogged along. Elwyn, in one boat, would pull over and stop at a ledge or sandbar where Hyde could hold the rod. Trimble would sight downstream and take the reading, then Loper would bring that boatload down past Elwyn's position to a point where Trimble could take a reading back upstream to Elwyn's station. And so it went. That day was the first time on the trip that they could see the bottom of a bucket after filling it with river water.

While carrying the line south up a creek by which they had camped, the survey team came across many v-shaped channels and potholes in the massive Wingate formation. Following behind the survey team, Miser reached a pothole a hundred feet long and sixty feet wide. The surveyors had gone around it by walking on solid, sloping sandstone at a point forty to fifty feet above the water. Miser tried going the same route and got most of the way before reaching a place that was so steep and narrow that he had to go very slowly. The farther he went the more frightened he became. Finally, deciding that life was too short to take a chance on such a place by himself, he backtracked. The survey party came back by another route to avoid recrossing the steep place where Miser had retreated from.

Later they came to the mouth of a canyon on the right and were wondering what the name of it should be. Loper told them about a man by the name of Wilson who had discovered a mesa and a way

to get up onto it. He said the mesa should be in that locality somewhere. Trimble named the canyon Wilson Creek and placed it on
the map as such.[1]

Wilson Creek was so choked with brush they had to find a way
up over the canyon wall on the east side and make the survey from
the rim. The sloping terrain across the canyon created an illusion
that made Allen wonder if the instrument had gone wrong. He dis-
puted the reading Trimble gave him, which caused a brief coolness
between them.

Some distance below Wilson Creek they came to an extensive
widening of San Juan Canyon. This was a surprise and an annoyance
to them, since it would require extra time to survey the area. They
were very low on grub again, and Oliver had made his last supply
drop. How far it was to the Colorado they did not know.

On September 30, while the surveyors worked downstream, Christensen and Miser hiked down to the mouth of a canyon coming in
from the left and located a camping place near an abandoned Indian
hogan and ramada.[2] Loper arrived soon afterward with the boats.
They carried the equipment some 100 yards to the campsite and
put up a tent. After supper the men carried the boats onto dry land
near camp.

A boulder fan at the mouth of the side canyon had clogged the
river causing a rapid with a fall of thirteen feet, so they called it
Thirteen-foot Rapid.

While the surveyors were at work Loper walked down the river
to see how far it was to the Colorado River, where a cache of food
was supposed to be waiting for them. He walked down the shore for
about two miles before his path was blocked by a ledge. There he
removed his clothes, making a bundle of them, then waded across
the river and continued on until his way was again blocked. He had
to wade back and forth several times before reaching the Colorado.
He arrived there and found the food cache about 1:00 P.M.

There appeared to be a storm brewing up the San Juan, so he was
in a hurry to get back. He knew that if the river raised a foot or more
he might not be able to make it upstream against the current. He
hurriedly put together a pack of about fifteen pounds of flour and a
few other items and started back.

On the return trip he had to go into the water and then out of it
many times. The evaporation caused him to become badly chilled,
even though he was moving with all the speed he could muster. He
began shaking all over and, to ward off the chills, he delved into his

pack and got out a bottle of vanilla extract, which he knew contained some alcohol. He drank about half of it.

In one place he got bogged down in some quicksand and floundered around until he finally got out and continued on. He said that if he had not made it out, no one would ever have found him. When he reached the place where he had undressed that morning he drank the rest of the vanilla extract and put on his clothes. By the time he reached camp he was perspiring freely and had no more chills.

It was after dark and the others were beginning to worry. They had expected him to find the Colorado in about five miles. Upon completion of the survey they found that it was twelve miles, so he had made a twenty-four mile round-trip. He had gone most of the way naked, too, so he had a nice case of sunburn.[3]

By midmorning of October 2 Trimble had finished working the canyon south of camp. The men carried the equipment and boats to the foot of Thirteen-foot Rapid while Christensen prepared lunch. At 11:25 they started downriver with Elwyn and Loper each rowing a boat while the rest of the party walked on shore and continued the survey.

On October 3 the skies were clear and the early morning temperature stood at sixty degrees. They surveyed the river and side canyons as they came to them. At one place they saw an arched-roof cave in Navajo sandstone. The river was falling, and it was again quite red.

They were delayed in one place where a side canyon and a low benchland had to be surveyed. They had to climb up a sloping bedrock by means of hand and footholds made either by cliff dwellers or gold miners. Elwyn carried the stadia rod, and they soon came to the edge of what appeared to be a shallow gulch with sheer sides. After Trimble had set up his instrument and sat sketching in the terrain across the gully, Elwyn shoved a large rock over the edge of the gully. It landed where he thought the bottom was, but to his surprise it then disappeared. He could hear it bouncing back and forth a time or two, then a splat as if it hit mud or shallow water.

It was only a short run to the Colorado, so Elwyn watched for the mouth of the gulch. As he was about to pass a sharp shoulder of the cliff, he saw it. Rowing hard, he managed to pull into the tail of the eddy caused by the jutting shoulder of the cliff. Landing the boat, he found the sandy mouth of a cave-like opening. He shoved an oar into the soft sand and tied the painter to it.

Those in his boat walked with him up the small stream for a short distance, finding it encased in a tunnel with a roof about thirty feet above the floor. They continued on for about a quarter of a mile to where the roof had broken down and sunlight came through. Great chunks of sandstone were in the streambed, but there was no rubble such as floodwater would deposit. Elwyn thought that he would surely come back some time to explore the place to its source. He wrote later that it was a great disappointment that he was not able to return and get pictures of it. As far as he knew no one else ever went into the place. There was no vegetation at the mouth of the canyon to indicate an extensive watercourse. It would be hidden from those going down the San Juan and might be missed by anyone able to go upstream, because they would be looking toward the far bend, wondering what was beyond. Now, with more than 100 feet of Lake Powell water over the little canyon, no one will ever be able to explore the place.[4]

The party reached the Colorado about sundown. They had traveled 133 miles of twisting river with walls as high as 1,300 feet and had dropped 600 feet in elevation while passing through both drab and wildly beautiful country. They had known heat, hunger, thirst, drenching rain, mud, and blowing sand. They'd had no sugar for about a week, no coffee for the last few days, and their supply of flour was completely exhausted. But their job was not done.

They made camp under a ledge on the left side of the Colorado upstream from the mouth of the San Juan. Boatman Tom Wimmer had left provisions there for them two weeks earlier. The bacon and hams were turning rancid and the potatoes were a rotting mess. But they had plenty of flour, dried fruit, coffee, and sugar, so they were in good shape compared to recent days.

Several miles up the Colorado from their camp was the Hole-in-the-Rock, down which the Mormon pioneers had blasted a trail and let their wagons down to the river on their way to settle Bluff. Loper and Trimble talked over how the party might visit the place. They decided that Loper and Elwyn should each row a boat upstream while the others walked along the bank.

The land party started out about 8:00 A.M. expecting to walk only five miles, the reported distance. Walking along the Colorado River was difficult because of the slippery, muddy banks, willow thickets, and steep, rocky slopes. They ate lunch at 11:30. By then they thought they had walked ten miles and were so tired that they about decided to turn back. The scaled distance, according to Chenoweth's map, turned out to be six and a half miles.[5] But they yelled and got an answer from Elwyn and Loper, so they continued on.

Elwyn wrote:

> I don't know who had the hardest trip, for at one place where a huge boulder lay in the river against the bank, I had to make several tries before getting past the rock.
>
> The men who walked were about exhausted by the time they arrived opposite the Hole-In-The-Rock. We rowed them across the river, where those with the energy climbed on up.[6]

The road through Hole-in-the-Rock was now impassable for even a horse. A clear stream tumbled from a big spring that gushed out of the bedrock a couple of hundred feet up the trail. A few trees grew along the stream providing some shade for the weary hikers.

In the winter of 1879–1880 the first colony of Mormons to settle Bluff constructed a road through Hole-in-the-Rock, a narrow slit in the canyon wall on the right side with an exceedingly steep gradient. The elevation at the top of the cliff was 4,900 feet, and the elevation at the river was 3,265. The length of the dugway from the top to the river was 2,600 feet, a descent of 835 feet in less than half a mile, indicating the steepness of the grade. They had to "rough lock" their wagon wheels and have men holding back on ropes behind to prevent runaways.[7]

Once at the bottom, the pioneers crossed the river in a ferry and swam the livestock across. They camped on a small flat on the left side of the river while constructing a road to the east that eventually went over Clay Hills Pass.[8]

After Loper quit placer mining on the San Juan in 1896, he lived with some of the Bluff pioneers who had been part of the Hole-in-the-Rock expedition. During that time he picked up a lot of history about that epic trek. He told the others what he could remember about it.

He said their hardships were many, but that those hardy Mormons would go through anything in the name of their religion. There was some difficult work to be done to get away from the river on the east side. Much of the road had to be blasted from rocky ledges. The whole journey took much longer than they had expected, and they often ran out of powder and had to send messengers back for more powder and other supplies.

When they were out of powder they built big bonfires to heat the rocks red hot. They would have all their containers filled with cold water standing by to dump on the hot rocks causing them to shatter. The fractured rocks could then be worked loose with pick and shovel to make the road.

A shortage of food developed, too. And, because of snow on the ground, the livestock had poor grazing.

Loper said, "There was one child born there—to Mr. and Mrs. Decker and the baby was christened—LENA—and in the course of time became the wife of Frank Hammond—I never heard of any deaths that occurred on the trip."

Loper was acquainted with many of those pioneers since he had lived among them in the home of Kumen Jones for two years. He said, "The memory of the many kindnesses and of 'UNCLE KUMEN AND AUNT MARY' will always be a bright spot in my memory and that old pioneer bishop—was one of Gods [sic] own people and one of the truest Christians it was ever my lot to meet."[9]

The Mormon pioneers did *not* make the steps that the surveyors found carved in the Hole-in-the-Rock crevice. The steps were chopped out later by Robert B. Stanton's men of the Hoskinini Mining Company so that supplies could be carried down to the river by manpower and pack animals.[10]

After hearing Loper's story, the men all rode back to camp in the boats. To relieve his blistered hands, Elwyn let Hyde and Miser take turns at the oars. Along the way they stopped at a drift pile and loaded wood to take back with them.

The San Juan was still running red with mud when they got back to camp. Elwyn was keenly aware of the unusual quietness of the Colorado. At this particular place there was very little fall, so the water did not make much sound. This was quite a contrast to the fast, noisy San Juan that had sung its wild song to them at every camp for two and a half months. Elwyn would miss it.

On October 5 Trimble and his survey crew worked around the confluence of the two rivers. Loper stayed in camp to mend his clothes. His underwear had been almost entirely replaced with flour-sack patches, and he used the same material for patching his overalls. His shoes were in better shape than those of the rodmen because his work was more with the boats than climbing rocky ledges.

Shortly after noon five men from the Chenoweth party, who had just finished surveying Cataract Canyon, stopped at camp. They were: Sidney Paige, geologist; Eugene C. La Rue, hydraulic engineer; Emery Kolb, photographer and boatman; Henry Rausch, Emery Kolb's assistant; and Ellsworth (Ed) Kolb, boatman. Loper and Ed

Kolb had been companions on a boat trip starting at Glenwood Springs, Colorado, so they were glad to see each other.

The Paige party brought a boat loaded with fresh supplies to leave with the San Juan team. They all seemed greatly concerned about the condition of Loper's clothing until he told them he had better ones in his duffel bag.

Elwyn's memoirs tell us:

> Someone noticed a newspaper in one of their boats and began to read the headlines. Every item was news to us, however, as we had seen no newspapers since embarking on our journey. Mr. Miser went on with the Chenoweth party, as his job was finished, the geology of the Colorado was already on record. We would miss the level headed, well-considered, opinions of this wise Arkensawyer.[11]

Kelly Trimble recorded an elevation of 3,240 feet for the mouth of the San Juan. E. C. La Rue claimed that was twenty feet too high. This set off a violent argument between Bert Loper and La Rue, since Loper was fiercely loyal to his boss. Repercussions would come later.

Miser left in a boat at 4:15 P.M. with Sidney Paige, Emery Kolb, and E. C. La Rue. They planned to stop at Aztec Creek for a hike to Rainbow Bridge before going on to Lee's Ferry.

CHAPTER 6

Cataract Canyon

While Kelly Trimble and his crew were surveying the lower San Juan Canyon, a party led by topographic engineer William R. Chenoweth had been busy surveying side canyons in Glen Canyon. Chenoweth had been assigned to survey Cataract Canyon on the Colorado, but had waited until September for a favorable stage of water to do it. He was now ready to begin that task, and with him were Frank Stoudt, recorder; Leigh Lint, rodman; Harry C. Tasker, rodman; John Clogston, cook; Ellsworth L. Kolb, boatman; Sidney Paige, geologist; and Eugene C. La Rue, hydraulic engineer.[1]

Emery Kolb and his assistant Henry Rausch, using Emery's boat the *Edith*, also went along to photograph the scenery and take movies of the boats running the rapids. The *Edith* was a survivor of the Kolb brothers' 1911 trip.[2] When Emery launched her at Green River she leaked so much she had to be taken out and repaired. Emery wanted to photograph the Land of Standing Rocks near the head of Cataract Canyon and was equipped to camp apart from the main party if a climb out of the canyon was necessary.[3]

Chenoweth had successfully completed a survey of the Snake River in Idaho in 1920, and Leigh Lint and John Clogston had been two of his crew members on that survey.

Three boats had been built for this expedition and paid for by the Southern California Edison Company. Two of them were of the Galloway type and were built on the same lines as the *Edith*, but larger, because ten men in all had to be transported down the river, and no supplies were available after leaving the town of Green River until the Cataract Canyon survey was completed. These two boats

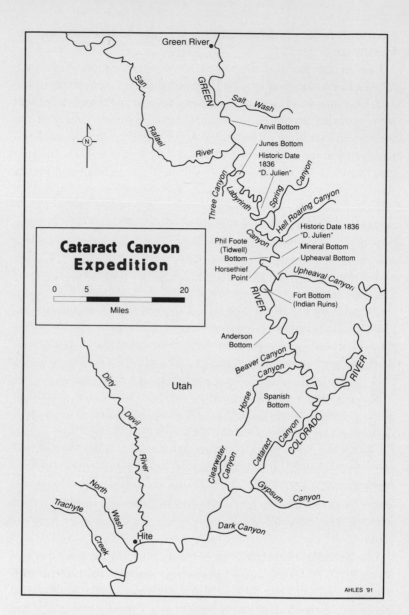

Green River

San
Rafael

GREEN

Salt Wash

River

Anvil Bottom

Junes Bottom
Historic Date
1836
"D. Julien"

Three Canyon
Labyrinth
Spring Canyon

Hell Roaring Canyon

Canyon

Historic Date 1836
"D. Julien"

Phil Foote
(Tidwell)
Bottom

Mineral Bottom

Upheaval Bottom

Horsethief
Point

Upheaval Canyon

RIVER

Fort Bottom
(Indian Ruins)

**Cataract Canyon
Expedition**

0   5   20

Miles

Anderson
Bottom

Beaver Canyon

Canyon

Utah

Horse
Canyon

Spanish
Bottom

COLORADO RIVER

Dirty

Devil

River

Clearwater
Canyon

Cataract
Canyon

COLORADO

Gypsum
Canyon

North
Wash

Trachyte

Dark Canyon

Creek

Hite

AHLES '91

were named the *L.A.* and the *Edison*. The third boat had different
lines from the others, being short and broad with deep sloping sides
and a flat deck, and was equipped with an outboard motor. Its shape
so amused the men that they at first dubbed it the "Tub." Later it
was christened the *Static*. All boats were of wood, flat bottomed, with

a ten-inch rocker both bow and stern. Emery Kolb's *Edith* was the fourth boat.

Late in the morning of September 10, 1921, Emery Kolb took movies of La Rue, Tasker, and Paige as they left Green River in the *L.A.* One man was seated in the rowing compartment and the others were sprawled on the cargo hatches. Kolb reported: "Many of the townspeople of Green River came down, partly to see the start and partly to feature in the movies. Some husky Paiute Indians camping nearby gave a western flavor to the scene." Emery Kolb and Henry Rausch left in the afternoon.

The three men in the *L.A.* arrived at the junction of the Green and Grand (Colorado) rivers on the afternoon of September 13.[4] The next day they climbed out of the gorge through a side canyon one mile above the mouth of the Green to the top of the cliffs 1,200 feet above the river. From there they had a grand view of the Land of Standing Rocks.

Chenoweth and the rest of the survey party were two days later leaving Green River. Lint operated the motorboat *Static*, and at first they tried towing the rowboat, *Edison*, behind. When that did not work too well, they lashed the two boats together side by side with a cork life preserver between to act as a buffer.

About midafternoon of the second day they overtook Emery Kolb in the *Edith*. Kolb had spent a lot of time taking pictures of the red-rock spires in the vicinity of the Double Bow Knot. They roped the *Edith* alongside and the passengers sprawled over the decks of the three boats. While they chugged along, Emery Kolb, an ex-lieutenant of the Signal Corps, began instructing the others in sema-phore by the oscillating-arm method. The Kolbs had learned in their first trip that no voice would carry for any distance in or near the rapids.

In a few hours the steady hum of the outboard motor gave way to a loud clatter. The water pump had not been designed for use with such muddy water, and the packing for the cooling system had burned out. From then on they had to syphon water from a five-gallon can to the engine's cooling system to keep it from overheating.[5]

Above the confluence of the Green and the Grand (Colorado) they hit a sandbar and broke the propeller shaft. After that they removed the outboard motor, stowed it in the boat, and reverted to using the oars. They arrived at the mouth of the Green about noon on September 15.

Right after lunch Chenoweth began the topographic survey along the river and to the 3,900-foot elevation. This survey, like that on the San Juan and in Glen Canyon, was being done to determine the storage basin of the proposed dam in Glen Canyon.

The *Static* was designated as the cook boat and given over to Clogston to arrange for the food and utensils that would come into daily use. Clogston was an experienced and exceptionally good camp cook. He had a wonderful sheet-iron stove, complete with oven and collapsible pipes. It was large enough that under Clogston's efficient management it turned out delicious meals sufficient for ten men, yet small enough to slip into a gunnysack and slide under the oarsman's seat. He had two boxes left over from the Snake River trip that contained the dishes, cleverly nested to save space but accessible. These boxes were hinged and equipped with straps for making portages or carrying when there was work away from the river. He had water buckets and a large pan, in which to clear the river water for culinary purposes, along with other conveniences, which all had to be stored in the holds of the *Static*.[6]

The party camped at the head of Cataract Canyon on the evening of September 15. At its head, the canyon, with its sloping brown and grey walls, was not especially impressive, having little of the symmetry and strength of some other canyons of the Southwest. Only at the top were the walls brightly colored. Forty-mile-long Cataract Canyon went from 1,300 feet deep at its head to over 2,000 feet near its mouth. It was the deepest gorge in all Utah canyon country. The Colorado dropped 425 feet in that distance—an average fall of more than ten feet to the mile. It had more than forty thundering rapids (sixty-four by some counts). All of the rapids below Mile 190 are now drowned by Lake Powell when it is full. Major Powell had named it Cataract Canyon in 1869 after his party had spent twelve grueling days portaging and lining the seething rapids.[7]

On the morning of September 16, Emery Kolb and Henry Rausch climbed the cliffs to photograph the Land of Standing Rocks and take movies from the rim while the other men portaged the supplies around Rapid Number One. Ellsworth Kolb ran the three boats through empty. Ellsworth ran Rapids Two, Three, and Four with full loads, getting a shower each time but having no mishap, while Emery trailed along in the *Edith* taking movies of the action. That day the surveyors carried the survey to a point just below Rapid Five. They made camp above the rapid.

Chenoweth party in Cataract Canyon. Left to right: Leigh Lint, William R. Chenoweth, Eugene C. La Rue, Harry C. Tasker, Ellsworth L. Kolb, John Clogston, Henry Rausch, Sidney Paige, and Emery Kolb. (Courtesy of Emery Kolb Collection, Cline Library, Northern Arizona University)

On the seventeenth Ellsworth ran the boats over six rapids. He would take one through and then go back for another. Rapid Five below camp was a bad one, and it did not seem possible that a boat could go through without upsetting. Ellsworth enjoyed running the bad ones. He ducked low to avoid being knocked out of the boat by the waves. La Rue took some moving pictures so they could see how it was done.[8]

In their account of the trip the Kolbs tell us:

The oarsman is seated with his back to the bow in the usual manner but the position of the boat is reversed when bad water is reached. Facing the danger, with bow pointed up stream, the single occupant retards the speed by pulling against the current. If rocks obstruct the channel, the flat-bottomed boat is easily turned at an angle with one or two pulls on one oar and a push on the other; two or three strong pulls on both oars take the boat out of one channel and into another, then the boat is straightened again with the current until a new danger threatens. Like a paddler in a canoe he faces the danger, but unlike the canoeman he travels slower than the current instead of going faster. This is the theory.

Great waves that crest over the boat and oarsman, blinding spray and conflicting currents that place at naught all his skill, and a multitude of difficulties that takes the oars and control from his hands, sometimes makes a different thing in practice. But it is the uncertainty of any game that thrills![9]

The next day La Rue decided to try his luck at the oars. He took one boat over small Rapids Eleven and Twelve, hitting a rock in number Twelve that gave him a pretty good jolt. The Kolbs and Rausch ran the other three boats through.

On September 19 they carried the survey to 16.6 miles below the junction. The boats were trailing the survey by two miles, having some bad rapids to pass. The Kolbs "spent half a day plotting a course through the twisting channels and boulder-strewn currents of this series of rapids." They made sketches showing the hidden rocks, which were located by trees on the shore. They memorized these sketches so well that they were able to run the boats through safely, although "they leaped, reared and dived like a bronco on a lariat." Two boats tapped hidden rocks but were undamaged.

On September 21 La Rue noted:

> Survey moved down to mile 21. We are camped just above Rapid 35. Passed over some good ones today. I rode the boat over some of them. Some bucking. Chenoweth has killed three rattlesnakes to date. Opposite our camp at Rapid 35 the walls are 2400 feet high. Tonight we set fire to great piles of driftwood. The flames were 30 feet high and lighted up the whole canyon. A number of pictures were taken by the light from the fires. All well except the cook.[10]

On September 22 La Rue reported, "All well including the cook." On the twenty-third they extended the survey five miles along mostly smooth water, their best day up to that time, and camped 29.62 miles below the junction. The two Kolbs and Sidney Paige climbed out to the top of the rim opposite camp to take pictures. They came back down in the dark, a precarious maneuver. When they reached the river they set fire to some driftwood to help light up the river. Those in camp built a big fire on their side, too, so that the three men could see their way across the river to camp. The swift current swept the boat some distance below camp, but they landed safely.

The next day La Rue stopped the party to survey a dam site, so they only moved three-quarters of a mile before making a new camp. They could almost see where they had camped the night before. La Rue, who took a bath in a clear pool in a side canyon that day, reported that the water was fine but almost as cold as ice. Emery Kolb and Rausch went on downriver in the afternoon to stop at Dark Canyon, about two miles below. The main party hoped to catch them the next day.

La Rue noted:

> We are camped tonight on a bar that is but a few feet above the river. The walls are sheer on both sides so we can't get higher up. I hope there is no flood due to hit here tonight; a small flood would drown the whole bunch, for we are 20 feet below the high water mark. Here's hoping we are still here in the morning.[11]

The dam site survey took all of the twenty-fifth and part of the twenty-sixth, when they moved on another mile to Rapid 44 and made camp. This looked like a bad one, so they portaged all the cargo around it. In late afternoon Ellsworth (Ed) Kolb ran Emery's boat through so Emery could take movies.

In camp that night Lint boiled his underwear in a bucket of water. But when Emery put a brown shirt in with it, Lint's underclothes, which went in a dirty white, came out a dirtier brown!

At noon on September 27 they reached Rapid 45 opposite the mouth of Dark Canyon, where their troubles began. This rapid had lashing reflex waves at the end that churned and foamed among the jagged rocks. Near the center was a sort of shoestring island of protruding rocks paralleling the left shore. A vibrating roar seemed to shake the rock walls to their foundations.

Ellsworth Kolb made the mistake of not removing the cargo from the *L.A.* Perhaps he was tired of portaging. Maybe he felt a certain amount of ballast would help in violent water. At any rate, the boat struck a rock near the head of the rapid and wound up caught between two rocks, partly on its edge. As the stern shot up, the bow went under, instantly filling the cockpit with water. The current held the boat pinned fast against the rocks.

Kolb worked hard to get it loose but with no success. What frustration he must have felt! He was offshore about fifty feet, so they were able to get a rope out to him. Then he rocked the boat while the eight men on shore pulled on the rope. They still could not move it.

They then rigged an A-frame to hold the rope above the water so Ellsworth could go hand over hand along the rope. He had quite a struggle in the swift water getting to shore. They worked with the boat for a couple of hours, then stopped for lunch.

After lunch Ellsworth decided to run the *Edison* through the rapid, this time emptying the boat first. Even so, he got hung up on more rocks near where the *L.A.* was resting. He climbed out on the rocks and teetered the boat until it came loose, then he jumped on it as it entered the steep part of the rapid. The waves were six to eight feet high, but he took her through and landed safely below the rapid.

Next he started through in the *Static*. This time he missed the rocks but got caught in some high waves that proved too much for that boat. The waves flipped her over with Ellsworth underneath. He soon worked his way out and grabbed onto the side-ropes. By then he was going down through the high waves of the lower end of the rapid. He tried to climb on top of the overturned boat but could not make it. When the boat was about to enter another rapid, he let go and swam to shore.

La Rue reached him first and, finding him safe, scrambled over the rocks as fast as he could to try to catch the boat. When it got caught in an eddy, La Rue got below it and remained there until the *Edison* could be brought down to rescue it. They hauled the *Static* ashore and righted her, then towed the two boats back upstream to camp. By then it was evening and Clogston had supper about ready.

The *L.A.* was still on the rocks, her hatches full and half covered with water. In the hatches were La Rue's grip and suitcase, as well as several bedrolls. But of more importance, the hatches held the map case that contained the results of Chenoweth's summer's work. Everything would have to stay in the boat until morning.

They divided up the bedding and contemplated their next move. It was apparent they would have to unload the *L.A.* to get her off the rocks. Before going to bed they made a pulley for an improvised tram to accomplish that job. The pulley was made by sawing a wheel from a five-inch cottonwood log and attaching boards on either side to hold the ropes in place and the bolt on which the pulley ran.

The next morning, September 28, all worked to unload the *L.A.*

and get her off the rocks. They attached a swing seat to the boards of the pulley. Emery, the smallest of the group, sat in the swing and pulled himself over to the boat. Then they hauled the pulley rig back and forth from boat to shore with sacks full of cargo until the *L.A.* was empty.

A lot of the cargo was wet. Watertight jars had saved La Rue's films, but his cigars and clothes were soaked. Paige's films, camera, and clothes were wet. Sacks of flour, sugar, cornmeal, and beans were a soggy mess after soaking in the hatch all night. Fortunately, Chenoweth's maps were dry.

They finally got the boat dislodged at 2:00 P.M., twenty-eight hours after she had hit the rocks. They remained there another night drying things out.[12]

They were now thirty-three miles below the junction. There was only one more bad rapid ahead of them before they would be out of Cataract Canyon.

The party next passed over three rapids. Then they stopped at the head of Milecrag Bend to survey a dam site, which took them until noon the next day.

Emery Kolb and Rausch had gone ahead of them the day before. When they came to the south end of Milecrag Bend they saw a desert bighorn, which Emery killed with a twenty-two rifle. When the survey party caught up, they feasted on mutton chops.

On October 2, a Sunday, the party ran the line to the Fremont River, where the survey of Cataract Canyon ended. Chenoweth had surveyed the next section of river while waiting for the right stage of water to survey Cataract Canyon. They reached Hite by noon and were the guests of Thomas G. Humphrey for Sunday dinner. In mid-afternoon, after filling up on peaches, watermelons, and tomatoes, Chenoweth, Paige, Ed Kolb, and La Rue went on in one boat. The rest stayed at Hite hoping to fix the *Static*'s engine.

Those in the leading boat traveled down sixteen miles to Red Canyon. They had most of their beds, but no grub except a can of soup and some peanut butter. After sundown they built a fire and were ready to open the soup when they saw another boat coming. It was Emery Kolb and Rausch. The other two boats were not far behind. By then it was getting dark, so those on shore built up the fire to signal the other boats where to land. With the party together again, they had a good supper by the light of the campfire.

On October 3 they camped at the mouth of Hanson Creek, where

The boat *L.A.* stranded on rocks in Dark Canyon Rapid. The crew made a pulley from a section of a five-inch cottonwood log and made a swing in which Emery Kolb went over to unload the boat so it could be lifted and pulled off the rocks. (Courtesy of Emery Kolb Collection, Cline Library, Northern Arizona University)

the party would split up. The Kolbs, Rausch, Paige, and La Rue would leave from this camp. Until about mid-December, Chenoweth and his crew would resume surveying the side canyons to the 3,900-foot level, advancing by boat down Glen Canyon. They unloaded all the boats so that personal belongings and equipment could be sorted out. Those remaining behind got busy writing letters and packaging exposed film to be taken out the next morning.

The five men leaving took two boats and made the twelve miles to Hall's Crossing by lunchtime, where they were met by Tom Wimmer and a man named Holland. Wimmer, from Green River, was employed by the government to bring in supplies to crews working along the Colorado. The two had hauled a load of supplies from Green River, the last stretch by team and wagon. The 1,500 pounds of supplies were for the Trimble party at the mouth of the San Juan. After loading the supplies in one boat, they made another sixteen miles before making camp.

At 2:00 P.M. the next day, October 5, they arrived at the San Juan where they found the Trimble party and delivered the supplies. The Trimble party got busy writing letters to be taken out.

H. D. Miser from the Trimble group left in the late afternoon with La Rue and the others who were leaving the river. They planned to camp at the mouth of Aztec Canyon in order to hike up to Rainbow Bridge the next day.

CHAPTER 7

San Juan Mouth to Lee's Ferry

On October 6 Trimble's crew began surveying side canyons that emptied into Glen Canyon below the mouth of the San Juan. The red-rock walls of Glen Canyon had numerous picturesque alcoves and water-carved glens, which led Major Powell to give the canyon its name. One of the more spectacular of these, the Music Temple, was located a short distance below the San Juan on the left side behind a low, willow-fringed bench on which grew a little grove of box elder and cottonwood trees. The vast grotto, carved out of rock, with a clear pool at the upper end, had been formed by dripping springs where ferns, columbines, and water plants bordered the seeps.

Major Powell wrote, "Here we bring our camp. When 'Old Shady' sings us a song at night, we are pleased to find that this hollow in the rock is filled with sweet sounds. It was doubtless made for an academy of music by its storm-born architect; so we name it Music Temple." [1]

Trimble's crew must have visited Music Temple, if only long enough to sing a couple of songs and to test the sound effect of the grotto against Powell's description. This remained a favorite stop for float parties until it was covered by the waters of Lake Powell.

The surveyors worked on down the Colorado another mile or so and camped on the right side above a nice sloping bedrock landing. Christensen had been suffering back pains for several days, so Hyde was doing most of the cooking. With the new boatload of fresh grub, they ate well and were in high spirits.

They made several more camps before reaching Oak Creek, where there was considerable surveying to be done. Christensen had been having stomach problems on top of his rheumatism and, according to Loper, "was not improving in his disposition at all."

On October 12 they moved from Oak Creek and camped on the right bank about a mile downriver. The next day, after the breakfast chores were done, Christensen and Loper took a walk up through a narrow canyon to where the survey team was at work. On the way up, Christensen kept complaining of a pain in his right side. After the two had visited with the survey crew for a while, they returned down the canyon. When they reached the river the two hot and thirsty men flopped down on their bellies and took a big drink of river water, then sat down in the shade of some willows to rest. In a little while Christensen leaned over and vomited up the water. Loper told him that he had all the symptoms of appendicitis. That night when the survey crew came in Christensen told Trimble he was quitting, giving appendicitis as the reason.

Allen, the recorder, had been sick for several days, too. Maybe he had a touch of homesickness since he had left a bride of a few weeks behind to come on the trip. He said he wanted to go home as soon as possible. Finally Trimble told Loper to take the two men out to Flagstaff and look for another cook and rodman. Elwyn could take Allen's place as recorder. On the morning of October 14 the three left for Lee's Ferry, the closest place they could exit Glen Canyon.

H. W. Dennis, chief engineer for the Southern California Edison Company, and T. G. Jardine, Trimble's boss in the topographic branch of the Geological Survey, were at the ferry with mail for the crew. Loper, Allen, and Christensen enjoyed letters from their families.

On the seventeenth Jardine and Dennis took the three men to Flagstaff by truck. Flagstaff, located along the Santa Fe Railroad at the base of the San Francisco Mountains, was the ranching and trading center of northern Arizona. At Flagstaff they luxuriated in a bath and a good supper in a first-class hotel. What a change after months under the sky!

By October nineteenth they located a new rodman and a cook. Loper wrote:

> Well we finally got what we were looking for and two good men too but I am afraid that their moral character was not up to much but as a cook it would be hard to beat the one we got for the job for he seemed to lie awake of nights concocting some

new dish out of the food we had I believe his name was Childers and the other was Pat Gallagher.[2]

When the group got back to the river a couple of days later, Loper was expecting to have to row back upstream. But Jardine and Dennis deemed it better to send a power boat. They loaded in extra provisions and towed the rowboat behind. In due time they reached camp, which they found just below the mouth of Aztec Creek.

On October 15 the survey crew had worked from the camp below Oak Creek on down to the mouth of Aztec Creek. The Hough party of the Coast and Geodetic Survey, which was doing work in Glen Canyon, too, had joined them there. The Trimble and Hough parties combined for a six-mile hike to visit Rainbow Bridge.

An unnamed young fellow in the Hough party fancied himself a walker and Elwyn, ever on the lookout for a challenge, paired off with him in a walking race. They kept about even until they entered Bridge Canyon a mile below the bridge itself.[3] There Elwyn saw that the trail narrowed along the sidehill so that only one person at a time could travel it. He made a sudden burst of speed and got to the trail ahead of the other fellow. That assured him of being the first to reach the great natural arch. The other man was right on his heels all the way, though, and the rest of the party was strung out for some distance behind.

Rainbow Bridge, one of the natural wonders of the world, was formed from the thick Navajo sandstone that dominated the area. The river survey parties were among the first Anglos to go to the bridge from the river.

The giant stone arch was first seen by white men on August 14, 1909. Professor Byron Cummings, of the University of Utah, and W. B. Douglas, a surveyor for the United States Land Office, were led to it by a Paiute Indian named Nasuah Begay.[4]

Elwyn and his friend from the Hough party climbed to the top of the cliff against which the bridge's south abutment clung, the cliff being about forty feet above the bridge. From there they had a grand view of Navajo Mountain and the intervening maze of rock-ribbed canyons. They tied a rope to a rock and let themselves down to where they could walk out on top of the bridge.

The next day Trimble's party ran the survey up Aztec Creek several miles beyond the mouth of Bridge Canyon. By late afternoon they were twelve miles from camp and had not yet reached the 3,900-

foot contour. They cached their rods and the survey instruments and made the long walk to camp.

Elwyn said he dreaded the long hike back the next day to the instruments. Their only consolation was that they had plenty of drinking water and a cool stream to wade in when their feet got hot and sore. When they reached the cached instruments they had to rest awhile before taking up their work.

The canyon had narrowed to where their footing was often on bare bedrock. They had worked only two miles more and reached the 3,900-foot level, so Trimble called in the rodmen and told them they could start back to camp. Elwyn said, "If the prospect of a fourteen-mile trek could be good news, that was good news." Already tired, they were very leg weary when they dragged into camp several hours later.[5]

On October 21 they took the day off. Finding some canned milk and chocolate among the supplies, Elwyn made a large bread pan of rich, creamy fudge. Sitting around and playing rummy all day, everyone ate more of it than they should. Some of them, including Trimble, got diarrhea. Elwyn was forbidden to make any more fudge.

On October 22 Loper and the new men rejoined the party. The new rodman was Pat Powell (whom Loper had called Gallagher) and the cook was Childers. Childers was a wonder and soon learned to cook in a dutch oven. Trimble was never very happy with Pat Powell, however, who turned out to be a troublemaker.

The job of recorder suited Elwyn fine. He had done some similar book work for Wolverton on the desert survey when he was just out of high school.[6]

Loper wrote:

When the recorder quit that job fell to Elwyn, and how good it makes a man feel to recommend a person and to always find that person on the job for I heard Mr. Trimble say that Elwyn was one of the best rodmen that he ever had and then to be able to fill the position of recorder and he was also some boatman and I kind a think that if he had been called on for something else he would have been on the job for that, too.[7]

The new cook made cake in the dutch oven, made jam from dried fruit, and made biscuits that were delicious. He was unhappy when left alone for very long, though. Once, when the others had been out all day, he said there had been nothing around except one bird, and he said it had made the most mournful cry he had ever heard.

Powell, the rodman, was a thorn in the boss's side, especially when he made snide remarks about Southerners. He and Hyde were at odds, too. He once offered to fight Hyde, one of them to take a knife and the other an ax. Elwyn thought that if Powell had made him that challenge, he would have called his bluff. Hyde let it pass, though he hated and feared Powell from then on.[8]

It took another month for the party to work its way down the river, surveying side canyons as they came to them. Klondike Bar on the right bank of the river, an important gold mining site in the 1890s, was staked by Louis M. Chaffin, William B. "Billy" Hay, and others. They named it for the gold rush to Klondike in the Yukon. Loper said there was some good money taken out by them and that after taking out the cream they sold the bar. A trail with chiseled steps led out to the canyon rim. Boaters on Lake Powell can still see some of the steps in the slickrock walls near Klondike Point.[9]

It took them several days to map the area along each side of Rock Creek. One day they had to use hand and footholds in sloping sandstone, which had been made by early-day miners or prehistoric man, to reach their work area on a benchland above.

A few days later the party took a day off to rest. Elwyn spotted deer tracks near camp, so he and Hyde decided to go deer hunting. Hyde had the gun, and Elwyn went along to help bring in the meat, if any. They followed the fresh deer tracks out of Rock Creek Canyon to the benchland above, upriver along the bench, then down to the river bottom. Then, to their surprise, the tracks led directly back toward camp.

Within 100 yards of camp, the tracks ended at the water's edge. The deer had apparently swum across the river to a brush-covered bar opposite camp. The two men had walked several miles and ended up where they started. Telling the others where they thought the deer had gone, they untied one of the boats and shoved off for the other side. Before crossing the river Hyde had suggested that they draw straws to see who would get the first shot. Elwyn won the draw.

Landing near a cutbank, they climbed up to more level ground where they came to a stand of young oak brush. Thinking the deer would be in the brush along the base of the talus, they walked along the outer edge peering into the shrubbery hoping to spot a buck. But they saw none the whole length of the bar. Then Elwyn worked his way back toward the lower end of the bar and flushed out a young buck. It bounded out into the shallow water, which extended out into the middle of the river.

Taking quick aim, Elwyn was about to shoot, when he saw Trimble in the line of sight across the river. Trimble was leaping in the air in his excitement and yelling "Shoot him!"

Elwyn waited until the buck was out of line with camp, then he fired. The buck's tail ducked, but he kept right on going.

"You missed him a mile," yelled Trimble.

Elwyn got off another quick shot. Wounded, the deer turned and started back toward him. Within a few yards of shore, it dropped into the water and began to float away. Just then Hyde came panting up. "You never let me have the second shot," he accused.

Elwyn jumped into the boat and grabbed the oars while Hyde untied the painter. They shoved off quickly and sped after the floating buck. When they caught up to the dead deer, they had to struggle to bring it over the side without swamping the boat. Then Elwyn rowed back upriver to camp.

Shortly after this Loper returned from a visit to Fowler's camp, downriver, where he had been visiting with Tom Wimmer, an old friend from Green River.[10] Wimmer had let him borrow an outboard motor, which made the trip back to camp quite easy. As he approached camp along a stretch of straight river, he could see the men in camp running back and forth from the river to camp and back again. He wondered what was happening until he saw the lungs and windpipe of a deer floating down the river.

When he arrived in camp he learned that there were still some deer across the river in the thick brush, but that Trimble would not let them kill any more. Hyde was rather glum, so Loper asked Trimble to let Hyde kill one and he would take it down to Fowler's camp. When Trimble agreed, Loper rowed Hyde to the opposite shore. In a few minutes he had climbed the slope to where he could see several deer. He picked out a fat buck and brought it down with one shot.

Next morning Loper put the dressed deer in the bottom of the boat. Then he loaded a pile of wood on top of it and headed for Fowler's camp. He knew there was no wood near Fowler's camp except willows, which make a poor campfire. When he pulled into camp he told the cook that he had loaded the wood and it would be up to the cook to unload it. The cook was glad to get the wood and started to unload it. When he came to the venison he gave a shout of surprise and pleasure. Fresh meat was a special treat to them at that time.[11]

The party now had company from time to time, since there was the group from the Coast and Geodetic Survey and other outfits working along this part of the river and boats of these parties would pass up and down the stream. Boatmen Tom Wimmer and Babe Howland had been hired by the government to supply these parties.

The Trimble party made two different camps on Wild Horse Bar, the first at the head of it beside a huge pile of driftwood, making it handy for firewood. The site was directly under a trail that had been made over the sloping bedrock by drilling holes in the sandstone and driving pins in the holes to support the logs and poles that went to make up the lower side of the trail. Wild Horse Bar was named for a lone dapple-gray horse that had lived on that bar for many years. Next the survey moved down to a grove of thick scrub oak that protected them from the wind.[12]

One night, after a light drizzle, the first real cold spell came on the river. Icicles decorated bushes the next morning. After that the half-quilts and canvas tarpaulins the men had for bedding were far from adequate.

On December 1 they broke camp at Rock Creek and moved down to the mouth of West Canyon. They called it Beaver Creek because Loper caught one beaver there after Tom Wimmer lent him some traps. He sold the pelt to Trimble for ten dollars, and that was the extent of his beaver trapping. They camped at West Canyon five days. At one place they crossed a lazy little side stream thirty-two times before reaching a spot where they could climb out and survey the upper benches. By that time ice froze in the pans every night. Elwyn said his skin grew thick to compensate for the lack of bedding. Trimble was the only man in the party who had either a coat or jacket. He saw Elwyn's teeth chattering one day and insisted he take the coat.

On December 6 they moved down to Fowler's camp. While they were there, Chenoweth's party came through. That group had finished surveying the side canyons of Glen Canyon above the mouth of the San Juan and were headed for Lee's Ferry. Chenoweth gave Trimble his remaining supplies before going on.

After leaving Fowler's camp the Trimble party surveyed on down the river, camping below the mouth of Sentinel Rock Creek.[13] This completed their survey. When they broke camp on December 15, they left their sheet-iron stove on a rocky point and headed for Lee's Ferry.

As Elwyn rowed along, Trimble sat in the stern of his boat. Even with his coat on he was cold, while Elwyn was warm from rowing.

"Blake," Trimble said, "let me row a while. I am freezing."

Elwyn let him have the oars, but in about fifteen minutes he fell farther behind Loper's boat. Besides that, his hands had begun to blister. "Take back your oars," Trimble growled. "I would rather freeze."

When they reached Lee's Ferry they pulled the boats out of the water and loaded them on trucks for the trip to Flagstaff. At Flagstaff the men received their pay and prepared to go their separate ways.

Elwyn and Hugh Hyde took a room together at the hotel in Flagstaff and were sitting talking just before bedtime when a knock came on the door.

"Let me in, Hugh," came the voice. It was Powell, who apparently wanted to bedevil Hyde one more time. He did not know that Elwyn was in the room. Hyde grabbed his thirty-thirty rifle, which stood nearby. "What do you want?" he demanded.

Elwyn spoke up then. "Go on away, Pat," he said.

"Oh, are you in there, Blake?" and he made some light remark and went on down the hall.

There was a cattle train on the tracks that would be leaving for Los Angeles in a day or two. Elwyn said:

> Some of the fellows made arrangements to ride the train, whether with, or without the knowledge of the train crew, I do not know.
>
> Pat wanted me to go along, to get Hugh and myself arrested, for me to steal Hugh's money and abandon him, just so he would learn about life. Of course I would not consider such a thing. Such animosity between the two was beyond me. Anyway I had my ticket by train, and was soon on my way.[14]

On the train ride to Gallup, Elwyn had time to reflect on the five months he had spent on the San Juan and Colorado rivers. He recalled the towering cliffs, the raging floods, the mighty sand waves, the river when it was so low, the rapids, climbing all those rocky ledges, the grandeur of that isolated area. These things had all made for a memorable trip. The linotype job he was returning to, or even the work on his homestead, would be tame by comparison. The trip had changed his whole outlook on life. He had developed more self-confidence, for he was sure he had done a good job. Moreover, he had been down the river. The sounds, the smell of the floods, and the stunning beauty of the canyons would remain with him forever. And, like many who would follow him, he felt he now owned a part of the river, and the river surely owned a part of him.

PART TWO
GREEN RIVER
EXPEDITION

CHAPTER 8

Green River to Red Canyon

In the late spring of 1922 Elwyn Blake received a telegram from Washington asking him to join the U.S. Geological Survey on the upper Green River. He was overjoyed at the offer and accepted it promptly.

The party, under the leadership of Kelly Trimble, would survey potential dam sites and map the river and the unsurveyed deeper canyons. They assembled July 8, 1922, and made camp on Scott's Bottom a few miles below the town of Green River, Wyoming. The party members were: Kelly W. Trimble, topographic engineer and chief of party; John B. Reeside, Jr., Washington, D.C., geologist; Ralph R. Woolley, Salt Lake City, hydraulic engineer and recorder; H. L. Stoner, Salt Lake City, field engineer for the Utah Power and Light Company, in charge of finances (the work was being done by the government and the expenses were born by the electric company); Bert Loper, head boatman; Leigh B. Lint, Weiser, Idaho; H. Elwyn Blake, Jr., rodmen and boatmen; and John Clogston, cook.[1]

All except Reeside and Woolley had been on either the San Juan or the Cataract Canyon surveys of the year before. Elwyn heard later that Trimble had wanted him for recorder, but that Woolley had insisted on that job for himself.

In 1914 the Reclamation Service had located a proposed dam site in Horseshoe Canyon below Flaming Gorge and mapped the reservoir basin from the dam site upstream to Green River, Wyoming. Flaming Gorge Dam was *not* built here, but in Red Canyon about twenty-five miles farther downstream. The Utah Power and Light Company also had surveyed portions of Gray and Desolation canyons for pro-

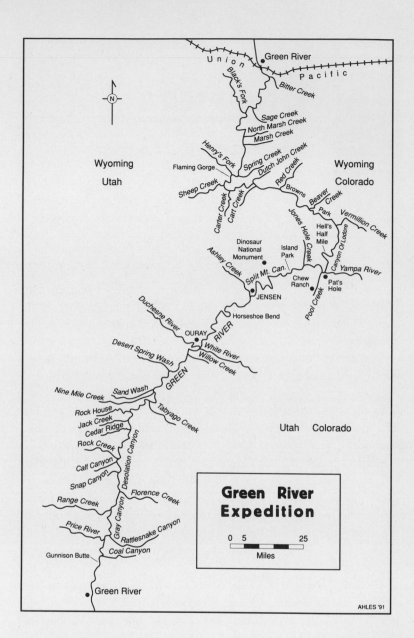

posed power projects. The purpose of the present expedition was to link these and other isolated surveys to complete a topographic map and profile of the Green River from a point near the Utah-Wyoming border to Green River, Utah.

Three boats for the expedition had been built in Wilmington, California, and shipped by rail to Green River, Wyoming. Two of

Green River 1922 survey party, left to right: John Clogston, J. B. Reeside, Bert Loper, H. L. Stoner, Leigh Lint, K. W. Trimble, Ralph R. Woolley, Elwyn Blake. (Courtesy of Special Collections, University of Utah Libraries; P0206 Utah Power and Light Collection, no. 1589G)

them were of the Galloway type, eighteen feet long and about four and a half feet of beam. The other one was sixteen feet long with a hull like a common flat-bottomed rowboat. The boats were similar to those used by the Kolb Brothers in 1911 and the Chenoweth party in Cataract Canyon the year before. The first to make this style of boat was Nathaniel Galloway, who designed and supervised the construction of boats for Julius Stone of Columbus, Ohio, for his trip through the Grand Canyon in 1909.

These boats were far different from those used the year before on the San Juan. They were decked over at each end with an open cockpit in the center for the oarsman. The end compartments were equipped with hatch covers fastened with wing nuts, and these covers had been made watertight by lining the contact edges with rubber. The frames of the boats were oak, and the two larger ones had ship-lap sides. The bottoms were flat and protected by oak strips running lengthwise.

When the boatmen looked over the two longer boats before unloading them, they seemed too large for one man to handle. For a while they considered having them cut down. But the plan was soon abandoned because when the boats were in the water they did not seem nearly as large and unwieldy. The names of the boats were left up to the boatmen, who chose *Utah*, *Wyoming*, and *Colorado*, and these were painted on the respective boats. Loper took the *Utah*, Elwyn the *Wyoming*, and Lint the smaller boat, the *Colorado*.

The party spent a week at Green River waiting for a shipment of life preservers and making final preparations for the trip. The evening before the start they were guests of a local service club, which gave a banquet in their honor. At the "bon voyage" by the club, the crew members listened to vivid tales of unsuccessful attempts to navigate the canyon by earlier adventurers, but this failed to dampen their spirits.

The boats were launched several miles below town to avoid a low cable across the river. Groceries, bedrolls, duffel bags, and survey instruments taxed the capacity of the boats. Loper and Trimble had to decide what personal effects could not be taken. Some of the men were resentful because extra shoes and other nonessentials had to be left behind. Elwyn had seen this happen the year before at the beginning of the San Juan River trip.

They embarked the morning of July 15, 1922, with three men riding on each of the large boats and two on the small one. The passengers sat on the hatches. They would be retracing the first leg of the trips made by Major John Wesley Powell in 1869 and 1871 and by Emery and Ellsworth Kolb in 1911. Loper was a friend of Ellsworth Kolb, and he brought Kolb's book about the 1911 trip with him for what guidance it might afford.

It was a long two-day row through slow water to reach the starting point of the survey. The barren wasteland through which the stream lazily meandered made this somewhat monotonous. The unaccustomed steady rowing brought on sore muscles and blistered hands.

They passed through the Green River Badlands, those strangely carved buttes composed of sandstones and shales, buff, red, gray, brown, turquoise, and black in color. Because the rocks were relatively soft, the hills were mostly rounded on top and had slight shelves where layers of harder sandstones occurred. The rolling hills between stretches of badlands cliffs were dotted with purple sage.

Elwyn marveled at some high buttes and the rock spires called fire-hole chimneys farther on. Little vegetation grew on the rocks, but willows appeared along the river in many places and wherever a tributary came in there were sure to be cottonwood trees.

The first afternoon they came to the Holmes's ranch where the Kolb brothers had been entertained in 1911. The Holmes well remembered the Kolbs and were glad to see this boat party. When it came time to camp that night they saw marshlands on the right side of the river, a sure sign of mosquitoes, so they camped on a barren gravel bench on the left side hoping to be out of range of the pests. But as the sun went down, a thin, black cloud rose from the marsh across the river and moved in their direction. How the mosquitoes had located them was a mystery to Elwyn.

There was no getting away from the pesky insects, even after the men moved up on a high hill a quarter mile from the river. They made a smudge by piling green material and cow chips on the fire. Finally a breeze drove the mosquitoes away and they were able to get some sleep.

Backwaters along the river provided excellent nesting areas for waterfowl. Soon after resuming their way downstream the next day they came upon a flock of Canadian goslings that were too young to fly. Some of the men ran down and caught and killed four of the young birds and took them along. They camped that night on the right bank just above the mouth of Henry's Fork alongside a big pile of driftwood.

Clogston, the cook, stated flatly, "I'll be damned if I'll have anything to do with those illegal geese." So Loper took it upon himself to tend to the birds. After cleaning them, he dug a hole about three feet deep, piled wood into the hole, and set it afire. When the wood was all burned down, he took a shovel and scraped the coals and ashes out of the hole. Next he put the dressed fowl into a big dutch oven, sprinkled the meat with salt and pepper, put on the lid, and set the dutch oven in the hole. Then he covered it all up with hot coals and ashes and left it overnight.

Next morning they had a dish fit for a king. The meat was falling off the bones and it smelled so good that even Clogston broke his word and fell to, enjoying the geese as much as anyone else.

On July 17 at Smith's Ferry, about a mile above the mouth of Henry's Fork, Trimble located a bench mark and began his first survey work. This kept Elwyn and Lint busy carrying rod. Loper was free for part of the day, so he took a trip up Henry's Fork to the little Mormon town of Linwood to mail some letters. He noted that the trees there were large and the buildings weathered.

That afternoon the party proceeded downstream. From Smith's Ferry the river veered straight into a slope of the Uinta range. As they rounded a bend, the north wall of Flaming Gorge suddenly appeared with its vivid colors of red, pink, yellow, brown, and ocher rising up the escarpment like a raging forest fire. Major Powell had given mile-long Flaming Gorge Canyon its name in 1869. Kolb had called it "the way to all the canyons." To Elwyn it was just plain awe inspiring.

Below Flaming Gorge the river turned directly toward the heart of the Uintas for a mile and a half. Then it doubled back on itself creating three-mile-long Horseshoe Canyon. The party passed on down to the original (1914) Flaming Gorge dam site, which was located near the lower end of the horseshoe. Box elder trees grew all through Flaming Gorge and Horseshoe canyons wherever the walls permitted. Pine and juniper trees dotted the slopes, extending down to the water's edge. The whole colorful landscape was mirrored in the clear, placid water of the river.

They arrived at the dam site by 2:40 P.M., and ten minutes later passed a deserted cabin that marked the end of Horseshoe Canyon. They made camp opposite a place known as Nielsen's Bottom.

At 7:15 A.M. on July 18 Loper ferried Trimble, Woolley, Elwyn, and Lint across the river for a couple of hour's survey work. Then he returned to camp, loaded his own boat, and helped the cook load the other boats. While the survey team was at work, Stoner and Reeside hiked back upriver to inspect the Flaming Gorge dam site.

As they floated down the river each boat had its own passengers. Loper carried Trimble and Woolley with him, Elwyn had Stoner and Reeside for passengers, and Lint, in the smaller boat, carried Clogston, the cook. The cook's boat always carried the food needed for immediate use. As the supply of food got low, they would replenish it from the supplies carried in the other boats.

On July 19 the party passed into Kingfisher Canyon, where they spotted many of the birds for which Major Powell had named the place. In this canyon they hit water so shallow that at times they had to get out and wade to drag the boats along. They ate lunch near Sheep Creek, a beautiful mountain stream coming in from the snow-capped Uintas to the west. At Sheep Creek Trimble and his crew had more surveying to do. Elwyn and Lint had their rodman jobs down pat. They were nimble as cats and could climb to the most difficult points with ease. Sheep Creek marked the end of Kingfisher Canyon. The scenery and the river seemed more captivating as they traveled along.

That afternoon they ran a little rapid, the first variation from the placid river they had traveled for four days and a mild foretaste of what was to come. It was so small that the boatmen paid little attention to it. Just below the rapid someone spotted a deer. Lint took two shots at it and both missed. They immediately stopped for lunch, sans venison.

Loper wrote:

> In looking back over the whole thing and taking the weather — the canyons — the placid river — the beautiful pines — the little rapid and the missed venison and the prospect of a 400 mile trip ahead sure makes one feel that this is a wonderful world to live in and the bunch of men that went to make up the personnel of the trip makes it so nice to be able to associate with them — we had a nice swim in Horseshoe Canyon at noon time and who was it said — backward turn backward o time in your flight make me a kid again and that is what a river trip seems to do to me and with one exception I do not believe I ever took a trip that did not seem to do that very thing.[2]

Such a mood comes on most of those who boat the river canyons. It expressed the way Elwyn felt, too.

For some reason Elwyn did not know the type of venture he was getting into. One day Loper casually remarked that the river dropped over 2,000 feet between Green River, Wyoming, and Green River, Utah.

"There must be some rapids then," Elwyn observed.

"There sure are," was Loper's laconic answer.[3]

Elwyn still did not consider himself a rough-water boatman. But if Loper and Trimble thought he could handle the job, he would give it all he had. Both he and Lint were good with the oars, but neither had experience in bad rapids. With Bert Loper as coach, they had no fear.

Fifty-three years earlier Major John Wesley Powell had made his first exploration of the Green and Colorado rivers. Several parties had made trips over the route since. None made the trip under the same conditions as the Powell expedition because, for the later ones, much of the uncertainty had been removed. Each profited from the experiences of those who had gone before them.

Loper wrote:

> The navigators of the Colo and the Green as a rule are prone to criticize the other fellow but if one is liberal in his criticisms he will be prone to do just the opposite for with every foot up or down there is a different river — there have been many UN-

JUST criticisms of Major Powell but there is nothing but praise from me and I could go on and on and make arguments but — not here — but I hope to do that thing some day — the first trip down this turbulent stream left every rapid of any note named and so that fixes it so we always knew where we were and what we were up against — the rapids are just as bad as ever and the river is just as beautiful and fascinating as it was 53 years ago but the records left by Major Powell have taken away much of that feeling of adventure that must have been felt on that first trip.[4]

At the lower end of Kingfisher Canyon a cone-shaped rock mass called Beehive Point came into view. When they reached it they had traveled seventy-nine miles, and the river in that distance had dropped 235 feet, a fall of a little over three feet to the mile. The elevation of the river at Beehive Point was 5,830 feet, and it marked the head of Red Canyon.

Posts on either side of the river and an old trail were evidence that this place had once been a crossing of some kind. A small open area below Beehive Point was known as Hideout Flat, a onetime retreat for cattle thieves. It would later be the site of a Utah State University forestry camp.

Elwyn sighted many beaver slides and fresh deer tracks along the banks as the boats drifted through Hideout Flat into Red Canyon. In Red Canyon what had been a mostly placid stream began giving way to rougher water. Where the river widened they came to several small, shallow rapids. With a little lower water the boatmen would have had trouble, for the rocks would have been at or near the surface. Loper knew of several parties who had run into trouble there.

CHAPTER 9

Red Canyon

On July 20 they entered Red Canyon, the first solid red-rock canyon of the Green River, with walls up to 800 feet high rising back to two thousand feet on the mountainside to the right. Its walls took on a deep rose color in the early morning light. They hit low water in a stretch of almost continuous rapids, and in one place Loper ran the *Utah* onto a gravel bar. It took him and his passengers several minutes to lift and pull the boat over to deeper water. Riding the white water down the churning and seething chutes made Elwyn's heart race.

They arrived at Carter Creek by 11:00 A.M. and made camp. This was a sparkling stream coming in from the right through a rugged, steep-walled gorge. The surveyors took the rest of the day to survey Carter Creek Canyon. The lower part of it was choked with cottonwood and box elder trees, along with much brush, making it difficult to traverse. The creek was running about 100 cfs. (cubic feet per second) of clear water and was teeming with mountain trout.

After work, while Loper nursed a headache, Elwyn and Lint went swimming. No camp suited them unless it had a good swimming hole. After the swim, the two joined the rest of the party, who had gone fishing. Kelly Trimble proved to be the champion fisherman with twenty-four trout to his credit. Elwyn caught five and Stoner four. In all it made a good mess of the speckled beauties.

Drinking water had been no problem on the early part of the trip since the river water was reasonably clear with no bad taste. But now storms on the barren drainage areas upstream suddenly turned the stream into a stinking brown river of mud. For the rest of the trip one of the priorities of a proper campsite was a source of good drinking water.

By midmorning of the next day they reached Eagle Creek, and in one hour the efficient team had finished surveying its canyon. Next they came to a half-mile-long rapid where huge boulders filled the channel, some jutting out of the water and many of them submerged only a few inches. It was time for Elwyn and Lint to get some instruction on running tough rapids.

Submerged rocks could not be seen because of the muddy water, but from the shore Loper pointed out how certain eddies and wave action marked their location. As the current met one of these rocks the water surged up and over it, then fell into a hole on the downstream side, ending in a tail-wave that broke upstream. Loper told Elwyn and Lint that the deeper the boulder was below the surface the farther downstream the back-wave would be. The submerged rocks were often difficult to spot from an approaching boat. For that reason Loper said a boatman should be ever alert. He said bad holes or other hazards could be marked ahead of time by a tree or a rock on shore.

Elwyn learned a lesson the hard way. Through inattention he let the *Wyoming* get hung up on a submerged rock in the middle of the river. The boat slid to a grinding stop with the prow high out of the water. Stoner and Reeside were on the boat with him. On top of that, Reeside could not swim and Stoner was not good at it. There was only one life jacket among them, and it was for the boatman. Passengers were supposed to walk around the bad rapids. Elwyn gave his life jacket to Reeside.

Loper was upstream and saw their predicament. He motioned that he would come by and try to knock the *Wyoming* loose. Taking the tie rope, Elwyn perched on top of the hatch cover and waited. The current was swift and as Loper maneuvered the *Utah* in close it bumped the *Wyoming* and moved it a little. Right after the moment of impact Elwyn leaped onto Loper's boat, landed safely, and took a swift snub around the hatch cover with the rope. As the painter tightened with a jerk, the stranded *Wyoming* slid into deep water.

Pulling the *Wyoming* close, Elwyn jumped back aboard, grasped the oars, and got things under control again. It was a good lesson, one which made him more cautious and respectful of the power of the river.

The party traveled five and a half miles before making camp. The river had a fall of eighty-four feet in that distance, 15.27 feet to the mile, much different from the three feet per mile of the first four days.

Next morning the surveyors worked their way down another mile to the mouth of Skull Creek. Trimble needed to connect his survey with a bench mark on top of a nearby mountain, so Elwyn and Lint carried rod up the mountain to the tie-point. They finished their work and were back in camp shortly after noon. After lunch they worked their way on down the river until rain clouds began to settle into the canyon. They made camp on the left bank of the river at 3:00 P.M.

The next morning, July 23, Loper crossed the river and climbed the mountain to a ranch Ellsworth Kolb had visited eleven years earlier. When Kolb had made the climb the ranch house was new, but when Loper reached the place it looked like it had survived some hard times.

At the ranch Loper had lunch with the family of James E. Swet, and the rancher agreed to take the surveyors' letters to the post office at Vernal, Utah, on his next trip out. Vernal was about forty miles away. Loper gathered wild flowers as he returned to camp.

July 24, Pioneer Day and a holiday for most Utahns, turned out to be just one more workday for the crew.[1] They broke camp and in about one and a half miles came to a hairpin bend. They stopped there to survey the mouth of a canyon coming in from the left side, then ran a long rapid around Hairpin Turn. At 11:00 A.M. they reached the mouth of Trail Canyon where scattered tall pines grew down to the shore.

On a benchland above the shore, watching their approach, stood a tall, bearded old man in patchwork clothes. He was as surprised to see them as they were to see him. They pulled in for a visit.

The gaunt old man was leaning on a scythe with which he had been cutting clover for hay. The men wanted to get a picture of him but were a little timid about asking. When they finally did, they learned that he was perfectly willing to have his picture taken.

His home was a crude hovel of boards over a small hole in the ground that was about the size of a large dog kennel and hardly big enough for one person. He had a paper sack for a hat, and his clothes were as meager as the house. They consisted of a shirt made from a grain sack with holes cut for head and arms, a ragged pair of overalls, and a unique pair of shoes. He had made the soles from pieces of cowhide about fifteen inches long with the hair on the bottom side. The uppers had been cut from old rubber boots and laced to the soles with rawhide strings. Dry grass stuck out around the edges, showing how the old fellow filled up the extra space in his oversized footgear.[2]

They invited the hermit to have lunch with them. He talked freely, giving his name as Amos Hill. He said he was seventy-one years old and had lived in the canyons about twenty years. Among other things he claimed to have gone through the Green River canyons on a raft taking a horse with him. Anyone who has been through the canyons would be justified in believing this to be impossible.

He said that he ran a few cattle and cultivated his garden patches in summer. In winter, when the river was low, he panned gold from the sand and gravel bars. The nearest post office was Linwood, some twenty miles or more up the river on Henry's Fork over a rough mountain trail. Vernal was about forty-five miles the other way. He packed his supplies in from either of these towns, making two or three trips a year.

His little farm was situated between Trail and Allen creeks, which were only a few hundred feet apart. Both creeks were small, and the old hermit diverted water in ditches from both streams to irrigate the few acres of fertile land that lay between them.

The party laid over at the hermit's place for part of the afternoon because of rain. He warned them about Ashley Falls a little farther downstream, but Loper and Trimble were already aware of this rapid. Elwyn listened carefully. When they moved on they left the steep-walled canyon behind and passed between a series of high rolling hills. Then, a little after 3:00 P.M., they reached Ashley Falls.

On June 2, 1869, Major Powell and his party had lined their boats over this rapid and made a trail among the rocks to transport their cargo to safer water below. On a rock high above the waterline by which the trail passed the surveyors found the inscription: "Ashley 1825." Powell named the rapid Ashley Falls. General William H. Ashley, the first white man known to have traveled this section of the river, did so in "Bull Boats" made from buffalo hides. He had painted the inscription on the rock in passing.

The survey party landed a safe distance above the swift water on the left side. They looked the rapid over carefully and then crossed to the right side for another look. The channel was almost entirely obstructed by huge, jutting boulders that had broken loose from the canyon walls. They found no abrupt falls as described by Ashley, Manly, and Powell, only a seething rapid plunging in narrow chutes between the immense rocks.

Elwyn wrote:

Bert Loper talking to Amos Hill, the hermit of Red Canyon — Kelly Trimble in the background. The hermit had come there searching for gold twenty years earlier where he eked out a living by raising a few cattle, a garden, and catching fish from the river. (Courtesy of Prescott Blake)

After inspecting "the falls" it was decided to run through between two protruding boulders near the south side of the steep drop. There would not be room to use the oars at one point, but with proper positioning, the boats would drift through, the boatman being ready to apply the oars as soon as there was room.[3]

They took every precaution for safety before starting the run. Each boatman wore his life jacket, the hatches were all tightly closed, and the other members of the party scrambled over the rocks to the foot of the rapid and waited with lines, ready for any emergency. A projection of the canyon wall obstructed the view from the starting place to safe water below. The boatmen decided to allow a ten-minute interval between runs, deeming that sufficient time for each man to get through.

Loper went first. He maneuvered his boat just right and sailed safely between the big rocks. Then, with a hard pull on the oars, he broke an oarlock. From there on it was a scramble to get the boat into

GREEN RIVER INVESTIGATION
BOAT "WYOMING" THROUGH ASHLEY FALLS
BLAKE - BOATMAN
JULY 24, 1922   31982

Elwyn Blake in the *Wyoming* running Ashley Falls. Since there was not room enough to use the oars between the two big rocks, the boatmen positioned the boats to drift through, being ready to apply the oars as soon as there was room. (Courtesy of Special Collections, University of Utah Libraries; P0206 Utah Power and Light Collection, no. 1052G)

an eddy near shore. Elwyn went next. He got thoroughly drenched as his boat went twisting up then down through the surging waves. He missed all the rocks, too, and pulled his boat into an eddy beside Loper. Lint ran last and got through with no mishap. After Loper repaired his oarlock, they were on their way again.

Ashley Falls had given the boatmen a good workout. It, and each new rapid they came to, increased Elwyn's whitewater experience and further toughened his muscles. They went on to Dutch John Canyon and made camp for the night. The river had dropped 11.5 feet to the mile in their course for the day.

On July 25 Trimble made a detailed survey of a possible dam site at the mouth of Dutch John Canyon. They finished surveying the dam site by 10:30 and then drifted down a short distance to Cart Creek, which had to be surveyed. While they were stopped for lunch, the fishermen in the party made another fine catch of trout. They cleaned the fish, then started their survey work, completing the job by about 5:00 P.M.

Below Cart Creek the canyon walls rose majestically 2,000 feet above the river. The cliffs were carved into large amphitheaters and buttresses in variegated colors of red, orange, and salmon. Green pines clinging to the steep slopes made a pleasing contrast to the brilliant-colored rocks. This eventually became the site of Flaming Gorge Dam, completed in 1963. The reservoir was first filled to its capacity of 3,749,000 acre-feet in 1974 and now inundates Henry's Fork where it enters the Green. The lovely Flaming Gorge, Kingfisher, Horseshoe, and Hidden canyons are all under water, and the little farm that was once home to hermit Amos Hill is flooded. The bad rapids at Ashley Falls, along with half of Red Canyon, are the deep haven of trophy-sized lake trout.

On July 26 the party passed over some good-sized, turbulent rapids. Loper's boat, *Utah*, struck a rock in one of them, so he had to pull ashore and unload the front compartment of the boat to calk the leak. As they floated on downriver, the canyon walls suddenly broke away into rolling hills, forming an open area about a mile long known as Little Hole. The term "hole" is used to describe valleys surrounded by hills or mountains where trappers "holed up" for the winter. Gorge Creek entered from the right at the upper end of Little Hole, and Little Davenport Creek came in from the left at its lower end. The river had dropped about seventy feet in the six miles traveled that day. They camped at Little Hole.

The next day Trimble had some flat country to work at Little Hole. This occupied the survey team for the entire morning. While they were doing this, Loper finished patching and painting his boat.

The river passed from Little Hole into another narrow canyon, but the walls were not as high as before and were more broken by ravines. About two miles below Little Hole the canyon became darkened by storm clouds. They made camp beside a clear stream coming from the right and put up the tents.

About half a mile up one of the ravines on the left side of the river was a rancher's cabin. During the evening the owner came to visit. He asked them to take a letter for him and mail it at the first place possible. During his stay he warned the party of a bad rapid ahead. He told them some precautions they should take to avoid the upset others had suffered when they did not realize until too late what was before them.

Loper dubbed this place Camp Piss Ant. He wrote, "Of all the camps this takes the plum for the ants are everywhere and there is no getting away from them." It rained most all night, but that did not seem to bother the ants. Trimble and the survey team had more flat country to work, so they did not move on until 11:30 A.M.

About a mile below their noon camp Elwyn began to hear a growing roar from downstream. Soon the water became placid, a sure sign of a dam in the river ahead. At length they came to the mouth of Red Creek and the worst rapid of the trip so far. Loper thought that a murderer had once lived at this site. Ann Zwinger refers to this in her book *Run, River, Run.*

Jesse Ewing had come to Red Creek to prospect in 1867. To help finance his operations he took on a series of partners. The partners' stays depended on how long their money held out. It is said that a young man by the name of Robinson became one of Ewing's victims. One account says that he was simply prospecting too close to suit Ewing and refused to move on. Ewing shot Robinson and slashed his body to ribbons before leaving it on the ice for the river to dispose of in the spring. Ewing reportedly told a group of miners, "If you guys want to see a handsome corpse, go up yonder on the ice and take a look."

Ewing eventually got lonely and sent away for a "coupon woman." She turned out to be Madame Forrestall, a former bootlegger to the Indians, whose outlook on life matched Ewing's. When a stranger fleeing from the law moved in with them to help Ewing in his mine, it soon became a love triangle. One day the handsome outlaw pleaded sickness and Ewing went off to work his claim alone. When he returned, "he was greeted by a warm blast from his own Winchester."[4]

Red Creek entered from the left and drained a large area of rolling hills. Its flow was torrential during floods, as seen by the debris and mud along its banks. The high-water marks through its canyon gorge were twenty to thirty feet above the creek bed. The Red Creek channel was strewn with large boulders embedded in the red mud, and a huge dam of boulders fanned out into the Green. This dam extended almost entirely across the stream, crowding the current against the opposite wall of the canyon and forming a raging rapid where the water finally tumbled over the boulder-clogged channel.

They camped at the head of the rapid and put up tents. The survey team spent the rest of the day mapping Red Creek, while Loper studied the rapid to look for a way through it. The rapid was in two sections, the worst being the upper one. In prowling around, Loper suddenly found himself in the midst of a big patch of poison oak. He immediately got out and luckily was not infected by the toxin.

After loading up the next morning Loper, Elwyn, and Lint took another look at the rapid from shore to plan carefully the route they would take. Their course would be a narrow one passing between some big jutting rocks.

The other men stationed themselves along the rocky bank to get pictures as the boats came down. Loper led off, made a good run through the twisting, rearing waves, and then rowed into an eddy just below the first drop, waiting there for the other boats. Elwyn made an exhilarating run, too, riding the rearing, plunging boat like a wild bronco. Then Lint came in the *Colorado*. Each boat made it through without mishap, although two of the boats scraped bottom on rocks. Had the river been only a few inches lower their problems would have been much greater.

Immediately below the rough part of the rapid the stream divided into two channels. The greater flow was in the left-hand channel and ordinarily they would have gone with that one. But the rancher had told them about a huge boulder blocking the lower end of it, against which the current swept before making an abrupt turn to the right. He had advised them to take the right-hand channel if possible.

Fortunately there was enough water in it to float the boats. They saw that it would have been nearly impossible to go through the larger channel without having the boat dashed against the big rock. The waves in the right-hand channel were plenty rough, but not as bad as in the upper part of the rapid.

Red Canyon ran for thirty twisting miles and ended three miles below Red Creek. The river in that distance had a fall of just a fraction less than twelve feet to the mile. Of all the rapids, the one at Red Creek had been the worst. If the water level had been a little higher they would have had no difficulty whatever. Thanks to Loper's coaching and their own quickness to learn, Lint and Elwyn were becoming two fine rough-water boatmen.

CHAPTER 10

Browns Park into Lodore

Leaving Red Canyon on July 29, the party came into Little Browns Park, where the river dropped eighty-seven feet in its twelve-mile length. At one place they saw mountain lion tracks in the sand. About two miles below their noon camp, on the left bank of the river, they came to the old Jarvie Ranch. They saw a waterwheel at the edge of the stream which had been used to lift out water for irrigation. The ruins of an old stone building stood where John Jarvie, who was the first postmaster of Browns Park, had run a store. Jarvie was murdered by a half-breed and his partner in 1909, and his body was set adrift in a skiff found later in Lodore Canyon.

A couple of miles below the Jarvie Ranch they came to the abandoned remains of Old Bridgeport where there had been a post office between 1881 and 1887. A large log house, blacksmith shop, and other buildings left mute evidence of more prosperous times. Another short-lived post office was established in 1889 at the Bassett Ranch in Browns Park with Herb Bassett as postmaster. The mail came in weekly from Maybell, Colorado.[1]

A mile or so below Old Bridgeport they came to the Taylor Ranch, where they obtained some vegetables. The boatmen took the ladies of the ranch for a ride on the river. Leaving the Taylor Ranch, the river entered Swallow Canyon over a wavy rapid. Everybody at the ranch came down to see the boats go through it. The party made camp immediately below the rapid. After pulling into shore and tying up the boats for the night, the three boatmen had a race to see who could be first into the river for a swim. While setting up camp they discovered mosquitoes, the worst of the trip so far. All they could do was swat and bear them.

Swallow Canyon was a short gorge connecting Little Browns Park with Browns Park proper, and the current through it was barely perceptible. The canyon walls were of solid rock that rose almost vertically for about 200 feet above the river. Hundreds of swallows had plastered their nests under ledges and in crevices there. Major Powell had given the canyon its name in 1869. Elwyn saw many other kinds of birds, too, including several varieties of owls.

On July 30 the group reached the Two Bar Ranch in Browns Park, where they made camp. They were now in Colorado. Browns Park was a broad, open basin about thirty miles long east to west, and a mile to five miles in width. It had rolling foothills and brush-covered bottomlands. (After many years of overgrazing, most of the streams in Browns Park have eroded into deeper channels resulting in a lowered water table. The once lush grasslands found there by the mountain men have given way to greasewood deserts.)

The river through Browns Park flowed sluggishly in a meandering course and small cottonwood groves dotted the area. In many places the stream had cut away its soft banks causing hundreds of cotton-wood trees to fall into the channel, leaving many snags sticking up in the river. But the boatmen had no trouble getting around the snags.

There were Canadian geese in abundance, too. Elwyn and Lint chased a small goose out into the stream. They tried to catch it but found this a frustrating endeavor. When they rowed directly at the little fellow it would swim desperately. Then, just as they were about to run it down, it would dive. The two were outmaneuvered each time, for they could never guess where the little gosling would emerge. At last it became exhausted, crawled out on the bank, and let those who had been watching pick it up. They took pictures of it and turned it loose.

In 1825 William H. Ashley, leader of a brigade of trappers, took a few picked men and drifted down the Green River looking for side streams that were rich in beaver. He noticed how the high mountains shielded the valley from winter's worst storms. The valley teemed with large numbers of antelope, deer, and mountain sheep that grazed on the rich valley grasses, making it a hunter's paradise. Ashley saw that this isolated valley would make an ideal wintering ground for trappers. Every year thereafter, from 1826 to 1840, trappers holed up for the winter in this hidden valley. The mountain men called it Browns Hole after Baptiste Brown, an early trapper who, along with an Indian woman, made his home there. In 1837 Philip Thompson and William Craig built a trading post there to trade with the trappers. They called it Fort Davy Crockett, although it was never a fort.

In the fall of 1840 Old Bill Williams, Kit Carson, Bill New, Bill Mitchell, and a Frenchman named Frederick trapped the Green and wintered in Browns Hole. After that year the fur trade dwindled sharply due to a scarcity of beaver and a change of fashion in London and Paris. Only a few trappers, Indians, and half-breeds hung on to make Browns Hole their home.

Browns Hole encompasses the point where Utah's eastern boundary and Colorado's western boundary meet to join the southern boundary of Wyoming. The Green River runs along the south end of the valley at the base of Diamond Mountain.

In 1869, not long after the railroad came to Wyoming, Major Powell began his epic voyage down the Green and Colorado rivers. He passed through Browns Hole but made little note except to change the name to Browns Park. On his second expedition in 1871 Powell found white settlers who had entered the valley with herds of cattle. He was able to get some supplies and send out mail with the Harrell brothers, the valley's first stockmen.

Over the next few decades the West's large cattle herds, mines, and railroads attracted rustlers and holdup men. Browns Park became a hideout and way station for many of these outlaws. In the heyday of the rustlers, stolen cattle could easily be driven over the line into another state if the law was on their trail. But for many years lawmen shunned this isolated valley. The Hoys (J. S., Harry, and Valentine) and the Bassetts, dominated by Herbert's wife, Elizabeth, were among the early settlers who were associated with or tolerated the various rustlers. Ann Bassett, later referred to as "Queen Ann," was the first white child born in Browns Park.

Negro Isom Dart was one of the characters associated with rustling who lived in Browns Park. Tom Horn, a killer hired by the Wyoming Cattlemen's Association, shot and killed Matt Rash from ambush, then shot Isom Dart as the black cowboy was answering nature's call at dawn. Other rustlers abandoned the valley quickly since none wanted to be next.[2]

In 1922, when the surveyors arrived at Browns Park, the Two Bar Ranch was headquarters for a cow outfit of that name. Stoner borrowed a horse from the ranch and rode to the post office at Lodore, Colorado, for the mail. Everyone had letters waiting for them, so they spent most of the afternoon reading and answering their letters. Elwyn was happy to have letters from his family. They were his lifeline to the outside world. He was even happier to be on the river than in Monticello with them.

There was no firewood near camp, so Elwyn, Loper, and Lint crossed the river in boats and brought some from the opposite side. After that the three of them went for a swim. There were not many days that the boatmen did not go swimming, sometimes several times a day. They considered it great fun to go up the river for a mile or so and then swim back to camp.

July 31 was Loper's fifty-third birthday. He started the day by writing more letters, one of them to H. D. Miser of Washington, D.C., the geologist who had been with them on the San Juan the previous summer. While waiting around for the afternoon mail, Elwyn helped load the boats to be ready for departure. After lunch Loper took letters over to the Two Bar Ranch for mailing. The people there asked him to hold the party at the river for a few minutes so they could take pictures of them leaving.

They started on down the river that afternoon and soon reached the mouth of Vermillion Creek, where Trimble picked up his point. From there they had a spectacular view of the mouth of Lodore Canyon. From a distance the opening looks like the letter v with the v slightly narrowed at the top. Its maroon-colored walls give the appearance of having been carved from living flesh. Several of the men took pictures.

It was twenty-three miles from Swallow Canyon to the head of Lodore, and the river had a fall of less than two feet per mile in that distance. The boatmen had plenty of stick work to keep the boats moving down the river as fast as they wished.

On the long row toward Lodore Canyon, Elwyn made the mistake of pressing too close to Loper's boat. This made Loper row even harder, turning it into a rowing race. The old boatman would not be outdone by any young whippersnapper. Stoner, who rode on Elwyn's boat, kept wanting to spell him at the oars. At last Elwyn let him take them. But try as he would, Stoner could not keep up with Loper. He soon lost so much distance that he gave the oars back to Elwyn.

In spite of the race, Loper took note of the scenery. He wrote:

It seemed to me that the river was trying to make its escape from Browns Park—seemed as though it was looking for a place to break through the mountains and when it reached the Two Bar Ranch it, very suddenly, made a right angle turn and headed direct for the mountain.[3]

On a bright sunny day it is hard to imagine the gloom that Major Powell described upon entering it in 1869. On a stormy day the mood could be different. Of course Major Powell and his men did not know what lay ahead.

The survey party entered Lodore at about 4:00 P.M. after rowing on the quiet water for several miles. It took quite a while and an agonizing effort for Elwyn to catch up to Loper again. Lint was well behind Elwyn when they landed to make camp.

When Loper pulled in, one of his passengers leaped ashore and snubbed the boat. Loper got wearily out and climbed up the bank to a flat place where he fell face down. He rested there until Clogston called supper. Elwyn followed suit. Both were exhausted. They did not even notice Lint when he pulled in.

The upper section of Lodore Canyon was composed of stratas of red, metamorphosed mudstones of the Uinta Mountain formation that tilt gently downstream. The upper part of the walls were almost sheer at this place. The lower slopes were dotted with dark-green pinion and juniper trees, lending a pleasing contrast to the scene.

Woolley described the canyon thus:

> The canyon is a rock gorge with jagged walls that rise almost vertically many hundreds of feet. The coloring is beautiful, comprising delicate tints of red, pink, and ocher, all blending into a wonderful picture in the soft light of the late afternoon and evening.[4]

While camped on a sandbar near the head of Lodore, the cook killed another fine goose, his aversion to such acts having slipped away. Storm clouds were moving in, so they put the tents up. That evening Lint took his rifle and went hunting and he soon killed a fat buck. The venison would be a welcome change from the diet of Canada goose they had enjoyed for the past several days.

A couple of miles after departing that camp they came to Winnies Rapid. It and the matching grotto on the right side were named for the daughter of A. H. Thompson, who manned the steering oar of one of Major Powell's boats. At the present water levels (late summer of 1990) a huge squarish rock in the middle of the narrowed channel splits it into two sections.

The surveyors ran through this short, wavy rapid with no problem, and in a little over a mile they came upon one rapid after another. On August 1, Loper wrote:

And so starts another month and it is some start with one of the very worst canyons of the entire series before us, but with the personnel of our expedition working perfect, with three good boats and with two of the very finest boys as co-boatmen there was very little to worry us so we made our start in good time.[5]

Some of the rapids were violent. The fifth one was formed by a huge boulder in midstream with smaller rocks scattered liberally about. The current swung around the boulder and formed a large whirlpool below.

Loper crossed the river to look over the channel from the left side. Elwyn could see no difficulty ahead, so he did not stop. With Reeside in his boat, he made the run on the right side. They both got drenched from the lashing waves and Elwyn had a hard pull in the huge eddy below the rapid but escaped without any damage and made a good landing. Neither he nor Reeside were wearing the life jacket. Lint ran his boat through the same channel as Elwyn and had no trouble.

Loper decided to run the far side of the rapid. The others could not see his run. They learned later that the swift current had caught the *Utah* and rammed her into the big rock, crushing a hole in the stern. The force of the blow had driven the iron handhold through the stern of the boat. Fortunately the hole was just above the waterline.

When Loper and Trimble caught up with Elwyn they both gave him a good chewing out for taking a passenger through the rapid, and especially for not using the life jacket. Another lesson for Elwyn in the ways of safe white-water boating.

Loper was probably already upset because of his own accident. He pulled over to the left bank and in about an hour had the hole mended. With the boat repaired, they proceeded downriver running the rapids as they came to them with no more trouble.

Within a few miles the men got glimpses of the canyon farther on down the river. The sheer walls were giving way to cliffs having a timbered talus sloping up from the river's edge. They ate lunch at a place where they could see a string of rapids below. In the afternoon they came to what they believed to be Disaster Falls, where Ashley upset a boat in 1825. The Powell party also lost one of its boats, the "No Name," there in 1869 when it smashed against a rocky island that split the channel.

The survey party found rock-filled, shallow channels on either side of the island. The boatmen got splashy, roller-coaster rides with plenty of thrills, but they got through without mishap.

About a half mile below Disaster Falls they came to the head of another roaring cataract. Loper decided that this was Lower Disaster Falls because the current had undercut the cliff on the right side, as pictured in Kolb's book.[6] If this was Lower Disaster, it meant they had already passed over Upper Disaster, as they had guessed. They made camp on the left side with the roar of the cataract in their ears.

While the cook prepared venison steaks for supper, the boatmen scrambled along the rocky shore studying the rapid. Around the campfire that night no one had yet figured out how to get the boats through.

Next morning they took another look at the rapid. Lower Disaster was situated at a sharp turn in the river, and most of the low water passed below the undercut sandstone cliff on the right side. The channel, before reaching the cliff, spread out in a fan shape, flowing over a shallow gravel bar before plunging swiftly into the undercut channel. Loper reminded Elwyn and Lint that when a boat strikes bottom the boatman loses some control of it. They decided there was not enough water over the gravel bar for a boatman to keep his craft off the rocky bottom. Besides that, it would be too precarious going past the undercut cliff. So they decided to portage.

They took their bedrolls and the more bulky gear out of the boats and carried them along the left shore to the foot of the rapid. This gave the crew an extra-good appetite for breakfast. After breakfast they "nosed" the lightened boats one at a time along the shore, wading alongside them in water just deep enough to keep them afloat yet keep them under control. When they got a boat past the danger point, one of the boatmen would climb into it and run it to the still water below.

On the right shore at the foot of the rapid the men found several rusted cans and the remains of an old campfire. Someone had passed that way in times past. By 11:00 A.M. they reached the mouth of Pot Creek, up which Trimble had to carry his line. (Today Pot Creek is a favorite camping place for raft parties.) At the last rapid before lunch Loper broke an oar and had to replace it with a spare from his boat. Their morning's work had taken them only a mile and a half.

That afternoon they went out of one rapid into another, but none compared to Lower Disaster. They camped at 3:50 P.M., having made 3.2 miles for the day. The drop in that distance was eighty-two feet, amounting to 25.6 feet per mile. Elwyn said that at one camp just below a roller-coaster rapid he and Lint had great fun "shooting the rapids" in life jackets.

The next day, August 3, they came within sight of Dunn's Cliff, a flat-topped part of the left wall. It had a capping of gray quartzite over the red sandstone through which the canyon was cut. The contrast of colors was striking. Major Powell had named this 2,000-foot-high cliff after one of his men, Bill Dunn.

At the foot of Dunn's Cliff the party came to Triplet Falls, three rapids in a distance of 800 feet. The rapids were swift and rough, bouncing the boats about in the waves. The stage of water was high enough, however, that the boats cleared the rocky bottom with no trouble.

CHAPTER 11

Hell's Half Mile to
Split Mountain

Not far below Triplet Falls the boats hit a stretch of still water, and all
through it they could hear an increasing roar from downstream. At
the end of this placid lake they pulled ashore. The river before them
plunged with a deafening roar into a wild stretch of white water.
Loper's copy of Kolb's book, and the pictures in it, served to identify this as Hell's Half Mile. Powell gave this rapid its name in 1871
at the insistence of John F. Steward. Almon Harris Thompson and
Francis Marion Bishop wanted to call it "Boulder Falls." The twisting, thrashing channel, clogged with foam-flecked rocks and filled
with churning waves, stretched for nearly one-third of a mile ahead.

As Loper and Elwyn sat atop a huge rock looking out over the
roaring cataract, Elwyn could see no possibility of running a boat
past the big rocks and through the curling back-waves, lashing side-
waves and twisting whirlpools without wrecking. It was apparent
to him that a portage would be necessary. The jumble of huge red
boulders along the left shore would make for a strenuous portage.

"It's going to be a tough job to drag the boats over that hill and
around this rapid," he remarked.

"We're not going to take the boats out of the water," Loper informed him. "We're going to run it."

Although Elwyn did not know it at the time, the rapid had never
been run. "How are we going to miss that rock?" he asked, pointing
to a jutting shore rock against which the current pounded.

"Just try and hit it," Loper said. "Then you won't go over the
big drop out there." He pointed to a huge submerged boulder in
midstream over which the water poured, dropping ten feet into a
big hole that caused a high back-curling wave below. It could easily

swamp a boat. Loper probably figured that the back-wash from the shore rock would keep a boat from smashing into it. Elwyn had unswerving confidence in Loper, so he accepted the fact they *could* run the rapid.

After studying the rapid carefully the boatmen unloaded the boats and screwed the hatch covers down tightly. Each boatman donned his life jacket, and when all was ready the other members of the party stationed themselves along the left bank at places of vantage. Some of them had loaded cameras and others had ropes to be used in case of mishaps.

Loper in the *Utah* went through first. Elwyn watched carefully as the boat plunged the nine feet of fall in the first four hundred feet. He saw Loper strain every muscle as he barely missed the midstream hole. With relief he watched him pull safely into an eddy along the right-hand bank to wait for the other boats. At that point the rapid was only half run.

Then Loper motioned for Elwyn to come through. He knew what he should do, but could he do it? As the current caught his craft, it seemed he was being shot directly toward the submerged rock he wanted to avoid. Those on shore thought he would surely go over it. He pulled desperately, raising half out of his seat, bending the nine-foot oars to near breaking point. Rearing, bucking, plunging, and twisting, the boat sped directly toward the big drop. Elwyn thought it was going over, but the boat finally yielded to his oars and came around toward the left shore past the big rock. The high leaping tail of the rapid was an anticlimax.

Lint in the *Colorado* was less fortunate. He came past the big hole with more margin to spare than Elwyn. But then he got hung up on a submerged boulder. All his efforts to dislodge her proved futile. After several attempts by those on shore, they succeeded in casting a line out to Lint. By hauling on the rope, they finally pulled the boat loose.

Below the first plunge of the rapid the river would have been spread out over a channel nearly six hundred feet wide during flood stage. But at the level of water on August 3, 1922, it was divided into two or three channels, all of them full of boulders. Except for a stretch of about forty yards of the remainder of Hell's Half Mile, the boatmen had no trouble controlling their boats. Along that forty-yard stretch the water was so shallow and filled with rocks that they "nosed" the boats through. After they reached the bottom of the rapid, it was obvious to them that the stage of the river had very much to do with their success. They could easily imagine what trouble they would have had if the water had been only a few inches lower. Every variation in the depth of water either creates new problems or does away with them entirely.

Their next job was to portage the cargo. Ralph R. Woolley wrote:

All afternoon the men toiled on the portage of supplies. [Along the left side of the river.] The trail led across a small ridge, across a deep red gully, into the high-water channel of the river, over this boulder-strewn course as far as possible, up a steep hillside of loose earth and rocks to a deer trail 75 feet or more above the river, and along this trail around a steep rocky point down to the sand bar, where camp was made. Forty three trips were necessary to place the cargoes below the rapid, and the course was close to a half mile long. Each load was about 60 or 70 pounds, and when the work was done every member of the party was quite exhausted. However, a refreshing plunge in the "swimming hole" just off the sand bar and some dry, clean clothes made a great change, and everyone had a good appetite for supper.[1]

After the portage, Loper made up his mind that in the future any rapid he would unload for would have to be an extra-bad one. He concluded that Hell's Half Mile was a most appropriate name for that rapid, and that anyone who loved rough water would surely get his money's worth there. He wrote:

When one reads the many hardships and the time the Kolb brothers had and put in in Lodore one will redily [sic] realize the unfavorable stage of the river they had. There is no one that knows the hardships of battling mud and slimy water rising and falling of the river and stormy weather more than I do for I have been through it all, but it is still a beautiful canyon and what a wonderful world this is to live in where a person can enjoy such wonderful sights and have such wonderful experiences. Who in the hell wants to be a white collar sissy when one can enjoy such grandeur and beauty such as this.[2]

On August 4 the party left Hell's Half Mile behind them and by late morning had reached what Powell called Rippling Brook. Here the lower slopes of the main canyon were heavily wooded with pinion and juniper and farther up with pine and fir. The Uinta formation had dipped under and been replaced by the Lodore formation. Deseret limestone showed above that.

The men hiked up Rippling Brook Canyon. Its clear stream issued from the right side of the canyon between sheer walls of sandstone. Box elders and cottonwoods lined the right side, and the left bank had gravel wherever it did not lap the base of the cliff. Elwyn and some of the others took a swim in one of the clear, deep pools.

During the hike up Rippling Brook, Elwyn got the scare of his life. A waterfall blocked the stream about a mile up the creek from the river, and it prevented anyone from walking farther up the stream-bed.

Several of the other men decided to go up to the falls for a shower bath. Loper and Elwyn climbed the talus slope to a ridge high above the gorge, where they sat down to rest and admire the landscape. They could not see the stream, nor could they hear the bathers below.

When Elwyn decided to move on up the ridge, he put his weight on a nearby rock to steady himself. He felt it slip from beneath his hand, and, with a quick jump, he gained solid ground. Looking back, he saw the rock go rolling, then bounding, down the slope.

As it plunged along the small boulder loosened an avalanche of other rocks that spun downward, bouncing high into the air. The rocks and dirt glanced off pine trees, went over the brink of the lower cliff, and disappeared into the canyon below.

Stunned, Elwyn pictured mangled bodies in the pool below the falls. He heard no sound from there, but saw dust drifting upward. In a shrill voice he yelled, "Anybody hurt?"

The answer came back, "Yes, we're all killed." What a relief! It could only mean no one had been injured.

The men below said the avalanche had leaped completely across the stream, stripping limbs from trees and crashing against the far wall. A fist-sized rock had landed on one man's shirt, barely missing a valuable watch. The total damage, a hole in one shirt. Elwyn was not very popular around camp for awhile.

Rippling Brook is now a favorite stop for raft parties who often hike up to the falls for a shower bath. Near Rippling Brook, at an elevation of five thousand feet, the survey party passed the halfway mark in the descent of the river. There would be another thousand feet to descend before reaching their destination at Green River, Utah.

The party made two or three more survey stops before camping near the lower end of Lodore Canyon. They had navigated and surveyed the 17.5-mile-long gorge in four days. The fall of Lodore was 269 feet, amounting to 15.37 feet per mile.

On Saturday morning, August 5, after traveling about two miles, they came to a strange formation on the right side where the rock strata was tilted almost to the vertical position. This was called the Mitten Park Fault. Beyond this the canyon walls began to break away on the left and the beginning of mile-long Steamboat Rock appeared on the right. Steamboat Rock is composed of Weber Sandstone and it is liberally streaked with desert varnish. This marks the end of the beautiful Canyon of Lodore.

The Yampa River empties into the Green from the left. Yampa is the Shoshoni name of wild caraway, a plant whose tuberous roots were a favorite food of the Indians. Major Powell called the area around the mouth of the Yampa Echo Park because of the many repeating echoes they heard from Steamboat Rock.[3] Locally the place is known as "Pat's Hole" for hermit Pat Lynch who lived in caves there from the 1880s to 1917.

Woolley gave an apt description of the area:

> Upon entering Echo Park the Green River flows southward at the foot of Steamboat Rock, which is about 700 feet high and a mile long; then it turns abruptly to the right and runs back in a northerly course almost parallel to its former direction for nearly another mile thus having the opposite sides of a long, narrow rock for its right bank. The tongue of rock resembles in general a huge ship and thus obtained its name. It has a mural escarpment along its entire east side, but is broken down in places on the west.[4]

They drifted down below the mouth of the Yampa and made camp. Loper was feeling sick, but Elwyn noted with admiration how Loper, in spite of his frequent aches and pains, kept the boats in good repair. And he never shirked the work of making a new camp or getting the boats loaded to go on again.

On Sunday while Trimble, Woolley, Elwyn, and Lint spent the day surveying, Stoner and Reeside hiked up to the nearby Chew Ranch. They returned about 5:20 P.M. bringing back some garden stuff and a hindquarter of mutton. Bert Chew, who came with them, went swimming with the boys, then returned home. In the evening they all engaged in a game of rummy.

On Monday, the seventh of August, they broke camp and ran down a mile to Pool Creek on the left, where Trimble spent the rest of the forenoon with the survey crew. After lunch they started on but had gone only about a mile when they came to some good springs. It was too good a place to pass up, so they made camp. This was on the right just below Mitten Park at the entrance to Whirlpool Canyon. Mitten Park was named for Pat Lynch's horse, Mitten. Loper still had his headache.

While at that camp Lint killed a two-point buck, so they had deer liver for supper. The Chew Ranch was up on a mesa a short distance from the river. Bert Chew came down again and had dinner with them. After dinner they gave him a short boat ride before he returned home.

The walls of Whirlpool Canyon were high and sometimes vertical, the canyon narrow, and in places the water filled the gorge from wall to wall. The red, pink, and ocher coloring of the pine-dotted steep slopes was similar to Red Canyon and the Canyon of Lodore. But Whirlpool was much narrower through its upper three miles and the walls were generally much steeper. The water flowed rapidly and was made to eddy and spin in whirlpools by projecting rocks and sharp curves.

On August 8 they surveyed along Whirlpool Canyon for another four miles. As they neared the Utah state line the canyon widened with space increasing between the streambed and the walls. High on the sides crags, pinnacles, and towers added to the architecture of the scene. Less than a mile into Utah they came to Jones Hole Creek on the right where a pretty crystal stream came in from a big spring about four miles above the river. It flowed with about 100 cfs. of water and was alive with mountain trout. They made camp on a sandbar just below the mouth of the creek and soon caught a fine mess of fish.

They found the remains of old campfires and rusty cans near camp. Elwyn supposed these camps had been used by parties exploring the river or by fishermen or hunters who had come down the creek.

The next morning, after a breakfast of trout, they surveyed on down the river about a mile to Sage Creek, which took an hour to survey. It was a small creek flowing in a rather broad canyon. They saw prospectors' tools, the remains of an old camp, and several prospect holes in the hillside a short distance into the canyon.

The party continued for a couple of miles before stopping for lunch. They were still fighting the boils and eddies of Whirlpool Canyon, and they hit some good rapids, one with a nine-foot drop

(Greasy Pliers) and another with a drop of ten feet (Dead Wombat).

Whirlpool Canyon ended three miles below Sage Creek where the cliff formations dipped sharply into the earth in a massive fault and the river entered Island Park. The nine-mile length of Whirlpool Canyon had a fall of ninety-eight feet, an average of 10.9 feet to the mile. They arrived at Island Park by 2:30 P.M. and camped on the right bank.

Island Park was named by Major Powell for the many islands along the course of the river in this stretch.[5] The area lay between the lower end of Whirlpool Canyon and the head of Split Mountain Canyon. The country surrounding Island Park was more or less open, and the river meandered through its seven-mile course. But the direct distance between Whirlpool and Split Mountain was less than half that.

The H. H. Ruple family was ranching in the upper part of Island Park and had taken water out of the river in ditches for irrigation. A deserted cabin about a mile northwest of the Ruple place marked the site of an abandoned homestead. Another shack stood at the edge of a cottonwood grove in the Rainbow Park area, with evidences of past attempts to cultivate the surrounding ground.

The many small ravines that drained into the park area carried water during spring thaws and local showers, but for the greater part of the year were dry. Several of these gulches showed evidence of occasional torrential flows. A wagon road to Vernal went along one of the ravines. McKee Spring, a small spring of clear water heavily impregnated with alkali, rose about a mile up the ravine. It flowed a few hundred feet, then sank back into the sand. They saw many Indian petroglyphs in the dark desert varnish on the smooth rock faces along that wash.

The Ruple ranch was located just below the surveyor's camp. Ruple came up to camp about suppertime and picked up their outgoing mail since he was going out to Vernal the next day. He promised to bring back any mail waiting for them there.

The wind started to blow and rain showers splattered them, so they decided to pitch the tents. They took their usual swim, then played rummy until bedtime. Most of them had become experts at this simple card game.

There was much open country to survey in the Island Park area, so they would be in this camp for several days. Although it was sprinkling lightly on August 10, Trimble and his crew surveyed until noon. When it started to rain harder they gave up and came in. They enjoyed lazing in the tents, listening to the beat of the rain, taking in the smell of wet canvas.

Before the heavy rain started Loper had gone down to the ranch to visit the Ruples. When they learned that he was an avid reader, they gave him a book entitled *Burning Daylight* by Jack London.

The Ruples lived on the ranch with their little girl and one hired man. Their garden produced enough fresh vegetables to supply a whole community. They invited the men to help themselves, so the crew made great inroads into the garden during their stay. When the party was ready to leave, Trimble asked Ruple what the bill was. He replied that if they had enjoyed the garden stuff that was pay enough for him.

The area around Island Park was a great circular country bounded all around by hills and mountains with the river meandering through it. Its course had many twists and turns with very little fall. Elwyn and the other boatmen used the oars freely in negotiating the river there.

The lower area of Island Park was separated from the upper part by a tongue of low rolling hills. The lower area was named Rainbow Park by Major Powell for the rainbow-hued Morrison formation through which the river passed. Beyond Rainbow Park was another small open area known as Little Park.

On the morning of August 17 the party entered Split Mountain Canyon. Here the sluggishness of the river disappeared, going back into the mountain spur through which it had previously cut the lower part of Whirlpool Canyon. When it reached the center of the spur it turned abruptly to the right splitting the mountain's Morgan formation longitudinally, thus the name Split Mountain Canyon. Powell first called it "Craggy Canyon" but later changed it to Split Mountain.[6] The canyon had a broad, flaring entrance, similar in structure to the mouth of Whirlpool Canyon. It had a rugged line of majestic crags and buttresses standing sentinel on each side.

Rapids followed one another in quick succession through Split Mountain Canyon. Although the water was swift, only two of the rapids were very rough. At the first one (now called Moonshine Rapid) the river channel was compressed into a narrow slit. It had a steep drop, so the current was exceptionally swift causing the water to billow with high choppy waves. The boulders in the channel were all a safe distance below the water's surface, though, and the boats shot through with almost express-train speed. Elwyn got a thrill from this ride. The other bad one (now called Schoolboy Rapid) occurred at a point where the river turned abruptly to the right causing the current to cross the canyon in a long chute at right angles and strike the opposite wall. There it had undercut solid rock, as it had done at Lower Disaster Falls, but with not as big an undercut. There was enough water outside the overhang that the boatmen, with a hard pull on the oars, could keep the boats clear and make the run safely.

The first day they made four and a half miles down Split Mountain Canyon. The Morgan formation had gone under, replaced by Deseret limestone, which resulted in more vertical canyon walls. The fall of the river was a hundred feet in that distance. They camped on a large sandbar at the foot of a splashing rapid. The eddy from the rapid would have made a good swimming hole except that the water was muddy.

A clear spring near the upper end of the bar furnished good drinking water, and the clean, white sand offered good places for beds. A large pinion tree added to the tapestry of the vertical rock cliffs rising immediately behind it. These cliffs created a spectacularly buttressed wall receding in the distance down the canyon. The coloring was dull gray with a little red and ocher, and the shadows in the late afternoon, extending artistically over the general scene, lent a charming effect.

Split Mountain Canyon was short, yet it had the greatest overall fall of any of the series of canyons they had traversed. In its eight-mile length it had a fall of 148 feet, an average fall of 18.5 feet to the mile.

The next day, while surveying the lower end of the canyon, one of the rodmen discovered a large cave about 150 feet above the river in the left wall. Everyone climbed up to explore it. To reach it they had to climb over a mass of boulders that had sloughed off the main cliff and nearly sealed the entrance. The cave was about twenty feet in diameter and roughly circular. The ceiling was eight to ten feet above the floor in the highest place and the floor was covered with sand as fine as the finest flour, forming a large mound in the center. Animal bones were strewn around, indicating that the place was a resort of some kind for wild beasts, which gave Elwyn the shivers.

As they emerged from Split Mountain Canyon they looked upon rather uninteresting country compared to the colorful gorge they had left behind. There were low rolling hills to the south with the Uinta Mountains in the distance to the north and west.

Farther on they stopped to inspect an old cabin that was nestled among some willows. While they were on the willow bar they jumped a deer, and Lint took a shot at it but thought he had missed. When they crossed the river after lunch they found the deer where it had fallen, mortally wounded, after having swum the river. They skinned it and saved the meat. Then the crew did some surveying before drifting on down the river to make camp on an island.

CHAPTER 12

Split Mountain to
Green River

On Saturday, August 19, the party left Split Mountain Canyon and
the island camp behind them. From there the river flowed with a
gentle current, meandering among low, rolling hills that had thin
vegetation but lacked in scenic interest. In midafternoon they came
to a ranch at Cub Creek occupied by a man named Butcher who,
with his wife and five children, four boys and one girl, came down to
the river to meet them. The ranch used water from Cub Creek for
irrigation.

After a short visit with the Butchers they moved on. Two miles
farther they came to some old placer diggings on the right side
where abandoned machinery along the banks told the story of more
blasted hopes. At another place they saw several old buildings and
the remains of a huge dredge that had apparently never been put
into operation. Everything was now dilapidated, a dismal reminder
of another expensive venture gone bad.

In this stretch Elwyn wished the river had some of the steep fall
of Split Mountain, for it took hard, monotonous rowing to make
headway. Loper said, "The fall along here could be marked by a
minus sign."

In its meandering the river passed within a mile of Dinosaur
National Monument. The quarry where the bones were being exca-
vated was located about six miles northeast of the village of Jensen,
named for Lars Jensen, the first settler there. Brush Creek entered
the river from the right about three miles above Jensen, and ranchers
used its waters extensively for irrigating the benchlands near town.

At midafternoon they came to a deserted ranch on the left bank.
They read some old letters they found there and decided the place

had belonged to a family named Thorne. Loper picked up a couple of old magazines to take along for reading material. He seemed to be the only one in the party with much time to read. When it started to rain they moved on down to an island near an old pumping plant where they made camp and pitched tents.

By 10:00 A.M. the next morning, Tuesday, August 22, they had made the run to Jensen, where a highway bridge spanned the river. The town had a general store, the last one on the highway east before reaching the small settlements in the Yampa and White River valleys of Colorado.

From Jensen the men hiked back to the quarry in Dinosaur National Monument and met Professor Earl Douglass, who told them that this quarry was a world-famous cemetery of giant prehistoric beasts and had furnished many significant specimens of dinosaurs. He said the bones were dug from the shale, then covered with burlap and a plaster-of-paris mixture, because, if left exposed to the air, the bones would deteriorate. Later the bones would be treated with a preservative that would harden and strengthen them.

Back at camp Trimble sent a man to Vernal, about ten miles away, to get their mail. By 3:00 P.M. they all had letters and spent the rest of the afternoon reading mail and writing letters. Loper wrote to the postmaster at Green River, Utah, asking to have the rest of their mail held there, unless it could be sent to the McPherson Ranch.

It stormed that afternoon and was so windy and wet that they gave up on playing rummy and just loafed in the tents until the storm passed. There was talk of a trip to Vernal the next day, so Loper, who carried no money, drew forty-five dollars from Stoner.

They found Vernal to be a nice little town of 1,200 with numerous shade trees in the yards. It had two banks, two drugstores, three hardware stores, two garages, and a few other businesses. Some streets had concrete sidewalks and drinking fountains. Vernal had been settled in 1879 and at first was derisively referred to as Hatchtown, then Ashley Center, and finally in 1893 was named Vernal for its verdant aspect in an arid valley.[1]

Trimble and Reeside visited the editor at the office of the *Vernal Express* who wrote a story for the paper about the party and its mission. The article stated that the job of the survey, which was under the direction of the United States Geological Department in cooperation with the Utah Power and Light Company, was to make a topographic survey of the Green River and its tributaries to locate dam sites for power and irrigation purposes and gather all other data concerning the flow of the river. The surveyors said they found many things different in the gorge than they had supposed from the many reports of previous expeditions, especially the height of the rapids, these in most cases being less than they had supposed.[2]

Elwyn spent the day puttering around just looking the place over. He bought a few things and played some pool. They all returned to Jensen by 5:00 P.M., well pleased with the trip.

The next morning, August 24, they had the boats loaded with new provisions and were on their way by 9:00 A.M. Below Jensen the river was exceedingly sluggish, having a fall of just over a foot and a half per mile for the next 132 miles. The same boats that had so recently behaved like wild horses now moved so sluggishly that the term "down" seemed to be a misnomer. They would see very little real canyon in that distance. This meant plenty of hard rowing for the boatmen.

The scenery was tame compared with that of the upper canyons. At 4:00 P.M. they reached the Alhandra Ferry. An hour later they came to another ranch and camped nearby for the night. They bought a supply of melons and tomatoes from the rancher, which tasted delicious in that hot weather. Next morning the family from the ranch came down to see the boats and watch the crew load up.

For miles through the Uinta Basin the Green River flowed in a channel with vertical cut banks. In some places the banks were as high as twenty feet above the water. The bars were fringed with willows and occasional small groves of cottonwoods. Back away from the banks were many broad stretches of nearly level country joined by rolling hills in the distance.

At Horseshoe Bend seventeen miles below Jensen the stream made a big loop with the two ends not over half a mile apart. A spur running south from Asphalt Ridge separated the ends of the loop. The distance around the loop by boat was about nine miles, and the fall of the river in that distance was less than ten feet. Since there was no surveying to do at that point, the passengers got off at the first end of the loop and hiked the half mile across the neck.

Elwyn, Loper, and Lint took the boats around, and, as they drifted along, indulged in some schoolboy antics by peeling off their clothes and taking a swim. It took them two hours and forty minutes to make the nine miles.

The river was so shallow the boats often grounded on sandbars, causing the boatmen no end of trouble. On the evening of August 25 they camped on a sandbar on the left bank. A strong north wind kicked up clouds of sand, so they moved the beds into a cottonwood grove. Despite the wind they took their usual evening swim.

Hard rowing the next day brought them to the edge of Leota Ranch, comprised of 1,600 acres, including groves of immense cottonwood trees along the river bottoms. They saw many trails where cattle came down to the river to drink. At one of these groves they stopped for lunch, and while they were eating a man came walking into camp. From him they learned that the land belonged to J. K. Ekker, Sr., formerly of Hanksville, Utah. Ekker had at one time owned a ranch and store in Hanksville, and Loper knew him well.

After lunch they ran on down to the Sheppard Ranch. There the passengers got out and walked on ahead to the Ouray Trading Post. Elwyn, Loper, and Lint came on with the boats and arrived there by 4:40 P.M.

The local Indians had come into the Ouray Trading Post for their monthly issue of rations and the men watched them curiously. Some of the crew bought Indian curios, such as beaded moccasins and belts. The Indian agent invited them up to his house for the evening.

The Indians did not want the surveyors to take pictures of them. Woolley fooled one group, who were drifting by in a boat, by pretending to be looking downstream while aiming the camera toward the river. As he saw the party in the view finder he snapped the picture and the Indians were none the wiser.

On Sunday, August 27, the crew passed the day loafing, reading, and writing letters. Elwyn and Leigh Lint hiked up the river about two miles and swam back, providing recreation for themselves and entertainment for the Indians, who sat along the high banks to see them swim back.

Loper ran into a man named Tet Taylor whom he had known in Moab twenty-seven years earlier. The last time they had seen each other had been in 1895 when they parted after having accompanied a trainload of sheep to Chicago.

Next morning they were again on the river. Immediately below the Indian agency at Ouray they passed the mouth of the Duchesne River, which came into the Green from the right. The Duchesne carried the biggest part of the runoff from the Uinta Basin. In 1825 General Ashley had left a cache of supplies at the mouth of the Duchesne, to be picked up when he returned from his exploration of the valley of the Duchesne. Major Powell had camped for several days there, too. The area, from the mouth of the Duchesne to White River, was a favorite winter camping spot for trappers, Indians, and early explorers. A short way below the Duchesne the surveyors passed the mouth of the White River coming in from the left.

The river ran approximately eighty-three miles through the Uinta Basin with an average drop of 1.87 feet to the mile. (By comparison, the Mississippi River drops four inches per mile.) The boatmen were faced with hard, steady rowing, with the August sun beating down, to reach the unsurveyed canyons below. Loper's left hand became blistered and sore. They camped on the right bank of the river after making twenty-three miles.

By 10:00 A.M. on the morning of August 29 they reached Sand Wash, a broad canyon about ninety-six miles above the town of Green River, Utah. The surrounding country was pretty drab with gray shale tali rising to flat-topped mesas. The only green vegetation was willows and cottonwoods along the river bottoms. They observed a strata of oil shale which prospectors had worked extensively. There was a ferry and a cabin at Sand Wash, but the occupants were nowhere to be seen. The survey team had an hour's work in Sand Wash, then they were back on the river.

They reached the mouth of Nine Mile (Minnie Maud) Creek by noon and stopped to do a little surveying. There they came across an abandoned homestead with a cabin, barn, corrals, and a small reservoir on the cleared ground. A mile-long ditch along the side of the canyon had been used to take water out of Nine Mile Creek. The entire area was encrusted with alkali. They decided the alkali was probably the reason for the place being abandoned.

With their work done by 2:00 P.M., they continued downriver. The cliffs were four hundred feet high and drably colored in layers of gray ocher and buff but were picturesque. Due to weathering they suggested Gothic cathedrals, castles, and turrets. They soon came to a little riffle, something they had not seen for some time. Elwyn and the other boatmen enjoyed the short respite from hard rowing. Soon after that, at the outside of a horseshoe bend, they could see Sumners Amphitheater, named for Jack Sumner of the first Powell expedition. The rim looked to be a thousand feet above them and the strata was of pale gray talus alternating with hard layers of chocolate-colored rock, tinged in places with apricot. After another six miles of rowing they came to a wash where Trimble had to pick up a point and start his survey again. They made camp at the mouth of this wash.

On Wednesday, August 30, while the survey crew was at work, Loper puttered with his boat and oiled his shoes. Then he helped Clogston load the boats. After that he took a walk to the top of the

canyon where he could see the river's loop below. He saw a bleak
landscape of buff sandstone and gray shales with hardly any vegetation. It looked uninteresting to him. He figured this must be the
beginning of Desolation Canyon, although just where the canyon
began was difficult to tell because of the absence of a well-defined
gorge. Actually, they were sixteen to eighteen miles inside Desolation
Canyon by this time.

Loper wrote in his journal:

> This is sure Desolation Canyon all right and that calls to my
> mind just how appropriate most all the names are that Major
> Powell gave different canyons and rapids. The canyon walls are
> a dull gray composed of sand stone and some oil shale and a
> little lime but no vegetation whatever— [3]

In reality a few dwarf gray bushes grew here and there, clinging
to the rocky slopes. The canyon walls became higher as the river
descended the canyon, and many side canyons cut the region into
a wilderness of gray and brown cliffs. Although the craggy cliffs
were ragged and barren, they were eroded into majestic pyramids,
spires, and other interesting land forms. In places the side canyons
were separated from one another only by narrow walls, which rose
hundreds of feet. Some of the walls were so narrow that the softer
rocks had crumbled away and left holes through the wall, making
side doors between the canyons. Heaps of broken rock lay against
the walls, and towers and peaks were all around. Away on the horizon
was a long line of broken cliffs, and in one of these cliffs, high above
the river, Elwyn noticed a large natural arch near the skyline. They
camped on the left bank at a place known as Gold Hole.

A storm came in during the night, blowing over the tents and soaking the men and equipment. Next morning, while the survey team
was at work, the rest of the men hung the beds out to dry.

About 11:00 A.M. another big storm came up, but by then they
had the boats loaded and the hatches screwed down tight. The men
sought shelter under some cliffs until the storm passed, ate lunch,
and went downstream about a mile and a half, when the skies darkened with the threat of another storm. Finding a good campsite, they
pulled in for the night.

On Friday, September 1, they passed some "hoodoo" pinnacles on
the left. These gargoyle-shaped towers are formed when hard cap-
rock protects the pillar of soft alluvium from erosion. They surveyed
four side canyons plus seven and a half miles of river—a very good

day—and camped on the right bank just below a natural bridge which Kolb had described in his book.

After another rainy night they ran down about four miles. Then it began to rain again, so they made camp at the mouth of Jack Creek.

About noon a man whose name they did not record walked into camp and ate dinner with them. He had walked from the town of Green River and was going to Ouray. After lunch he asked for some grub and was on his way.

Between periods of rain Elwyn, Reeside, and Stoner climbed up the side of the canyon to a natural bridge. At this place the sandstone cliffs were reddish-brown and dotted with dark-green pinion and juniper trees, not so desolate as the name of the canyon implied. Looking down the river, they could see a stretch of white water, the first they had seen in many days. This signaled the approach of the white-water section of Desolation Canyon.

On Sunday, September 3, the crew took the day off to wash clothes, shave, and clean up. They finished the day reading and playing cards. It was fine weather until bedtime, when more rain fell. The fall rainy season had really arrived.

It rained again at breakfast, so they were in no hurry to load up. When it cleared a little, Trimble took the crew and surveyed up Jack Creek. That afternoon they surveyed down the river for about two miles, in spite of a light shower.

Next day they worked side canyons and by 3:00 P.M. reached Flat Creek, a small stream coming in from the right. The extra men made camp while Trimble and his team surveyed the side canyon. During the day they had covered five and a quarter miles of river, running several small rapids. The fast water gave the boatmen welcome relief from the continual rowing. Still, because of a stiff, upriver wind, it was hard rowing between rapids. The boatmen were ready to make camp.

On Wednesday, September 6, they had so many side canyons to survey that progress was slow. They ran several rapids—one of them rough—traveling only four and a half miles before camping on the left bank.

They were definitely in canyon country again since the boatmen had to negotiate sizable rapids at the mouth of almost every side canyon. The roughness of a rapid depended on the number and size of boulders that had washed into the river channel from the side canyon. Many of them required extra caution to avoid rocks in the shallow water. They ran all of the rapids without trouble, and the passengers were able to remain on the boats through most of them. They covered another four and a half miles with an average drop of 13.5 feet to the mile.

On Friday, September 8, a strong wind blew up the river all day making for hard rowing. They traveled about two and a half miles before noon and about the same after lunch. Trimble accidentally mashed a finger, which made work painful. The boaters ran a large, splashy rapid (Steer Ridge Rapid) that afternoon and reached Rock Creek by 4:00 P.M. Rock Creek, fifty-four miles upstream from Green River, Utah, flowed a stream of cool, crystal-clear water that originated in some large springs about two miles from its mouth. Willows and cottonwood trees lined the river on the right side.

The Seamountain Ranch was located below the mouth of Rock Creek, which provided irrigation for the farm. Dan Seamountain raised alfalfa, a garden, and a small orchard of peaches, apricots, and apples. The family got its supplies either by packtrain along a trail down the canyon to Green River, or out of the canyon over the mountains to Sunnyside, a mining town in Carbon County, Utah. The Seamountains saw the surveyors at work and came down to the river to visit them. Flossie, Dan's wife, had once been a clerk in the bank at Green River, Utah, so both Elwyn and Loper knew her. After a short visit the party went on down the river a couple of miles and camped on the left side below a small stream.

On Saturday, September 9, they worked on down the river to Three Canyons, where Trimble had some surveying to do, which he finished by noon. From Three Canyons a break in the cliffs allowed them to see a mountain peak off to the right with tall pines and aspens growing on its slopes. While the surveyors were at work, Loper took a walk down the horse trail over the hill past the second rapid.

After lunch they ran on down one and a quarter miles below Three Canyons to the last dam site. By 2:30 P.M. they had finished surveying it. The boats hit some rough rapids that afternoon. In one of them Loper's boat slammed into a rock and gave him the worst jolt of any bump on the entire trip.

They rowed for another nine miles where the lower slopes and middle cliffs were a deep purple—too colorful for the name Desolation to apply anymore. At a hook in the canyon they came to the ranch of James McPherson, who irrigated his farm from Florence Creek, a small side stream coming in from the left. It was at Florence Creek that outlaw gangs once crossed the Green on their way to Browns Park and the Hole-in-the-Wall hideout in Wyoming.

McPherson often swapped fresh horses with Butch Cassidy's Wild Bunch and supplied them with grub, saying he got along better with the outlaws than with the posse that chased them.

Besides hay for his stock, McPherson raised abundant crops of fruit and vegetables. A trail led down the canyon to Green River, Utah, and pack mules were the only means of transportation for the rancher. Still, the McPhersons had all sorts of heavy farm machinery—wagons, a large steel range, and many other heavy and cumbersome articles. All had been packed from Green River to the ranch by the mules.

The peaches grown on this ranch were of the finest quality, so good they found a ready market in Chicago and other cities. The fruit brought top prices, carried to Green River by mule train and shipped east by rail.

The men received a cordial welcome from Jim and Tora McPherson, who invited them to supper that evening. Some of them had letters waiting. McPherson told them they could have all the peaches they wanted and Tora gave them four loaves of homemade bread, which they all enjoyed.

Sunday, September 10, was a day off, so they rested, shaved, and did their washing. Elwyn, Lint, and Loper went up to the orchard, filled a two-and-a-half-gallon bucket with peaches, and started back to camp. But before reaching camp they had eaten all the peaches, so they went back and filled the bucket again. They also brought back melons and tomatoes. The three boatmen took their regular dip in the river, but the water was so cold they made it a quick one.

On Monday, September 11, they loaded up with more peaches, melons, and tomatoes and were on their way again. The scene below McPherson's Ranch was of pale green cottonwood trees along the river, purple and maroon slopes reaching up over half the height of the canyon walls to jagged, tiered sandstone cliffs above, all dotted with dark-green pinions and junipers. Their first excitement came at the long, rocky rapid at the mouth of Florence Creek. Loper thought the river was a little low for safe boating since there were a lot of big rocks dangerously close to the surface. Trying to dodge the rocks, both Elwyn and Loper got hung up a couple of times but were able to work the boats free and go on through without damage.

A mile below the ranch the river plunged into the drab sandstone and shales of Gray Canyon. Major Powell first called it Coal Canyon, then Lignite, and finally Gray because of the color of its walls. They hit another difficult rapid (probably Wire Fence Rapid) about a mile below Florence Creek, but all came through safely. Below that they hit several more stretches of rough white water, but nothing slowed them down.

In Gray Canyon the physiographic features were somewhat similar to those at the head of Desolation Canyon but it looked much more desolate than most of Desolation Canyon. The walls increased in height as they descended the canyon. At Coal Creek, and for several miles below, the river flowed in a narrow, box-like gorge with vertical walls that broke back into rough, barren slopes. In many places the inner gorge was as much as 100 feet deep. Vegetation was confined to a fringe of willows along the riverbank and an occasional cottonwood tree.

There was a big rapid at the mouth of Coal Creek and another at the mouth of Rattlesnake Canyon. Just below Rattlesnake, Trimble and Woolley located the connecting point of their survey. They tied into this point and surveyed on down another half mile, where they made camp on the right bank. Elwyn and Lint hiked back up to the head of Rattlesnake Rapid and entertained themselves by running it in their life jackets.

On Tuesday, September 12, they all crossed the river to where Trimble picked up his lines and started the last leg of the survey. At noon the McPhersons passed by on their way to Green River. Tora only stayed on the ranch during the summer and she was going out for the winter.

About eighteen miles above the town of Green River, the Price River joined the Green from the right. During flood stages the Price River carried a considerable flow and large amounts of debris. But during the dry season practically all the flow was diverted for irrigation in the upper part of its basin. All that reached the Green River was a small stream of muddy water with a disagreeable odor. It was a foretaste of what *could* happen when most of a river's water was diverted from its natural course. They had lunch at the mouth of the Price River and by night had surveyed another 4.7 miles.

The last big rapid in Gray Canyon (Swasey Rapid) was just opposite Gunnison Butte. This landmark was named for Captain Gunnison of the U.S. Army, who surveyed westward and crossed the Green River below there in 1853.[4] This high pinnacle could be seen from the town of Green River and had long been a prominent landmark. Elwyn had hiked up to this rapid when he was a teenager living by the Green River. At that time he had thought the rapid could never be run. Now an experienced white-water boatman, he and the others ran it taking hardly any water. After the run they made camp on the left side of the river just above Willow Bend. It was the last camp of the trip.

About six and a half miles below the mouth of the Price River the Green emerged into Gunnison Valley. The mapping from there to the mouth of the Green River where it joined the Colorado, a distance of 117.3 miles, had been done in 1914 by the Reclamation Service. On September 13, when Trimble tied his survey to that of the Reclamation Service at Gunnison Valley, his job was over.

Eleven miles farther down was the town of Green River, Utah, a station on the main line of the Denver and Rio Grande Western Railroad. The fall from the end of Gray Canyon to the city of Green River was forty-one feet, or 3.73 feet to the mile.

On Thursday, September 14, as they prepared for their last short run, one of them discovered a rattlesnake among the rocks. Someone hit it with a rock but did not kill it, and it scuttled away. They finally discovered it under a flat stone not two feet from where Reeside was standing. One man turned the rock over and another dispatched the rattler. When they were ready to leave, Clogston left the sheet-iron stove in place with a roaring fire in it. Maybe they were so anxious to get going that they didn't want to wait for it to cool off. That sort of thing would not be allowed today since all garbage must be packed out. The park service urges travelers to leave nothing behind but footprints.

The boats made good time and they soon reached the Green River Dam. Because of the low stage of the river they had to unload men and cargo from the boats at the dam. Trimble telephoned into Green River and had George Franz come out to get the gear. The barely submerged plank top of the dam made a wet platform over which they slid the empty boats. That left the three boatmen with empty boats to row the last eight miles.

At Elwyn's suggestion, they stopped at Block's ranch, where they received a warm welcome. The Blocks remembered Elwyn as a neighbor in his teenage years and were glad to see him. During the visit they treated the boatmen to their fill of watermelon. They tarried so long that when they got going again Loper was suddenly in a great hurry. He had only gone a little way when he saw his wife Rachel standing on the bank of the river in company with Jack Douglas and his wife. He immediately landed the boat and took Rachel on board.

A truck was waiting for them at the landing just above the railroad bridge. They took the boats out of the river and loaded all three onto the waiting truck. That evening they had one last dinner together at the Midland Hotel.

The next day they said their farewells and most went their separate ways. Loper's home was then in Green River, so Elwyn stayed to visit with him and Rachel for a day or two before going on to Monticello. He was in no hurry to go back to "regular living."

Elwyn and Loper relived the expedition, telling Rachel all about the exciting times they had been through. Elwyn could not hide his pleasure when Loper told Rachel that he was now a first-class, rough-water man, as good as any around.

PART THREE
GRAND CANYON
EXPEDITION

CHAPTER 13

Lee's Ferry to Soap Creek

In 1921 the Colorado River Basin states formed the Colorado River Commission, chaired by Secretary of Commerce Herbert Hoover. Their aim was to determine how the water of the Colorado River was to be divided. The final meeting of the commission was to be held in Santa Fe in November 1922. In that summer, before the November meeting, several reclamation and utility company people decided to gain some publicity for the commission by giving the delegates a boat trip in Glen Canyon, believing that some on-site background would help the delegates in their deliberations.

Eugene Clyde La Rue, chief hydrologist for the United States Geological Survey, who had been working on plans for the Colorado River for many years, organized the trip. He had a special interest in the plans for the river, believing that of all the proposed dam sites one in Glen Canyon just above Lee's Ferry and another in Grand Canyon at Diamond Creek would best serve to control flooding and generate electric power.

Lewis R. Freeman, a free-lance journalist and explorer, heard of the Glen Canyon trip and got in touch with La Rue. He wanted to be part of it, having already explored several rivers, including the Columbia, and written stories about his experiences. La Rue believed Freeman could help generate the publicity they were after, so put him on as a boatman.

Under the leadership of Tom Wimmer, a crew took four boats out of storage at Lee's Ferry and put outboard motors on them. In two weeks they got the boats up through Glen Canyon to Hall's Crossing. There they picked up the main party, which had come overland with

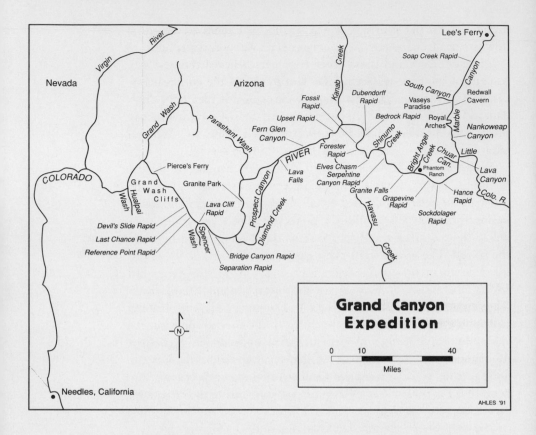

Grand Canyon Expedition

0   10   40
Miles

AHLES '91

La Rue from Salt Lake City. Included in the party were Dr. John A. Widtsoe, apostle of the Church of Jesus Christ of Latter-day Saints, former president of the University of Utah, and Utah's delegate on the Colorado River Commission; Arthur Powell Davis, director of the United States Reclamation Service (now the Bureau of Reclamation); Colonel Claude H. Birdseye, chief topographic engineer of the United States Geological Survey who would be in charge of the Grand Canyon Survey; Clarence Stetson, secretary of the Colorado River Commission and a representative of Herbert Hoover; Herman Stabler, chief engineer for the Land Classification Board of the U.S. Geological Survey; and various other officials.[1]

From Hall's Crossing the party floated down Glen Canyon. Along the way La Rue showed them all the scenic and historic places, including a hike up to Rainbow Bridge. He took pains to show the dignitaries his pet dam site, which was located about eleven miles downstream from where Glen Canyon Dam was eventually built.

Director Davis and some other engineers believed the best way to control the river was by a high dam in one of the gorges below Grand Canyon. La Rue tried to sell them on his idea for a high dam in Glen Canyon to even out the flow of the river. Hydroelectric projects below there could then be constructed at sites to be chosen after completion of the upcoming Grand Canyon survey.

At Santa Fe the Colorado River Commission hammered out the historic Colorado River Compact. By terms of the agreement, the water of the river was divided equally between the upper and lower basins. The commission chose a point near Lee's Ferry, one mile below the mouth of the Paria River, as the dividing point between the basins. The government put a gauging station at Lee's Ferry to measure stream flow, and they designated that site as Mile Zero from which all mileage, both upstream and down, would be measured.[2] The commission could not agree on how much of the river water each of the seven states would get. That would have to come later.

Freeman was quick to capitalize on the news of the signing of the compact. In a few months he turned out several articles and a book entitled *The Colorado River Yesterday, To-day, and To-morrow.* His flamboyant articles about the trip helped land him a job as boatman on the 1923 expedition.

The only remaining unsurveyed stretch of the Colorado River system was through Marble and Grand canyons. Colonel Claude H. Birdseye organized the expedition to fill this gap. It would be a major scientific endeavor, since up until that time only twenty-seven men were known to have traversed the length of Marble and Grand canyons, and of them all only Major John Wesley Powell and Robert B. Stanton had had any scientific background.[3]

Colonel Birdseye was well qualified to lead the expedition, having surveyed Mount Rainier, the crater of Kilauea in Hawaii, and other notable sites. He was a top-notch organizer, and he worked all winter and spring on the endless details of outfit, personnel, and schedule. He believed in the theory that every member and everything essential to the success of the expedition should be included, but anything not essential should be excluded. He decided he would need a topographic engineer, a hydraulic engineer, a geologist, a cook, a rodman, and a boatman for each of the four boats. This brought the party to ten. Herman Stabler assisted in the planning by compiling a manual of navigational information from all available reports and accounts of previous expeditions.

A research crew, after months of tentative trials and experiments, designed waterproof bags and boxes. All the tubs, sinks, and basins in the Geological Survey wing of the Department of Interior building in Washington, D.C., served as testing tanks. They came up with an inner sack of rubber covered with an outer one of double-tied, water-proofed canvas for protection of bedding, duffel, and provisions such as flour, sugar, and dried fruit. Attempts to make watertight instrument and camera boxes from galvanized iron failed because the metal tended to bend under pressure. Wooden boxes with covers held down upon rubber gaskets by brass catches served better. The researchers selected almost everything in the outfit by test and comparison from the best that could be bought or made.[4]

Birdseye was charged with making an unbroken traverse and level survey line through Marble and Grand canyons and running the survey line up side canyons. In addition, the party would survey possible dam sites under the direction of the hydraulic engineer, E. C. La Rue.

In July 1923 Elwyn got an offer from Colonel Birdseye to act as one of the boatmen for the Grand Canyon Survey. His spirits soared. He accepted immediately, and with happy anticipation left Monticello on July 10. Traveling by automobile and stage over dirt roads and then by rail, it took him four days to cover about 300 miles. Flagstaff was a lumber-mill town of a little over three thousand population with one- and two-story business houses of red Moencopi sandstone lining Santa Fe Avenue (Route 66), running east and west, and San Francisco Street, running north and south. At 6,900-feet elevation, the town was nestled in tall ponderosa pines at the base of Mount Elden with the San Francisco peaks rising beyond that to the northwest. Flagstaff was the trading center for northern Arizona ranchers as well as for Navajo and Hopi Indians from the nearby reservations.[5]

Elwyn was intrigued by some small wagons drawn by scrubby Indian ponies rattling along the streets. Chubby papooses peeked from cradleboards as their vividly dressed Indian mothers hawked pottery, blankets, baskets, and silver jewelry on the sidewalks.

Soon after breakfast the next morning Elwyn met Colonel Birdseye. The tall, white-haired party chief took him down to see a new boat that had been made especially for this expedition. Besides the new one, they would use three boats that were in storage at Lee's Ferry.

When Elwyn asked Colonel Birdseye if Bert Loper would be going on the trip, he was disappointed to learn that his old friend and companion of the two previous expeditions would not be along. He found out later that Birdseye had asked La Rue about hiring Bert Loper, but La Rue had said Loper was rather old for the job. Loper was fifty-four, but his age may not have been the real reason for La Rue's comment. Both men were domineering and opinionated, and La Rue's rebuff may have resulted from the violent quarrel the two had had in Glen Canyon two years earlier. So instead of Loper, Birdseye had opted for Emery Kolb as head boatman.

Kolb, a wiry, dark-haired little man weighing no more than 135 pounds, had boated through Grand Canyon with his brother Ellsworth in 1911–1912. He and Ellsworth (Ed) operated a photographic studio at the head of the Bright Angel Trail on the South Rim. They showed movies daily of their 1911 trip and sold scenic pictures of the canyon. They also took pictures of tourists who were about to descend the canyon trail on mules and had them developed by the time the people returned.

Elwyn spent the first day helping to make boxes for the cooking utensils. Leigh Lint, of Weiser, Idaho, with whom Elwyn had boated the Green River the previous year, came in that evening. Twenty-year-old Lint was a beefy athlete who could tear the rowlocks off a boat. The two roomed together and went to a picture show that night.

Lewis Freeman of Pasadena, California, arrived the next afternoon. He had once been a star athlete at Stanford but had let his weight balloon to over 250 pounds. He showed up nattily dressed in knickers, knee stockings, two-tone oxfords, and carrying a walking stick. This pompous appearance did not endear him to the other boatmen, who considered him a snob.

On the following day La Rue and Dr. Raymond C. Moore (from the University of Kansas) came in on the afternoon train. La Rue, at age forty-four, was tall, thin, and wore a small black mustache. He suffered intermittent stomachaches and was unduly cranky when bothered with them. He had qualified for the position because of his many years specializing in problems of, and working on, the Colorado River.

Moore was an acknowledged authority on the geology of the

middle Colorado canyon. A former athlete, toughened by many a hard summer's fieldwork, he was in prime physical condition.

Emery Kolb drove over from Grand Canyon with his wife, Blanche, and daughter Edith. He had thought this trip would be an excellent opportunity to take more pictures with better equipment than he and his brother Ellsworth had used on their 1911 trip. Birdseye had put the damper on this in a letter dated February 10, 1923, warning, "Unless you consider the success of the government expedition to the entire exclusion of your private interests, we will secure another boatman." The USGS, he said, meaning La Rue, would take its own movies for its own publicity purposes.

This had upset Kolb no end. "I feel," he wrote back, "it would be self-extermination to take part in a trip where others obtain motion pictures, as it is in such pictures, more than anything else, we make our living." Kolb had asked for a thousand dollars per month and the right to take moving pictures. Birdseye would not agree to that, but finally allowed Kolb to take along one small movie camera with the understanding that he would only use it when it did not interfere with his boating responsibilities. He wanted Kolb for the trip because of his knowledge of the Grand Canyon. As a second choice he would have taken Bert Loper, who wanted the job badly. In the end, Kolb accepted Birdseye's terms, but it would rankle him throughout the trip.

Frank B. Dodge arrived on horseback from Mesa Verde after taking a week to ride across the Navajo reservation. He was thirty-one, short, stocky, powerful, and growing bald. Born on the island of Oahu, he was an excellent swimmer and horseman. He had worked for the Geological Survey in Hawaii. Frank Word, the cook, arrived from Los Angeles.

Topographic engineer R. W. Burchard, who would do most of the mapping work, came in by train. He was a powerful Texan who had already surveyed the lower stretches of the Colorado River from thirty-five miles inside the Grand Canyon to the Boulder Canyon dam site and on to Needles, California. He had a powerful physique, great endurance and a cool head.

The monthly salaries of the nonscientific members of the crew were as follows: Kolb, $500; Freeman, $250; Blake and Lint $200. Dodge signed on at $150 per month but said he would have gone for nothing. His pay was raised to $200 midway in the trip. Frank Word signed on for $125 per month, but this was raised to $150.

Freeman, the official diary keeper, got extra pay because he was an able journalist. He took the first typewriter through the canyon, whipping it out as soon as he landed at a new camp, pecking away on it while others gathered wood and set up camp. Dodge said, "Where I'd walk off with 100 pounds at a portage it was all Freeman could do to carry himself around."

On July 17 the crew spent the morning loading the new boat and other equipment onto trucks for transport to Lee's Ferry. At noon the whole party sat down as dinner guests of the Rotary Club of Flagstaff.

Before the group left the hotel, introductions were made all around. Freeman passed out pamphlets to each one saying, "This will serve to introduce me," or words to that effect. Elwyn glanced at the paper, which he remembers as saying something like: "Lewis R. Freeman, author, explorer, champion athlete." Dodge took one look at it, wadded it up, and threw it on the floor. He wrote later that he did not resent Freeman's pompous airs the way the other boatmen did. He figured that exaggeration and flair helped Freeman sell his books and articles.

Early on July 18 the party headed for Lee's Ferry with Dodge and Elwyn riding on the front fenders of one of the trucks. At every stop they placed gunnysacks on the fenders while they were off them so the sun would not make the metal too hot to sit on. They reached "The Gap" on the Navajo Indian Reservation about 3:30. Having no lunch with them, they went on to Cedar Ridge, where they had supper and stopped for the night.

The caravan consisted of three trucks and three touring cars. Kolb's wife, Blanche, went along, as did their vivacious daughter Edith and her friend Catharine Pahl of Los Angeles.

The next day the party encountered some bad road caused by washouts from recent flooding. They were able to make repairs with picks and shovels. On the upgrades the weight of the boat projecting back from the bed of the truck hauling it tended to lift the front wheels off the ground. Freeman's excess poundage (he rode on the front fender of that truck) helped to overcome this problem.

The caravan approached the river on the old Mormon dugway that threaded along the base of a chocolate-colored ledge called Lee's Backbone. Across the river to the north Elwyn could see a distinctive whitish knob of the Chinle formation standing out against the pink sandstone cliffs. Kolb told him this marked the mouth of the Paria

River, where the old home and farm of John D. Lee were nestled in the cottonwoods. They arrived at Lee's Ferry before noon and camped near the Edison boathouse located on the left bank a couple of hundred yards below the ferry.

Lee's Ferry was the only place for hundreds of miles up- or downstream where the Colorado River could be approached without a descent into a forbidding canyon. With Glen Canyon above and Marble and Grand canyons below, it was also the only place where the river could be reached from both sides. The crossing was discovered in the 1860s by Mormon explorer Jacob Hamblin, who later told John Doyle Lee how to find it. Lee, a fugitive from federal authorities for his part in the Mountain Meadows Massacre, established a small farm and ferry there in the fall of 1871, first using one of Major Powell's boats that had been stored there for the winter. Even today Lee's Ferry has the only road to the river for launching boats between Glen Canyon and Lake Mead.

The party learned from a man named Cockroft, the hydrographer who was stationed there, that the ferry had sunk three days previously, carrying down a couple of cars and giving some Boy Scouts from Minnesota a good scare. Cockroft said he had had a rather busy time fishing the youngsters out with his canoe.[6]

The Colorado was 800 feet wide at Lee's Ferry. Lint, Kolb, and Elwyn dived in and swam across the river. Kolb returned on a canvas boat which Dodge had rowed across.

Later that day the boatmen began the much-needed repair of the three old boats which were on loan from the Southern California Edison Company. The boats, made of pine, were of the Galloway design, but made heavier for carrying more freight. Two of them were seventeen and a half feet long with just under five feet of beam and each weighed about 700 pounds. Hatch covers measured about eighteen inches by three feet two inches and were held down with wing nuts. The third old boat was sixteen feet long and of a different design (probably the "Tub" or *Static* used in the 1921 survey of Cataract Canyon).

The new boat was eighteen feet long, made of oak, and weighed 800 pounds. It had a four-inch rake (the amount of overhang or incline from perpendicular at the bow), its bottom was protected with two-and-a-half-inch slats spaced two inches apart, and it had thin sheet copper at the chines (the intersection of bottom and sides).

Each of these boats was equipped with a three-quarter-inch lifeline that led all around the gunwale (the upper edge of the boat's side) through iron eyes. The rope was stopped by turksheads (turban-shaped knots worked on the rope with a piece of small line) at both sides of each ring. The oars were copper-covered at the tips. A metal handle, or portage bar, was fitted to the sterns, and all the boats had air tanks for safety and buoyancy. All were without keels.

The fifth boat was a fourteen footer made of canvas. It had tire inner tubes on each gunwale for bumpers and oil cans fitted inside for buoyancy. Life preservers for everyone were of cork with a kapok collar. Of the four wooden boats, the new one handled the most easily.

The survey party spent from July 20 to 31 extending the topographic surveys up the Paria River and in the area around Lee's Ferry. The four boatmen, Emery Kolb, Elwyn Blake, Leigh Lint, and Lewis Freeman worked on the boats, caulking, white leading, tarring, coppering, and soaking them.

The men set up a radio and heard a concert from Los Angeles. Moore fashioned a loudspeaker out of a funnel and a tin baking-powder can that made the concert quite audible forty feet away. Freeman noted that the radio continued to function right through a violent thunderstorm. He said, "Static would crash in the ears simultaneously with the flash of lightning, but hardly a word or a note would be lost."[7]

One day Lint decided to swim across the river and upon approaching the far shore got caught in a whirlpool. Apparently he did not know enough to dive through the bottom and out. It pulled him down into the vortex, where he was barely able to keep his head above water. In a panic, he called for help. Dodge happened to be nearby with the canvas boat and heard the call. In a minute he was beside the exhausted Lint, who grasped the stern of the boat. Dodge towed him to shore where Lint climbed into the boat for the return trip. He was too exhausted to want anything for supper and went straight to bed.

On July 26 Freeman recorded:

Boat nomenclature has finally been worked out. Each craft is to be named after one of the canyons of the lower river, these being allocated as follows: The new boat is called the *Grand*; the red 18-foot boat, the *Glen*; the green 18-foot boat, the *Marble*; and the 16-foot boat, the *Boulder*; the folding canvas boat takes the name *Mojave*, from the canyon below Topcock. Fiske, who was once a sign painter, inscribed these names on both bows of the respective boats before launching.[8]

Boatman assignments were as follows: the *Marble*, Emery Kolb; the *Grand*, Lewis Freeman; the *Boulder*, Leigh Lint; the *Glen*, Elwyn Blake; and the *Mojave*, Frank Dodge.

Normally Colonel Birdseye would record while Burchard did the surveying. But after the boats were refurbished Birdseye and Burchard each surveyed a different area to more quickly finish their work around Lee's Ferry. Elwyn acted as recorder for Colonel Birdseye. On the first day the ground got so hot he could not sit on it.

They came in about 2:30 P.M. and launched the *Boulder*. Then they went swimming to cool off. Elwyn got out before the others, whereupon they tried to throw him in the river. He had done some wrestling while in the army, so they only succeeded in getting his clothes dampened from their wet swimming suits.[9]

On July 27 Colonel Birdseye, Charles Fiske, and Elwyn did some surveying in the hills south of camp. By about 10:00 A.M. the rocks were too hot to sit on. Once again Elwyn had to stand up to do his recording. The temperature hit 109° F that day, so everyone in camp went swimming in the evening.

On July 29 Elwyn recorded for Colonel Birdseye again. The thermometer registered 110 in the shade. La Rue and Moore went up the old dugway in the Dodge car. They hiked along the cliffs trying to find a way down to Soap Creek Rapid but did not succeed. After putting some finishing touches on his boat, Elwyn joined Lint to haul a boatload of wood for camp. Elwyn worked all day without a shirt, getting a bad sunburn.

The passengers got their boat assignments that day. Elwyn would take Frank Word, the cook, and the cooking outfit on the *Glen*. Lint, in the *Boulder*, would carry Birdseye and Burchard and the instruments. Freeman, in the *Grand*, was to take Moore and La Rue as passengers. Dodge got the canvas boat, *Mojave*, for carrying the rod. Kolb, in the *Marble*, would have no passengers for the present, only supplies.

That evening they enjoyed fresh vegetables and roast beef for supper—the last of either they would have for some weeks. Right after supper two canvas boats pulled down the river past camp and landed on the opposite bank. Dodge crossed over and found they belonged to Dave Rust, who had brought a party of eastern college students down from Hite. Rust, who lived at Kanab, Utah, was a friend of Emery Kolb. Kolb said Rust knew the middle Colorado region very well, both historically and by traveling it. He said Rust had waited for him and Ellsworth here at Lee's Ferry in 1911 and warned against running Soap Creek Rapid. They ignored his advice and upset twice. Rust talked interestingly of John D. Lee, Father Escalante, and many other river subjects.[10]

On July 31 they had a "shakedown cruise" of all the boats to make sure they were in good order. In the afternoon they began stowing cargo into the boats. Freeman had almost a full load in the *Grand* by evening. He gave it a tryout by pulling up the river to the spring with La Rue and Edith Kolb as passengers. He found that it was very different from handling the empty boat. He decided she was surely going to have a willful way in rough water, especially with two passengers on the decks.

Elwyn, like the others, spent the day preparing for the start next morning. Both La Rue and Kolb took movies of the outfit preparing to leave and a simulation of the actual start. Kolb, his daughter Edith, and Elwyn went to the spring for drinking water since the river water was too muddy to drink without settling. A still photo of the crew did not have Dodge in it, because he was sleeping off a bout of the evening before with Cockroft's fig wine.

On August 1 they finished packing the boats and were on their way by about 9:30. The holds of the boats took an astonishing amount of cargo, and everyone was relieved that the volume of cargo did not force them to remove the airtanks for further room.

Kolb led off with his daughter Edith and her friend Catharine Pahl on board. The girls went with him as far as the end of the dugway and had a thrilling ride in the Paria Riffle. Freeman went next with La Rue and Moore as passengers, followed by Elwyn in the *Glen* loaded with the cook and his kitchen equipment. Dodge followed in the canvas canoe. The last to shove off was Lint in the *Boulder* with Burchard and Birdseye on board.

The survey crew started work below the south end of the dugway using an alidade, plane table, and stadia rods, as had been done by the previous two year's expeditions. Birdseye began to run the river line with Burchard recording and Dodge holding the rod. Dodge used the canvas boat to get to his stations. It appeared to be useful for that, at least in the quiet water.

Kolb's wife, Blanche, and Roger Birdseye each drove a car over the dugway and picked up the girls. Roger, a cousin of Colonel Birds-

The Birdseye party, taken just before their departure at Lee's Ferry. Left to right: Leigh Lint, Elwyn Blake, Frank Word, Claude C. Birdseye, Raymond Moore, R. W. Burchard, Eugene C. La Rue, Lewis Freeman, and Emery Kolb. (Grand Canyon 314, U.S. Geological Survey)

eye, was charged with getting supplies to the expedition at appointed intervals along the canyon.

During the afternoon the *Marble*, *Glen*, and *Grand*, with their usual passengers, drifted ahead of the surveyors. Dodge would land the *Mojave* and hold rod for the surveyors wherever they needed a point. Lint, in the *Boulder*, landed Birdseye and Burchard wherever they had to set up the plane table and alidade.

Marble Canyon is a box-like gorge having nearly vertical red walls rising from the river's edge. The walls are not actually marble but are composed of gray Kaibab limestone stained red by the ferrous-laden formations from above. The red walls are liberally streaked with desert varnish. The party passed through two small rapids before noon.

They stopped for lunch "at a so-called bridge site, a narrow section with abrupt walls nearly 500 feet high." After looking it over, Freeman noted: "If a bridge is ever built here it will almost surely be a record-breaker for height." [11] The Navajo Bridge, 834 feet long and 467 feet high, was completed at this site in 1929.

The men ate lunch on a sandbank and enjoyed a birthday cake Cockroft's wife had given Frank Dodge just as they were leaving.

Kolb and Elwyn each got some drinking water at a seep on the left side of the canyon, making a ticklish climb to get it.

They camped for the night on the right shore above Badger Creek Rapid. Badger was a nasty looking jumble of furious waves. Badger Creek Rapid, 7.4 miles below Lee's Ferry, had a fall of thirteen feet in about 100 yards. Powell had estimated it at eighteen feet and the Kolbs at twenty. A big whirlpool made a wide sweep against the left bank and outside of this the current set strongly to the right across the head of the rapid where it tumbled into a nest of boulders. The tongue, that narrowing chute of relatively smooth but fast-moving water leading into the rapid, passed down the right side of the eddy, surging steadily against the set of the current to the right. It looked as if a boat would have a rough time getting through.

Because of the abrupt drop of the rapid, the tongue was not visible for more than 50 to 100 feet ahead. The boatmen knew the approach would call for some expert maneuvering. After looking it over, they expected the boats to take some water. Maybe a boat or two would capsize. Tomorrow would have the answer.

A heavy shower fell after sundown. The resulting cascades were magnificent to behold as they plunged over the 600-foot-high cliffs to the canyon below, some dissipating into lacy spray before reaching the canyon floor.

They strung the aerial and tuned in the radio. Someone had read an article that said it would be impossible to get reception in the bottom of a deep canyon, but the radio came in clearly from stations at Los Angeles and Salt Lake City. Almost immediately after turning on the radio they learned of President Warren G. Harding's continued illness. He had fallen sick in Seattle upon return from a trip to Alaska. The doctors suspected food poisoning, and the President was taken by train to a hospital in San Francisco. "Uncle John," a Los Angeles radio commentator, promised to send a special message to the Colorado Canyon party the following night.

Next morning the boatmen tossed driftwood into the water and watched its course into the rapid. They packed up and loaded the boats immediately after breakfast. Kolb, Lint, and Elwyn crossed the river to look over the possibility of running the rapid from the left, finally deciding that the center would be the best route to take. They portaged the canvas boat around the rough water to a point near the foot of the rapid, where Dodge stationed himself to be ready to help if a boat got upset or swamped.

Kolb elected to go through first. He dropped into the tongue of the rapid just about as he had planned and shot past a big rock, missing it by half an oar's length. But he failed to reckon with a more deeply submerged one just below it, and the bottom of the *Marble* struck it a sharp blow. The boat was thrown partly out of control, and it hit the next line of waves almost sideways. It had only partly swung back when it went into a hole below another big boulder. The boat and boatman disappeared in a cloud of spray, but reappeared an instant later, riding buoyantly through the rest of the rapid. Kolb pulled in and landed upon the beach of the left bank.

Lint ran through next in the *Boulder*. He was able to keep the lighter boat under complete control and landed in an eddy on the right.

Freeman found the *Grand* aground when he went to push off. He floundered around in the mud for several minutes before he was able to work it out to deeper water. Casting off, he drifted down the tongue, got a little too far to the left, and was caught in an eddy. His boat was carried back upstream along the bank, circling round and round. He bent to the oars and pulled out at the head of the eddy and swung into the current again. He then dropped quickly down along the right side of the tongue and hit the first big wave stern on. He felt a solid jolt as the water came rolling into the cockpit. By pulling to the right as chance offered, he missed the hole below by a comfortable margin and worked over to land below the *Boulder* on the right bank.

Elwyn ran last. He was drawn a little to the right of the tongue and dropped into a heavy wave that seemed to sweep completely over the *Glen*, hiding her from sight for a full second from those on shore. Diving and plunging in rough water for the next 100 feet, Elwyn then pulled out under good control. They decided later that, as the rocks under the waves to the right of the tongue were well covered, the better course would have been to ride over them rather than to crowd the rocks on the left, as Kolb had done.

All passengers walked around the rapid. Raymond Moore, while talking to Elwyn later, remarked, "Blake, if you tell me you can take a boat up the side of that cliff, I'll believe you. It wouldn't be any more difficult than running that rapid."

Although it was not yet noon they decided to have lunch before going on. As Kolb started to pull across to where the other boats had landed, he found about five inches of water in the *Marble*'s stern compartment. After he landed, they hauled her out onto the sandbar where they found a hole in her bottom that called for repairs.

The metal map case was in the bottom of the hatch and enough water had leaked through the rubber tape at the cover to ruin most of the map paper. Birdseye decided to use celluloid for mapping the rest of the trip. An hour and a half later the *Marble* was again ready to launch.

They boated on down 3.25 miles to the head of Soap Creek Rapid, surveying as they went, and discovered that Soap Creek was two miles nearer to Badger Creek than was shown by existing maps. They found an abundance of driftwood on the right bank and decided to camp there, 100 yards above the head of the rapid. While some of the crew set up camp, Burchard and Birdseye surveyed Soap Creek Rapid, finding that it had a fall of eighteen feet, twelve feet of it in the first 100 yards. Modern river maps show it with a fall of sixteen feet, but rapids sometimes change over the years due to scouring or added deposition.

That evening the men set up the radio and almost immediately learned of the death of President Harding, just forty-five minutes after it occurred. The doctors now said he had died of pneumonia, although an autopsy was never performed. "Uncle John" repeated that message eight or ten times during the evening and once said he was directly addressing "that heroic band of engineers braving death in the rapids of the Colorado," or words to that effect. The radio came in plain, though faint.

Although the rapid looked to be a terror, the tired boatmen did not worry about it. At least Elwyn did not. He now considered himself a rough-water man equal to whatever the river could throw at him, if he was careful.

CHAPTER 14

Soap Creek to the
Little Colorado

On the morning of August 3, 1923, they loaded the boats in expectation of running the rapid. At the last minute Kolb decided to cross the river for one more inspection of it. He returned to announce that he considered running the rapid to be too dangerous—a boat would be almost certain to upset in one of the first two big waves, and after that to drive upon some rocks not visible from the left bank.

Earlier boaters had come to grief in Soap Creek Rapid. The Kolb brothers had upset both of their boats there in 1911. Colonel Birdseye supported Kolb. He said it would not be warranted to take chances with the outfit, especially so early in the voyage.

Elwyn and Lint were keenly disappointed with this decision. They both agreed that if Bert Loper had been head boatman there would be no portaging. They felt let down at missing the chance to make what might have been the first successful run of this notorious rapid. They had to follow orders, though.

Kolb decided they should also portage the boats past the worst of the rapid. The method of portage was the same in the case of each boat. The *Glen* was the first to go. Elwyn took her a couple of hundred feet under oars, then they lined her another 100 feet to where she was unloaded. They lined her empty for fifty feet more to the head of the portage.

The portage was across large boulders on the right side, over and between which logs were laid at short intervals to prevent the boats from being crushed in sliding down. It was heavy work, but with everybody pitching in they got the job done. At the end they lined the boat over a five-foot waterfall to a quiet cove that was protected by two huge boulders. There she was reloaded.

Soap Creek portage proved to be so arduous that only one other portage of boats was made on the entire trip. (E. C. La Rue 343, U.S. Geological Survey)

After the *Glen* was reloaded Elwyn backed her out of the cove between the two large boulders and ran the rest of the rapid, passing through a couple of hundred yards of surging but not dangerous water. Pulling the *Glen* into an eddy on the right bank where the cook was waiting to start dinner, Elwyn beached her and began unloading the cook's equipment and supplies.

The crew took the *Grand* down the same way before lunch, and the *Marble* and *Boulder* in the afternoon. There was enough time left for a good swim and a couple of hours' rest before supper. They camped on the sandbar where they had eaten lunch, since the site offered plenty of wood and clear water.

Colonel Birdseye wrote, "It was killing work to portage the wooden boats. We probably could have run it safely, for we ran worse rapids later on, but did not think it wise to take any unnecessary chances so early in the trip."

That evening they heard on the radio that President Warren G. Harding's funeral was set for Friday, August 10. They also heard a detailed description of his funeral cortege.

Elwyn chuckled when he heard a letter from Freeman read over the radio. In it he said Blake had special instructions not to lose the cook.

They pushed off at 8:00 A.M. the next morning. The river at this point was 250 to 300 feet wide and the rose-colored, black-streaked cliffs towered 1,000 feet above them. There was swift water to the first bend.

About a mile below Soap Creek they passed over a riffle where, on July 10, 1889, President Frank M. Brown of the Denver, Colorado Canyon, and Pacific Railroad had been thrown from his boat and drowned while attempting to survey the proposed river-level route. Had he been wearing a life jacket he would no doubt have survived.[1] From there the river followed a winding stretch of canyon filled with deep water, swirling eddies, and great surging boils.

The boats rolled heavily in the boils, and at times the eddies spun them completely around. There were several sharp chutes of hard-running water, but none to warrant the name of rapid so freely used by Powell and his successors. Birdseye had decided to rate as a rapid only those with a descent of six feet or more in a comparatively short distance, with exceptions made in case of places dangerous to navigate irrespective of fall.

During the day they ran between 1,300-foot-high cliffs where the river was narrow and deep. Just before noon they stopped at the head of a cataract which Birdseye named Sheer Wall Rapid because of the sheer walls through which it passed, making it impossible to walk around. After lunch they made a safe run of the rapid in spite of some dangerous rocks in midstream near the foot of the swift water. They found the fall of the rapid to be nine feet in a thousand.

The boatmen ran the rapids stern first, facing downstream, so they could see where they were going. All wore their life jackets. Passengers lay face down on the hatches, clinging to the lifelines.

In the next few miles the canyon displayed places of rare beauty with many caves formed by the undercutting of cliffs. At one place the forward boatmen rowed into the deep shade afforded by a wide overhanging cliff where it was delightfully cool. They paused to rest and sing songs, which echoed from the opposite cliffs.

At about 3:30 P.M. the men heard the din of another rapid ahead. It sounded like a big one. This proved to be House Rock Rapid at Mile 16.7. They were relieved to find only great surging waves, but no dangerous rocks. They ran the wooden boats through the billowing waves, while Dodge took the canvas boat along the quieter water near the shore. Geologist Moore rode on Lint's boat, the *Boul-*

Frank Dodge with stadia rod on station at Sheer Wall Rapid. (Courtesy of Prescott Blake)

der, lying face down on the stern hatch. Several waves broke over the stern of the boat, drenching him thoroughly. Both the *Grand*, manned by Freeman, and the *Boulder*, manned by Lint, landed so far downstream that they had to be towed back up to the campsite.

Kolb dug a shallow well in the sand, but waves from the river washed into it before the water had settled. They were too tired to set up the radio. Elwyn, Lint, and Kolb slept under an overhanging ledge.

Next morning the river was smooth for the first few miles. They passed a huge rock about fifty by eighty feet in size at the waterline in midstream. It protruded thirty feet above the water. Dellenbaugh had described this huge boulder in *A Canyon Voyage*, an account of Powell's second trip, and Ellsworth Kolb had mentioned it in his book. The place was called Boulder Narrows.

There was smoother water below the big rock, and Elwyn knew that smooth water was usually a sign of a rapid ahead. This was no exception. They soon reached North Canyon Rapid, which had a fall of eleven feet. It looked dangerous.

They stopped for lunch in the shade of 2,000-foot-high cliffs near the head of the rapid. Kolb and his brother had lined their boats over this rapid in November 1911. He looked it over carefully from both banks and studied the layout of the rocks above and below. It looked runnable.

After lunch Kolb, with Lint on deck, ran the rapid. Lint wanted a close look at the rocks before taking his own boat through. By skillful maneuvering at the head of the rapid, Kolb avoided all the bad rocks. The huge waves tossed the *Marble* about like a cork and at times she seemed almost to fly out of the water. The next moment she was nearly smothered under. After the run, Lint scrambled back over the shore rocks to his own boat.

Elwyn went second, then Lint, and finally Freeman. The first three boats went between the rocks at the head of the rapid. They made the run nicely in spite of the upstream wind that lashed foam and spray in their faces. Freeman missed the deep channel and hung up on a rock. His boat swung around but suffered no damage. All landed safely.

After running the rapid the boatmen picked up their passengers, who had walked around it. A half mile below they ran 21 Mile Rapid, ran farther on, and pitched camp on a rocky shore on the right bank. Luckily there was a sandy bench nearby where the beds could be unrolled.

La Rue took a movie by flashlight of the "gang" around the receiving set. Then everyone listened to the radio. They had suspended its 200-foot aerial from the canyon wall by a cord about 300 feet long. They heard "Uncle John's" words regarding the funeral train carrying the body of President Harding through Wyoming. The train had been delayed fifteen minutes because of a broken rail.

On August 6 they had an eventful boating day. They ran some medium-sized rapids and a number of riffles. In nearly every instance the head of one was in sight of the foot of the last. They ran only three miles all day, with a descent of fifty feet, one of the greatest average falls in Marble Canyon.

As the *Grand* approached the second rapid, with Moore and La Rue riding, Kolb, who had landed to look it over, signaled for Freeman to go on through without stopping. It was a straight run down the middle with no chance of rocks — only big water. Kolb directed him to pull down the tongue and then to the left. Feeling there was no real menace, Freeman did not pull to the left hard enough. As a result some great side-running waves came rolling over the *Grand*, completely filling the cockpit. She still rode fairly steadily, but was so low that all of the succeeding waves swept her fore and aft. The boat was still manageable enough, however, that he was able to row her into an eddy at the left bank well above the head of the next rapid. It took ten minutes of bailing to get the cockpit dry again. The watertight camera box under the seat proved as good as its name. But Freeman's small camera, which was not in the box, got thoroughly soaked.

It required skill and hard work to keep the boats out of trouble. Early in the trip the passengers got a genuine thrill riding the plunging boats through the mountainous waves while lying prone on the hatches, clinging to the lifelines. Later, after becoming accustomed to riding rough water and getting soaked, they vied with each other to make the plunge with a lighted pipe or cigarette without losing the light.

Dodge tried to run one rapid in the canvas boat, but it capsized. He swam out, dragging the boat with him, and righted her without assistance. Dodge was the strongest swimmer of the party and afraid of nothing wet. He lost his hat in the upset, but did not lose the oars or the stadia rod. He decided to line or portage the *Mojave* past subsequent big ones.

They were able to run 25 Mile Rapid safely because the high stage of the river covered all the bad rocks. But Kolb accidentally broke an oar, which gave the Colonel some concern because the boat barely escaped smashing into a cliff before he could put a spare oar into place. On July 16, 1889, Henry Richards and Peter Hansbrough of the Brown-Stanton party had drowned here when their boat hit an overhanging ledge and overturned. Had they been wearing life jackets they, too, would no doubt have survived.

Elwyn took some water over the side while running the next rapid, and he broke an oar just as he made the last heavy pull for a landing. It would have shocked the Colonel had he known that Elwyn broke it deliberately. Elwyn thought it was a good idea to make the weak oar useless rather than have it break while running a worse rapid.

Because of someone's neglect, they had no spare nine-foot oars, so they hoped to have spares brought in at Hance Rapid. Kolb, the smallest man of the crew, had ordered eight-foot ones, while the others used nine footers. Elwyn would have to use eight-foot oars for awhile.

They camped on the right bank near some good springs above another roaring cataract. Just below camp Kolb located the cave where he and his brother had camped in 1911. The men found some steel traps, old tools, and cooking utensils on the cave floor which had been uncovered by floods since the Kolbs passed that way. La Rue took pictures of the cave.[2] They named the rapid just below camp Cave Springs Rapid because of the fine springs near the cave.

On August 7 the first order of business was to run this rapid. Dodge, Burchard, and Kolb started to line the canvas boat past the big boulders at the head of it when suddenly the boat capsized, filled with water, and was swept against a half-submerged rock. The surging current was too much for the frail craft, wrapping it around the protruding rock, tearing out the floorboards, and sweeping them away. Efforts to free the boat only succeeded in tearing the *Mojave* to pieces.

Kolb and Lint then ran the rapid in close succession. They both landed by a big whirlpool on the left side. During the run Kolb had some difficulties and was carried almost against the cliff. He had a hard time pulling into safe water. Freeman came through next and made a good landing, although he broke an oarlock in making a hard pull. Both Elwyn and Kolb had broken oarlocks earlier in the trip, testifying to the flimsiness of the welds.

Elwyn then pushed off and hit the big water intending to land where the others had. However, when he was partway through the rapid, Colonel Birdseye signaled for him to come in to shore and pick up Dodge at a turning point. He had all he could do to buck the powerful whirlpool and crosscurrents to get close to shore. He finally had to straddle the prow of his boat and catch fingerholds in crevices and on projections of the bedrock. In this way he pulled the boat up to where the backwater caught the *Glen*, propelling her in the direction he wanted to go. When Dodge was through holding rod for the Colonel, Elwyn picked him up and ran the *Glen* on through the rapid.

They hated to lose the canvas boat. It had been a great convenience to have it for the rodman, and it had given them a feeling of safety to have it at the foot of a rapid ready to rescue any boat that needed help.

After the canvas boat was lost, the cook was transferred to Kolb's boat. From then on Elwyn would have Dodge, the rodman, as his passenger. He would have to land Dodge wherever a rod station was needed, which meant every few hundred yards for the entire length of the canyon, no matter how difficult the task. Lint had a similar chore in landing the instrument men at alternate stations.

They ran two more large rapids and several small ones that day. Freeman noted, "The *Grand*'s passage was dryer than usual. The splash did not even put out La Rue's pipe. This had come to be the accepted test of a good run."

The lower walls of the canyon here were of Redwall limestone that rose nearly straight up for 350 feet. Above the red Supai formation rose another 700 feet, rising from there through Hermit, Coconino, Toroweap, and Kaibab formations to the rim 2,300 feet above. During rainstorms spectacular volumes of red-colored water cascaded from usually dry washes over the limestone below, giving it an outer coating that looked like red marble. The action of the river water had given it a fine polish, further increasing its marble-like quality. This had prompted Major John Wesley Powell to name it Marble Canyon.

They camped on the right bank by a small spring of clear water thirty miles below Lee's Ferry. La Rue wanted to survey two dam sites in that area, so he and Moore carried rod until suppertime while Birdseye and Burchard did the surveying. They heard no rapid's roar that night to remind them of the power and danger of the Colorado. This may have been the setting for Elwyn's poem, "Night on the River," which reads:

> The sun long since, has dropped behind the cliff;
> Dark shadows of the night have come once more.
> All sound has ceased, save from the restless stream,
> Where quiet gurgles tell of pebbly shore.

The flickering fire no longer leaps with flame;
It slumbers now, beneath an ashy quilt.
While silent men, tired from the day's hard row,
Lie here and there, their beds spread on the silt.
Above, high on the dim, far canyon rim,
Sits rows of silent figures, looking down;
Of men, and beasts, and reptiles, there on high.
Carved by wind and rain and frost,
From the bedrock crust of this old sphere.
They seem to watch the river's deepening courses
As it labors day by day, and year by year.
There's peace this night. No roar of Rapid's boom
Is heard between the towering silent walls;
For once, no cataract is near, upstream or down.
It is the peace of silent, cloistered halls.
Night on the river may be calm as this,
But then it may be fraught with danger sound,
As waters rise, and crash frail boats about,
While shouts rise high, above the rapids pound.
Nights often stygian black within the gorge,
But when the desert moon shines large and bright,
Voyagers often lie awake, enthralled
By the magic of a desert-river night.

The next morning, August 8, the surveyors finished mapping the second dam site before the boatmen pushed off. The boats were in shade until 11:00 A.M. because of the high walls of the canyon. They encountered no large rapids that day. At Mile 31.5 they came to South Canyon, where Stanton and the remaining members of the Brown-Stanton expedition had climbed out from the river in 1889 when they abandoned their trip after Brown and two crew members had drowned in rapids above.[3]

At Mile 31.7 they paused to survey dam site number three and explored a large cave (Stanton's Cave) near there. But they found no evidence of the earlier exploration.

About 500 yards below the cave they sighted a green spot at the base of a red cliff where the river turned to the left. On closer observation they saw a veritable hanging garden of maidenhair ferns, moss, scarlet monkey flower, columbine, and poison ivy. Through the greenery they could see silvery streams of water spouting from the canyon wall. Some of the fountains issued from very high up.

One large stream of clear, cold water gushed from the cliff about seventy-five feet above the river level. Four or five large falls and many smaller ones occurred in a space of about 100 feet. It was a most pleasing contrast to the almost-barren canyon through which they had just passed.

They landed at the base of this lovely garden and climbed under the falls for a refreshing shower bath in the cool, clear water. Then they filled their canteens before crossing to a gravel bar opposite the spectacular group of fountains to take pictures. Major Powell had named the place Vasey's Paradise for his friend George Vasey, a famous botanist, who had been with his party in Colorado in 1868. It had been described by Powell, Dellenbaugh, and Kolb.

The afternoon journey was through one of the most picturesque canyons imaginable where they saw many caves and sparkling springs. Redwall Cavern, at Mile 33, was 250 feet across the mouth, 200 feet in depth, and 150 feet high, according to Elwyn (although it looks more like 50 feet high). The floor was a succession of terraces of smooth, hard sand, rising like the tiers of seats in a stadium until the highest touched the vault of the limestone roof. Freeman estimated that the amphitheater would hold 10,000 to 15,000 people. Powell had guessed its capacity at 50,000, probably overestimating its size.

At another place Elwyn heard water splashing but could see no waterfall. Upon rowing the *Glen* closer to the canyon wall he saw a small opening a few feet above the river's surface in a chimney formed of travertine. Inside the travertine tube he could see cold, clear water plunging to the river from ten or fifteen feet up on the face of the cliff. By grasping the edges of the opening, he and Dodge were able to hold the boat stationary in the quiet water and fill their canteens.

Toward evening they came to a weird-looking formation on the right side of the river. At this place (Mile 35.6) some high towers, a small natural bridge, and a wild jumble of windows, gables, turrets, and buttresses rose above a small riffle. There was one hole through a rocky roof looking out to the sky. Freeman noted, "During several hours about midday this must let a beam of sunlight through to dance upon the riffle, which was trying to undermine its foundations under the right wall." Freeman named the place Goblin's Castle.

They camped opposite and a short way below Goblin's Castle on a limestone ledge at the head of a rapid at Mile 35.7. There was no sandy beach or soil of any kind, just a series of stone terraces or shelves. Some were wide enough for two bedrolls to be laid side by side, but most were scarcely wide enough to accommodate a single bed. Each man sought a low or high berth according to his inclination.

By now the party had drifted into barely perceptible factions. Three of the boatmen, Elwyn, Lint, and Kolb, rolled their beds close together whenever possible and shared much of their leisure time. Freeman and the professional men, Birdseye, Moore, La Rue, and Burchard, seemed to have more in common and they formed another loose group. Dodge and the cook, Word, were somewhere between.

From the beginning there was no love lost between Kolb and La Rue. La Rue seemed unduly brusque to those around him when he suffered bouts of the stomachache. Kolb took this as a personal affront. He also deeply resented La Rue being the official photographer for the expedition, believing that picture taking in the Grand Canyon was his personal domain. Friction between the two persisted.

The day's run had disclosed very few places with so much as a sandspit or bit of soil. In many places the cliffs rose sheer from the water's edge. They set up the radio that night and were still able to get good reception.

The next morning, August 9, Moore discovered some new fossils (or rather hitherto undiscovered ones) near the previous night's camp. With an early start the party was soon into another rapid (Mile 36). All rode through on the boats. Billowing waves washed over the decks, the boats shipped some water, and everybody got wet, but all got through with no damage. Sometimes Dodge spelled Elwyn at the oars in the quieter water. Since losing the *Mojave*, he missed having his own boat.

The canyon walls were still high, colorful and picturesque, with several large alcoves lined with ferns and wild flowers. They saw some beautiful arches on the right side at Mile 41.2. Birdseye named them Royal Arches because they reminded him of the Royal Arches of Yosemite Valley. Near there the Muav Limestone began to appear under the Redwall formation. Late in the forenoon Moore reported the first appearance of Bright Angel Shale.

At one place La Rue spotted a doe and her fawn downstream. He set up his movie camera and signaled for those below to drive the animals past him so he could get pictures. When the deer saw they were trapped between two groups of men on shore, they took to the river and swam to the other side. Lint tried to catch them in his boat, but they could swim faster than he could row.

Most of the day's run was through very quiet water. Because of threatening clouds they quit early and made camp on a sandbar above a rapid at Mile 43.75. A house-sized boulder lay mostly submerged in midstream near the foot of the rapid. The river current dashed against the boulder with great force causing a geyser. Birdseye at first called the place Boulder Rapid but later changed it to President Harding Rapid in memory of the late president. Kolb did not remember having seen the big boulder on his voyage of 1911.

A gusting wind came up while they were unloading the boats. Rain began to fall while they were stringing up the radio aerial and dusk brought a heavy downpour. There was no natural shelter, so Freeman stripped and placed his clothes under a tarp to keep them dry. Kolb crawled into the fore-hatch of his boat and pulled the hatch cover over.

Elwyn and Lint stood in the front hatch of the *Glen* with a tarp over their heads until rain began to trickle down their backs. Then they too lay down in the boat and pulled the hatch cover into place, leaving a small crack held open by a piece of driftwood so they would have air. They both went to sleep and slept until awakened by Kolb. The rain had stopped.

When they emerged from their cozy retreat they observed La Rue, clad only in a shirt and with a piece of canvas over his head, hovering over a smoldering fire. He looked miserable. Freeman was wearing only a life preserver. After coaxing the fire into a more healthy blaze, everyone rolled out his bed and got into it to keep dry.

It was sprinkling again on the morning of August 10. They did not move on because President Harding would be buried that day. They stayed in camp as a salute to him. The river continued to fall despite the rain. Freeman felt so clean after his rain bath the night before that he did not spoil it with his customary dip in the river. Everyone got busy with mending and laundry. Later some of them played an improvised game of tennis-handball.

A search along the left-hand cliff for Peter Hansbrough's grave met with no success. It is there, however. Later river runners located it below the rapid. Peter Hansbrough, a member of the Brown-Stanton expedition, which had no life preservers, drowned when his boat overturned on July 15, 1889. His body was found and buried at Mile 44 and the promontory opposite was named Point Hansbrough in his memory.[4]

Lint and Elwyn went up a side canyon where they filled the water

Elwyn Blake writing
in his diary in Grand
Canyon. (Courtesy of
Ida Blake Westwood)

bags and canteens with clear water from a stream that poured over a
cliff more than 100 feet high. Then Elwyn mended his shoes, which
were beginning to disintegrate. La Rue and Kolb each took some
movies. Later Dodge set fire to a big pile of driftwood. Kolb crossed
the river to look over the part of the rapid below the big boulder.
Then he, Lint, and Elwyn went swimming.

Next morning the first order of business was to run the rapid. They
decided the reason Kolb did not remember the big boulder in this
rapid was that it had lodged there since his trip in 1911, as evidenced
by a large gray scar on the cliff above. The large block of limestone
lay in the center of the river near the lower end of the rapid. They
surmised that if a boat hit this rock it would surely turn over.

The passengers went ahead on foot while the boatmen crossed the
river to inspect the rapid. La Rue set up the movie camera at a good
vantage point opposite the big midstream boulder. Kolb made the
first run and got through nicely. Aside from the rock, there was no
real danger. Then Lint took the *Boulder* plunging through. He came
a little closer to the rock, but made it by safely. Elwyn followed.
He noted:

As I approached the largest wave thrown out from the mid-stream obstruction, I leaned away from the back curl so as not to take any water. The wave hit the tilted boat solidly, and with power. Suddenly I felt myself flying through the air. The next thing I realized I was swimming beside the plunging boat, which was still right side up. I swam to the boat and crawled in to find that one oar had been swept overboard. A spare oar was soon in place.[5]

Those on shore noted that the *Glen* was driven down against the back-thrown side-wave and missed capsizing by a hair. Freeman could see all of the inside of the boat from his position above the rapid as it was thrown on its beam by the blow, and Kolb, from below, said he saw all of the bottom. Elwyn turned a complete somersault as he was thrown cleanly out of the boat. The *Glen* righted herself in time to ride the second wave above the big whirlpool behind the rock. Kolb picked up the floating oar that Elwyn had lost.

Freeman made the run without accident, though he did get into dangerous water. Elwyn had hopes of a good movie of his peculiar accident. When he asked La Rue about it, La Rue said disgustedly, "Nothing ever happens to you, so I never had the camera going."

For the first time they saw trees of good size on the Kaibab rim above them and mesquite trees along the river. The mesquite grew wherever there was soil enough for a roothold, scrubby on the talus, of good size at the mouths of side canyons and on bars.

They saw no large rapids during the day, although the river had considerable fall. They passed three large caves on the right bank at Mile 46.5. These caves were beautifully arched and pillared. Birdseye called them "Triple Alcoves."

Saddle Canyon on the right side was filled with a rock slide at the 3,200-foot level, so the surveyors did not have to traverse up it very far. During the survey they saw another doe and fawn. They made camp on the right side above Little Nankoweap Wash, having traveled eight miles that day to a point 51.6 miles from the mouth of the Paria.

For the first time they did not get KHJ (Los Angeles) on the radio. They did get the *Deseret News* of Salt Lake City (KZN). It came in better than at anytime since leaving Lee's Ferry. "Barney Google" came in strong and clear.[6]

On the morning of August 12 they did some surveying. Lint carried rod up the Little Nankoweap where they traversed it up to the 3,150-foot contour. They then crossed Nankoweap Creek at Mile 51.8 and surveyed it to the same level. Nankoweap Creek flowed a clear stream of about three cfs. La Rue measured the flow of every stream they came to. Freeman noted, "The two miles surveyed revealed many pretty groups of cottonwoods along the streams with occasional cold springs."

At Nankoweap Kolb, La Rue, and Elwyn made a steep, one-mile climb to explore and photograph some Anasazi ruins perched under a high cliff 600 feet above the river. From there they had a spectacular view of the canyon and river below. Today a well-worn trail to these ruins testifies to their popularity with river travelers.

On a sandy beach at the mouth of Nankoweap, La Rue picked up a Log Cabin syrup can he had thrown into the river at Lee's Ferry on July 24. He had scratched his name on the can, so he knew it was the same.

Nankoweap Rapid, with a fall of fourteen feet (twenty-five on today's river maps), had some big waves but few rocks. Every boat took some water as they plowed through the lashing waves. After bailing out the boats they went on four miles to Mile 55.7, where they camped above some roaring whitewater.

Kolb had gone ahead with Elwyn's boat, the *Glen*, which contained the cook and his gear, to make camp, while Elwyn took Kolb's boat and the rodman to continue the survey that day.

The next morning the instrument men, Colonel Birdseye and Burchard, worked Kwagunt Creek near camp while the boatmen ran the rapid.

Freeman recorded:

> For some distance above the Kwagunt the left hand walls of the canyon have been almost sheer from the river to the highest rim of the Kaibab. These are the most imposing walls we have yet seen, and can have few rivals in the whole Colorado Canyon series. The outer rim of the Grand Canyon proper is higher, but there is always the broad bench of the Tonto platform between the upper cliffs and the inner gorge.[7]

In looking over Kwagunt Rapid it appeared almost as rough from one side as from the other. The most favorable course seemed to be down the tongue near the left-hand bank. Kolb, Lint, Freeman, and Elwyn ran it in that order. All had a bumpy passage but none was in any difficulty except that Lint broke an oar. They each drifted along the left side of the tongue to miss two big corkscrew waves that looked equal to upsetting a boat. This still left a jumbled line of combers that tossed the boats about merrily and doused those aboard. They had to pull away hard to make the eddy on the other side. It was apparently much rougher than the Kolbs or their predecessors found it due to the considerable amount of debris and boulders that had washed into the river during a torrential flood from the Kwagunt.

Elwyn crossed to the left side of the river to pick up Moore, who had been dropped there to do some geology work. While there, Elwyn received a semaphore message that there was a spring below him and that he should fill the water vessels. He found the spring and it was a beauty, bubbling forth clear and cold. He filled a can, took a deep draught, nearly gagged, then spit it out with a startled exclamation. It was saturated with salt. He filled a pail with the nice-looking brine and took it across the river. The first man to taste it gave Elwyn an indignant scowl. The others sipped lightly, made wry faces, and spit it out.

The surveyors worked on downriver passing several midstream boulders during the morning, but encountering no large rapids. Freeman, La Rue, and Moore went on ahead and stopped at the mouth of the Little Colorado River, Mile 61.5. La Rue had intended to measure the flow of the Little Colorado but it was in flood, pouring yellow water into the main stream, too deep for him to wade. It was even dirtier than the Colorado. Those on that boat had lunch on a shelf of rock near the water level. Today, except during times of flood, the Little Colorado is a lovely scene of turquoise-blue water tumbling over rocks into gem-like pools, the color due to springs of copper sulphate and other minerals about twelve miles above the mouth.

Kolb took the cook on the Glen and went ahead of the surveyors in search of a camping place. The survey team made the afternoon run through a succession of small rapids. There was usually a huge whirlpool at the foot of each, so it took some hard rowing and expert maneuvering to land below the rough water. The team reached the Little Colorado about 3:30 P.M. but, with no campsite to be seen there, they went on a couple of miles and caught up with Kolb at a suitable campsite.

The walls of the canyon were very high. Cape Isolation, (now Solitude) opposite camp was 3,440 feet above the river. In ancient times the Colorado Plateau, which surrounded Grand Canyon, had been uplifted to the shape of an inverted bowl. The river had cut its canyon as the plateau gradually rose. At the same time it had been eroded by thousands of side canyons draining into the river, exposing rock formations that would normally be thousands of feet beneath the earth's surface. The Moenkopi Shale seen at Lee's Ferry had given way to other formations — the Kaibab, Taroweap, Coconino, Hermit Shale, Redwall Limestone, Muav Limestone, Bright Angel Shale, and Tapeats Sandstone in succession.

They had entered into what was then the Grand Canyon proper, since Marble Canyon ended at the mouth of the Little Colorado. (In 1975 the boundaries of Grand Canyon National Park were changed to reach from Lee's Ferry to Lake Mead.)[8]

They had good radio reception in spite of the great canyon depth. Birdseye reported the length of Marble Canyon as a fraction over sixty miles and the elevation of the mouth of the Little Colorado as 2,745 feet. Both figures were slightly less than previous estimates.

The men inspected the boats just before retiring and found them high and dry because of a drop in the river. About an hour later they heard the boats bumping together. The river was up again. They tied the boats to a long rope through a small hole in the base of a cliff, then went back to bed.

CHAPTER 15

Lava Creek to Trinity Creek

Geologist Raymond Moore told the men that the deep gorges ahead would expose more geologic formations that had been pushed up from deep inside the earth. He said Grand Canyon was the only place in the world where so many layers of the earth's crust were exposed.

Elwyn noticed that new formations had emerged that slanted gently upward from the river's edge as they traveled downstream. At Mile 63 red shale beds slanted away from the river and sheer walls rose farther back. Beyond that, great temples and buttes could be seen. He looked forward with excitement to what lay ahead.

On August 14, Kolb in Elwyn's boat was the last to leave since the cook needed to clean up and pack his cooking gear. They ran several rough little rapids and bucked a number of frightful boils, rowing through whirlpools that almost seemed capable of sucking a boat under. The rowing was very difficult at times.

Just after lunch they reached Lava Creek, where the lava and sandstone walls were more broken up. At Mile 68 dark purple lava showed at river level with varicolored pink and slate shale beds slanting back above it. The river was almost a continuous riffle from Lava Creek to their next campsite above Tanner Creek Rapid. The rapid roared its welcome with big lashing waves.

It rained hard before dark, and a brilliant double rainbow appeared as it was clearing up. La Rue described the fury of the storm. "The thunder roars up and down the canyon like 1,700 big guns cut loose at once." They were camped near Comanche Point and in sight of Desert View, where Grand Canyon Drive then ended. They lit two large fires to signal anyone who might be watching from the rim that they were several days ahead of schedule. Later they learned that a guide at Desert View on the South Rim had seen the fires and the boats.

On August 15 they broke camp early, running Tanner Creek Rapid below camp with no more trouble than getting doused with muddy water. They passed over several swift riffles before reaching Unkar Rapid shortly after noon. Unkar was a rough one, having a twenty-one-foot drop in less than half a mile. It ran in a semicircle against an overhanging cliff where monstrous waves were formed, with smaller ones along the right side where they ran. They managed to avoid the worst waves and all got through with only a muddy bath. But Colonel Birdseye got a ducking when Lint ran into a submerged rock while landing below the rapid.

Along the shore was a huge pile of driftwood that covered about two acres. One of the men set it afire and, when last seen, it was burning furiously. This was the twenty-fifth large rapid they had recorded so far.

They traveled on for two more miles and made camp at the head of a large rapid at Mile 75, which is now called Nevills Rapid. It had been a hot day with no shade since the sheer canyon walls had given way to more sloping inclines. They found clear water in 75 Mile Creek and everyone enjoyed bathing in it.

La Rue noted:

> All are well except Colonel Birdseye has a bad toe, infected and swollen double its normal size; The cook, Frank Word, has trouble with his eyes, which makes him feel miserable, and Kolb has a touch of lumbago. A bad night for lumbago.[1]

The boats were sitting in mud the next morning, since the river had dropped and the boats had been moored in shallow water. In the rapid below camp they encountered some of the largest waves yet seen. Kolb wanted to portage the supplies and boats partway, but the rest of the crew persuaded him that it could be run safely. The boatmen had a rough ride and when they were through all had cockpits full of water, but they made it without upset or damage.

About an hour later they made camp on the left side at the head of Hance Rapid. It was named for Captain John T. Hance, miner, rancher, tourist guide, and master storyteller. He was the South Rim's first settler and had carved a trail down Red Canyon to the river at the rapid bearing his name. The surveyors expected Roger Birdseye to bring them fresh supplies down this trail.

Their oarlocks had been poorly made and by now nearly all were broken, so they planned to have new ones made before attempting to run this dangerous rapid. Kolb knew that Harvey Machine Shop at the South Rim could do the job.

Colonel Birdseye was suffering increased pain from his infected toe. Kolb, after several jabs with a novocaine needle, lanced the infected digit. Then Kolb, Lint, Dodge, and Elwyn started to walk up the trail to the top of the rim to notify Roger Birdseye that they were nine days ahead of schedule and to get the new oarlocks.

They left camp about 3:30 P.M. Dodge only went about a mile and a half, far enough to get a good view of the canyon, then returned to the river. The other three reached the old Canyon Copper Company diggings about dark. They found a spring below the old mining camp and refilled their canteens. The trail from the mine to Horseshoe Bench had been blasted out of solid limestone for the most part. It was in poor repair and very steep.

Arriving at the top of Horseshoe Bench, they stopped to rest and talked about sleeping there but decided to go on and look for a better place. There were miles of steep trail ahead of them, with a rise of about 2,500 feet, and they felt they had already put in a hard day's work. Yet they kept plodding upward, stumbling along in the dark.

As the hours wore on they could look upward and see the skyline above. At each resting place they would think that the rim above was surely the top, but there was always another bench above. Several times one of them would fall asleep when they stopped to rest.

At last they sensed a leveling off of the trail because they were stepping higher and walking was much easier. They had reached Grand View Point, 5,000 feet above and sixteen long trail miles from the river. They hiked another mile and a quarter to the closed Grand View Hotel. There they awakened Dick Gilliland, the caretaker, who put them up for the rest of the night. They got to bed at exactly midnight.[2]

Back at the river Birdseye was still feeling miserable from the infected toe. In the evening La Rue and Moore listened to the radio until 10 P.M. La Rue was just going to bed when Moore came to his bunk and asked him to come up to his bed in the rocks because he thought he had heard a rattlesnake. La Rue put on his shoes and by flashlight climbed over the rocks to Moore's bunk. There was a rattler there sure enough, and it was a big one. La Rue found it about one and a half feet from the head of Moore's bed. He tried to pin the snake to the rocks with a stick, but it got away. So Moore moved his bed down to the sand.

The noise and light woke up Colonel Birdseye whose bed was in the rocks not thirty feet away. La Rue told him that he had just tried to kill a big rattler but it got away. The Colonel did not sleep anymore that night since every noise he heard sounded like a rattlesnake.

Next morning, August 17, the three men at the rim had breakfast with the Gillilands. Afterwards Dick Gilliland drove them to Grand Canyon Village where Emery Kolb's wife fixed them another breakfast. Their exertions of the night before had sharpened their already healthy appetites.

The first order of business was to get new oarlocks made. Kolb went to the Harvey Machine Shop to take care of that. Elwyn and Lint collected their mail and read the welcome letters from home. At 11:00 A.M. Edith, Kolb's daughter, took them to the Kolb studio where Kolb showed them pictures of the brothers' 1911 trip through the upper Green River and the Grand Canyon. Later Edith drove them out to Hermit's Rest for sight-seeing. It rained most of the time they were gone. That evening the Kolbs put on a birthday party for Lint.[3]

While Elwyn, Lint, and Kolb were at the South Rim, Birdseye stayed in bed by the river and rested his foot. Burchard and La Rue, with Dodge holding rod, ran the survey line downstream about half a mile. Then they started to survey a dam site at the mouth of Mineral Canyon. About a half mile below Hance Rapid they found a steel boat cached under the rocks well above high water.

Burchard measured the fall of Hance Rapid and recorded it at twenty-eight feet. He predicted trouble in sheer-walled Granite Gorge below there because the high water would make it difficult to find places to set up the plane table.

The next day La Rue and Burchard completed a detailed survey of the dam site at Mineral Canyon. In doing so they had a difficult time climbing along the canyon walls. About 3:00 P.M. Lint and Elwyn passed them on the trail above while returning from Grand View and El Tovar. They announced that the packtrain would be down in about two hours. They said ladies would be in camp, too, so the crew should put on some decent clothes and cut out all rough language.

Before leaving Grand Canyon Village Elwyn and Lint had collected the new oarlocks and a supply of food ready for the packtrain to bring down. They had walked down the trail ahead of the packtrain, which was in the charge of Roger Birdseye. With Roger, besides the mule handlers, were Charles Fiske, National Park Ranger,

Dick Gilliland's wife, and Edith and Emery Kolb, who all rode mules. The women were going down to watch the boats run the rapid.

Hance Trail had been out of use for years so, in preparation for resupplying the expedition, it had been necessary for Roger Birdseye and Fiske to locate and rebuild the trail. Elwyn and Lint went ahead of the pack outfit, often running where the trail was not too steep. They arrived at the river about two hours ahead of the pack-train, a little footsore but feeling fine otherwise. The party enjoyed a fine supper that night—real potatoes and fresh fruit. Those who had stayed at the river soon settled down to read letters and newspapers. The river was still abnormally high for that season of the year.

On Sunday, August 19, the party enjoyed grapefruit for breakfast, then prepared to run the rapid. The boatmen deemed it too rough to risk running with loaded boats. The portage of cargo would be easy this time because the wranglers would use pack mules to haul the loads from the head of the rapid to a sandbar below the main part of it.

After the boats were unloaded they were taken out on the beach and inspected carefully for damage. They ran a line along the bottom of each with just enough slack for a man to hold to in case of an upset. Freeman wound the handles of his oars with rubber tape since he had been having trouble gripping them with wet hands.

Large boulders were scattered through the head of the rapid, and there was a bad hole in midriver halfway down. This limited the possible courses to two—one on either side of a large rock showing just above the water at the brink of the first fall. The boatmen decided that the important thing was to keep away from the big wave below the hole. They felt certain that getting into the big hole above the wave, the bottom of which could not be seen from the highest vantage, meant at least an upset, if not a smashed boat.

They watched a floating log as it passed close on the right side of the dividing rock. It floated into the middle of the big wave they wanted to avoid. They figured that, by making a long, hard pull away from the middle wave, with no bad luck a boat could clear this most troublesome obstacle. So that was the course Kolb decided they should run.

Kolb ran first with Lint riding along to get a close view of the rocks before taking his own boat through. Kolb borrowed nine-foot oars from Freeman to increase his pulling power. With the roar of the rapid in his ears, the boat rising and diving in the angry waves,

Loading up pack mules for portage at the head of Hance Rapid. This beach is now covered with a grove of tamarisk. (Grand Canyon 332, U.S. Geological Survey)

he shot by the edge of the huge hole and missed the big tail wave. His boat did get a hard slap from the side of the big wave in passing. Lint said he hung over the big hole and could see way down into the bottom of it.

Dodge was waiting in the water at the foot of the rapid to throw a line to help them land. But Kolb could not get near enough to allow Lint to reach it, so he was unable to land on the beach where they intended to camp. He brought the unruly craft in about 100 yards below.

Edith wanted to ride the rapid, so Kolb consented to let her ride on Lint's boat. He set up his movie camera while Lint began the run in the *Boulder* with Edith on board. Lint's oars were kept busy during the wet run through the billowing white waves. He missed the biggest wave by a safe margin, but nearly capsized when another one slopped over them. "Edith was wet but game, showing good nerve."[4] She was probably the first woman to run a dangerous rapid in Grand Canyon.

Elwyn followed them at an interval of about 100 feet, making a good run but getting plenty wet. He landed on the beach beside the *Boulder*. Freeman then made a sloppy but successful run, barely making it to shore at the head of the swift water below. He told it this way:

The difference in the way the empty boat pulled and handled was evident as soon as I pushed off. With more confidence in my ability to control the boat, I ran closer to the midstream boulder than I otherwise would have, passing an oar's length to the right of it. This left me well set for my pull away from the big wave below. Wave after wave that would have swept the loaded boat from end to end, she now lifted over buoyantly. Shipping no more than spray, I passed the big wave hole by about fifteen feet and pulled into the beach after a comparatively dry and easy run.

The part of the rapid we have run has a fall of about 25 feet, leaving not over 3 or 4 for the riffle below. Powell estimated the whole rapid at this point as having a fall of 40 feet. He portaged here on both voyages. The Kolbs portaged one boat and ran one. Ours is probably the first party that has run all its boats.[5]

Kolb took movies of the other three boats running the rapid. They later judged that Hance Rapid was one of the worst they encountered on the river. (This author would have to agree, having spent nearly six hours there in June 1990, on a raft draped around a protruding rock.) Just after the first boat came through Ellsworth Kolb arrived with the new nine-foot oars they had ordered, which had been sent to Flagstaff by mistake. He left as soon as the others had made their run. The two women went back out with Ellsworth. They planned to camp on the trail. Blanche, Kolb's wife, would meet the three at about 1:00 P.M. the next day at the head of the trail.

Freeman actually brought his boat in so far below the intended landing place that it had to be towed back up to camp. His clumsy handling of the boat had not been lost on Colonel Birdseye. At this point he apparently considered replacing Freeman as a boatman. In his autobiography Elwyn says:

After the run Colonel Birdseye called me into his tent and asked me what I thought of Freeman as a boatman. I got the idea that the colonel was contemplating sending him out and, possibly, making a boatman of Frank Dodge. I could not bring myself to giving an opinion which would be the deciding factor so gave my opinion that: "His muscles seem to be a little slow."

"I think his brain's a little slow," the Colonel said. He then consulted with Moore and La Rue about the matter, dismissing me presently.[6]

On August 20 the pack mules got loose at daylight and started up the trail for home. The packers hurried to head them off, coming back with them about 1:00 P.M. They got the packs loaded and were off for the rim by 3:00 P.M. Birdseye called this day Sunday and took another day's rest since the whole crew was very tired.

The boatmen took advantage of the time to paint their new oars with linseed oil, and Kolb set his oarlocks a little farther toward the rear of his boat. In midafternoon Lint, Kolb, and Elwyn went up the wash a short distance where they found some shade. There they slept, read, and wrote letters as the fancy hit them. Later the three went to camp and dug some shallow wells, then pulled the boats up farther since the river was rising.

Later in the day Colonel Birdseye and Moore played bridge against Burchard and La Rue until the wind and rain broke up the game.

Elwyn's August 21 notes read:

> We took down the tent flys and packed up preparatory to moving. We then put the boats into the water and found that the bottom of Leigh's boat had drawn away from the bulkhead so that water could seep from the cockpit into the forward hatch. The *Boulder* was then dragged out of the water and a number of screws were placed through the bottom of the boat into the bulkhead, making an effective repair.[7]

Upon getting under way they entered the Granite Gorge with walls at some places only about 125 feet apart. The walls of the inner gorge were composed of black Vishnu Schist about 1.8 billion years old and pink Zoraster Granite said to be about 1.5 billion years old. As predicted, they had trouble getting footing for plane table and stadia-rod stations because of the sheer walls and swift water. Despite this they surveyed a dam site along the way.

Freeman noted: "A light drizzle of rain was falling as we entered the Granite Gorge, but even with that the walls had a less sinister aspect than one would gather from Powell's descriptions. A mile in heavily swirling water took us to the head of Sockdolager."[8] Sockdolager, meaning a knockout punch, was named by Major Powell.

The rapid could not be inspected from shore because of the cliffs on either side, so they ran it with full loads and with all passengers on board. Previous explorers had grossly exaggerated the fall of Sockdolager. Dellenbaugh reported a drop of eighty feet in a third of a mile. The fall amounted to only nineteen feet, most of which occurred in the first hundred yards.

Kolb and Word, the cook, went through first in the *Marble*. They were out of sight in the waves half the time but got through in fine shape.

Elwyn wrote:

> There was a long finger of granite extending from the eastern cliffs and angling into the river about half way through. As a "shot" from the head of the rapid to the foot would be too long for the instrument the feasibility of trying to land behind the finger was discussed. Such is the position of a boatman who carries the instrument or a rodman that he must attempt the impossible and must land every half mile, or rather within a half mile of the last point in the survey line, regardless of the type of water or shoreline. I said I would attempt to pull in below. As the twenty foot waves began combing back over the stern of the *Glen* I thought I had bitten off much more than I could chew. I pulled toward the granite finger as best I could, and managed to thrust the prow into the surging backwater below.[9]

The water surged against the rock, casting spray into the air, then receded with a sucking power. As the boat rose on the surge, Dodge leaped to a precarious little ledge where he held the painter while Elwyn poised for the jump. They stayed in place until readings were made, both from above and after the instrument had been set up below. Thus they escaped the necessity of trying to climb back along the opposite shore from below the rapid, which would have been a tiresome and dangerous undertaking and would have involved much lost time.

Freeman with La Rue and Moore went next in the *Grand*. She took practically no water. After making the shot with the instruments, Birdseye and Burchard brought up the rear in Lint's boat. They all got a good ducking. Birdseye said he nearly broke his neck looking up from the rear deck to see the tops of the onrushing waves. He said the ride was a thrill but that previous explorers had exaggerated the danger of the rapids. The waves were enormous but the channel was free of rocks, so the only danger was from an upset.

They found no sandspits big enough for a campsite until about 5:00 P.M. when they were opposite the mouth of Vishnu Creek at

Mile 81. The ominous thunder of a rapid floated upstream to them, so they decided to camp at this place. Luckily they found mesquite wood and a pool of clear rainwater nearby.

The river dropped two feet during the night and the boats were again high and dry. Soon after embarking they reached Grapevine Rapid a half mile below camp. Grapevine had a fall of sixteen feet in several hundred yards. The river was high, so it covered most of the rocks. Still, the waves billowed high and there were large whirlpools and eddies below.

Kolb went through first followed by Elwyn with Dodge on board. The *Glen* heaved and plunged in the steep choppy waves causing her to take some water. The *Grand*, with Freeman at the oars, came through next, followed by Lint in the *Boulder*. Some of the men who were watching from twenty feet above the river reported that all of the boats were out of sight for several seconds at a time. The big whirlpool at the foot of the rapid carried the *Boulder* around several times.

The survey crew made a cross section for a dam site after lunch. La Rue took movies of the survey crew at work, with life jackets on, perched on a narrow ledge right at the edge of the turbulent river. They ran several small rapids, then came to the only sandbar of any size seen during the day. Birdseye decided that they should camp on the bar rather than risk having to cling to a narrow shelf of rock all night farther on. The spot was 1,200 feet below Clear Creek on the left side. Two of the men stretched the radio aerial from a seventy-five-foot-high shelf of rock down to the campsite. While putting it up one of them loosened an eighty-pound rock which fell to the wet sand within a few feet of where Elwyn was walking.

Colonel Birdseye, La Rue, Moore, and Burchard played bridge that evening. Kolb and Elwyn tuned in the radio. Reception was clear but faint, so Elwyn went to bed early.

On August 23 they passed between walls more abrupt and higher than any they had seen in the inner gorge. The engineers surveyed three more dam sites during the morning. At one point they encountered the largest whirlpools they had yet seen. Freeman, who did not have to land his boat, let it drift along to save strain on the oars. The current carried her round and round and from one cliff to the other. He said, "At places the surge of the water back and forth was like the slopping of the surface of a violently rocked trough." He said he was more conscious of the power of the river in those stretches of savage swirls than in even the hardest of rapids.[10]

Elwyn noted that landing places were few and hard to reach. He and Lint had to land at frequent intervals regardless of the kind of water.

Shortly after noon they passed under the frail-looking Kaibab Suspension Bridge, which afforded the only good means of crossing the river in the whole Grand Canyon area. They stopped at a point just above Bright Angel Creek, where they found Donald Dudley in charge of the U.S.G.S. gauging station. They stored their beds and dunnage at the gauging station preparatory to climbing out to the South Rim. Dudley informed them that the river was flowing at more than 25,000 cfs. and that it had been up as high as 34,000 during the previous week. This meant that the river had been at its highest during the days they were running Hance and Sockdolager rapids, which was a good thing because fewer rocks were exposed.

That afternoon Kolb, Lint, Dodge, and Elwyn took Kolb's boat and crossed the river a half mile below Bright Angel Creek. They pulled the boat well out of the water and tied it securely before starting up the trail to the South Rim.

The rest of the party had supper at Phantom Ranch, a Harvey Resort[11] located half a mile up Bright Angel Creek. Freeman, Word, and Moore started up the trail about 8:00 P.M., reaching the south rim at 7:00 A.M. the next morning. Birdseye, Burchard, and La Rue camped at the hydrographer's home near the mouth of Bright Angel Creek and prepared to walk up the trail the next morning.

Elwyn reported:

> Emery knew of a secret trail over the bed rock and ledges which he said would save us about four miles on our way to the rim. In places there was [sic] only toe and handholds where a slip meant a drop of several hundred feet. We reached the foot of Bright Angel Trail in about forty minutes of breath-taking climbing. We now had a broad mule trail to follow and started toward the rim.[12]

At one place Elwyn, Lint, Kolb, and Dodge came to a clear stream that plunged over a series of falls from the higher cliffs. At the base of one fall was a shimmering pool large enough to swim in. Kolb called it the "Bath Tub." They paused there long enough for a refreshing plunge. After that they hiked on up the "Cork Screw," and then on to Indian Gardens, where they paused for a cool drink from a large spring. While at Indian Gardens they visited briefly with an old prospector who lived there.

When they reached a point within about 1,000 vertical feet from the rim they heard someone calling from above. Kolb soon recognized the voice of his brother Ellsworth. When they reached the head of the trail at 7:40 P.M. they were met by Ellsworth and by Emery's daughter Edith, who informed them that supper was ready.

After enjoying the fine home-cooked meal, Dodge, Lint, and Elwyn rented a cottage with four beds. The night seemed cold compared to the river temperatures they were used to, so Dodge used the bedclothes from the extra bed to keep warm.

The next morning Dodge, Lint, Kolb, and Elwyn were eating breakfast at the Bright Angel Cafe when a rotund man sat down next to Kolb. Kolb got up and introduced the man as the governor of Arizona. Dodge, thinking it was some kind of gag, got to his feet, bowed, and made a frivolous acknowledgment. He was a little embarrassed when Kolb finally convinced him that the man was, in truth, Governor George Wiley Paul Hunt. Before becoming governor Hunt had been a cowboy, so he probably enjoyed the incident.

As soon as the post office opened they collected their mail. Then Kolb's wife, Blanche, drove Lint and Elwyn out to some of the more interesting overlook points along the rim.

Colonel Birdseye and Burchard arrived at the rim riding mules, but La Rue had stayed at camp. At 4:15 P.M. all those at the rim were guests of the Kolb brothers, who showed movies of their 1911 trip from Green River, Wyoming, to the Gulf of California. They also showed pictures of the 1921 surveying expedition in Cataract Canyon.

On August 27 Elwyn and Lint made ready to return to the river. They made one last trip to the post office then waited at the Kolbs until Emery was ready to go. Edith walked down the trail with them. She waited while the men made their way up to the boats and brought them on down to where she was waiting to cross the stream.

Herman Stabler arrived from Washington and joined the party that day. Stabler, who represented the Land Classification Board, came down with the packtrain. He would remain with the party for the balance of the trip.

La Rue had stayed at the hydrographer's house to measure the flow of Bright Angel Creek and do other work. His wife had joined him there.

A Fox News film representative by the name of Shirtliff was waiting at the river to take pictures. He rode through the riffle with

Freeman taking movies while riding in the rear hatch of the boat.

Birdseye and Stabler rode mules down with the pack string. They arrived at the mouth of Pipe Creek by noon. Burchard surveyed the line from Bright Angel Creek to Pipe Creek, arriving there at 1:00 P.M. La Rue's wife rode down to Pipe Creek in Lint's boat. She and Edith Kolb then returned to the rim with the pack string.

The party camped at the mouth of Pipe Creek where loads were rearranged. Dodge, Freeman, Kolb, Lint, and Elwyn returned to the "Bath Tub" and had a fine bath. Then they gathered wood and carried it to camp. They set up the radio and tuned in station KHJ to hear Freeman's report of the trip. Freeman said, "We shall be more heavily loaded than before—not just what one would prefer on a falling river. The latter has but little over half the flow it had when we arrived at the suspension bridge five days ago."

On the morning of August 28 Bert Lauzon, a man who had accompanied the Kolbs on the latter part of the voyage in 1911–1912, arrived at camp, along with Postmaster Kitchner. They had left the rim about 4:00 A.M. in order to be at the foot of the trail in time to see the boats go through the rapid. As it turned out the river party was delayed in starting until after 10:00 A.M., so the observers need not have hurried. The surveyors spent the morning mapping a dam site just below the mouth of Pipe Creek, then a long section beside the river.

Several tourists arrived in time to witness the running of the rapid. Pipe Creek Rapid had a fall of eight feet in one-third of a mile so the waves were not bad. The Fox newsman took movies of the boats going through the rapid which would be shown in movie theatres throughout the country. Kitchner and Lauzon returned to the rim immediately following the run.

The boaters went on to near Horn Creek Rapid before eating lunch. They suspected that Horn was a bad one by the roar that bounced off the canyon walls. It turned out to have a short but savage drop, which called for careful reconnoitering before the run.

A large granite boulder lay in midstream, making a choice between two channels necessary. Dodge and Elwyn landed on the left side of the river while the rest of the party landed on the right. They eventually decided to run it on the left side to avoid some of the big combing waves.

Kolb, Lint, and Freeman ran through in close succession. A big wave turned Kolb's boat on its side, but it did not capsize. He had to drop the oars, though, because the thrashing and wrenching given them by the violent waves split the gunwale and bent one of the heavy oarlocks. Kolb got a bruised hip out of it.

Elwyn was the only one who allowed a passenger to ride through. Dodge held on with all his strength to keep from being torn from the boat. Near the foot of the rapid the *Glen* got into a backwater that was running like a millrace. Elwyn made two attempts without success to thrust the boat out into the main current. It worried him when the boat was twice propelled at terrific speed toward a projecting rock ledge. Each time, at the last second, the backwash flung the boat away preventing a smashup. On the third pass Elwyn jumped for shore with a rope. He slipped on the slick rock, bruised his palm, skinned a knee, and fell half in and half out of the water. But he held fast to the rope and managed to get a handhold in a crevice of the rock.

Elwyn held the boat while Dodge bailed water from the cockpit. Then he climbed back in and made a last mighty attempt with the oars. He was relieved to feel the boat slide free of the backwater. From there the boat whisked away toward the base of an overhanging cliff, which he managed to avoid.

The surveyors carried the line to a point opposite Trinity Creek, where they intended to camp. A dust storm came up and blew sand into their eyes and ears, so they pulled across the river and landed a mile below. Kolb nursed his lame hip and Elwyn his skinned knee. Radio reception was better than ever.

CHAPTER 16

Trinity Creek to Specter Chasm

On August 29 the party ran a riffle below camp. Beyond that the river was smooth and deep with few places to land. Then they passed over a small rapid into quieter water. From downstream they could hear an ominous roar. In a little while they came to Monument Creek Rapid (Granite Falls). They stopped at the head of the rough water where the boulder fan from Monument Creek had narrowed the river causing it to plunge over a jumble of huge boulders, many of which protruded above the surface. The boatmen discussed the possibility of running through a narrow channel between the rocks but quickly discarded that idea. It was plain that they could not avoid the big waves. Freeman noted, "The rapid is in no sense a 'fall,' however, as there is no abrupt drop, and such a name is a palpable misnomer."

Following lunch they crossed the river again to take a last look at the right channel. A heavy rain shower came up while they were there. They kept dry by crouching under a projecting ledge. Afterward all passengers climbed past the rapid over low cliffs on the left bank.

The best course turned out to be the simplest—down the tongue on the right, pulling away from the big waves against the cliff. Kolb ran first. Elwyn followed. Lint and Freeman came after them. Rising on the spray-lashed crests, then wallowing in the troughs, each battled his way through. Kolb's boat went too close to the cliffs for comfort but came through in fine shape. His boat took less water than any of the others. The combined fall of the two, almost-continuous sections of the rapid was nineteen feet.

They made the remaining one-mile run to Hermit Creek in about an hour and pitched camp. Because of a late afternoon storm, Hermit Creek was running a good flow of dirty water. The rapid looked almost as rough as Granite Falls.

Colonel Crosby, superintendent of Grand Canyon National Park, had put together a large party of Arizona State and Park officials who wanted to watch the boats run this rapid. He came down the Hermit trail from the rim with a ranger and Roger Birdseye about 4:00 P.M. Roger brought in new oars and supplies. They expected a big group in camp the following morning. Shirtliff, of Fox News, came in that afternoon, too, as did Blanche and Edith Kolb. The Kolb women were camped at Hermit's Rest, about a mile and a half up from the river.

For some time Kolb had been brooding over his festering argument with Birdseye about picture taking. He did not like the idea of Fox News and Santa Fe Railroad people taking movies of the run through the rapids, considering this as an unwarranted intrusion on his own photography business. He told Birdseye he was quitting that afternoon.

In an insert to his diary Birdseye wrote:

> At this point Emery Kolb announced his intention of quitting, at first giving no reason. There had been constant petty friction between Kolb and the crew of the Grand—La Rue, Moore and Freeman—most of it due to Kolb's extreme jealousy of anyone who writes about or takes pictures of any boat trip through the canyon. He considers this his special prerogative. It is quite true that he and his brother Ellsworth had some rather hard knocks from the Harvey Co. and the Santa Fe R.R., and have had quite a fight for existence as scenic photographers in the park. Nevertheless the Kolb Bros. fail to realize that in this progressive age they must survive by competition and not by adopting a "dog in the manger" attitude. La Rue and Kolb mix like oil and water and have had a little friction, but not enough to force my notice. Kolb has picked on Freeman incessantly and the latter has shown a fine spirit by not saying a word. Freeman brags a little about his past explorations and his writings and all this seems to have grated on Kolb's sensitive nature. The moving picture venture of the Fox News and also La Rue's operations with the little Sept camera have also displeased Kolb who at first asked for exclusive moving picture rights. He has feared that the Harvey Company would get the pictures and

run them as a free show at the El Tovar Hotel and thus ruin his business which includes two moving pictures a day at his studio.[1]

There seemed nothing to do but to make the best of a bad situation. Several difficult rapids lay ahead, and none of the party had ever seen them except Kolb. Birdseye told Kolb to go. He would let Dodge take the fourth boat. He decided not to have a head boatman but let the four boatmen try to work out a harmonious procedure among themselves. He expected to rely largely on Lint and Blake, who had had more experience in rapids of this kind than Freeman. It was his opinion that Lint handled his boat better than anyone in the party, including Kolb, but he was too young for the responsibility of head boatman. Besides that, Kolb had apparently soured him on Freeman, so there would continue to be friction.

Blanche and Edith Kolb came down to camp and were very much shocked when they learned how Kolb had acted. They implored him to try and get his job back. At 8:30 that evening Kolb came to Birdseye and begged to be taken back. The Colonel told him it was too late. He had already made a deal to apportion Kolb's salary between the lower-paid boatmen, Lint and Blake, and Dodge, the rodman. It would have meant a $150 raise to Dodge and lesser amounts to Lint and Blake. But these three yielded to the entreaties of the women and agreed to support Kolb in his efforts to come back.

Kolb then asked Birdseye to try him as far as Bass Trail. He said that Blake, Lint, and Dodge wanted him to come back. Dodge wanted badly to have a boat of his own but agreed he would give up the chance if Kolb would stay. When Birdseye consulted with Freeman, he magnanimously said, "By all means."

Birdseye then talked it over with Stabler, who also advised him to give Kolb another chance. He then told Kolb that he could stay if he promised to act decently and make no more criticisms or remarks about any of the other men.

When Kolb told his wife and daughter of the boss's decision, Edith fainted. They had to bring her around by using ammonia and the "snake-bite" bottle. Edith stayed in camp that night while Elwyn and Lint escorted her mother back up to Hermit Cabin, a mile and half up the creek. It started to rain just as the two began their return. A faulty flashlight was all they had to light the trail. It had to be held "on" by constant pressure of the thumb. When one's thumb gave out he would give the flashlight to the other, and when that one could no longer hold the button down he would hand it back again.

During the evening Shirtliff of Fox News and La Rue each took flashlight movies of the radio set in action. In doing so they set the flare too near Birdseye and Stabler, and the two were almost overcome by the fumes.

The next morning, August 30, Edith seemed OK. Blanche Kolb, Ellsworth Kolb, Santa Fe Railroad officials, Harvey Company officials, and others from Hermit's Camp began to arrive before breakfast. When all were assembled, thirty-four spectators had come to view the running of the rapid.

Faced with so many people to cook for, Word balked and also threatened to quit. His temper was already on the ragged edge because of sore eyes—the glare of sun on the water kept them continually inflamed. With some coaxing from Colonel Birdseye he grudgingly fixed breakfast. However, he gave notice that he was leaving the party at Bass Trail, the next stop. Birdseye sent out for a new cook to join them at that point.

After the movie machines were set up, Kolb and Lint ran the rapid. Ellsworth Kolb had returned to the Hermit Creek camp, but he arrived back at the river in time to set up a camera and get movies of the run. The Fox newsman made several shots of the crew and boats before the boatmen embarked. Kolb seemed to be in good humor again and posed for him and the Santa Fe movie operators.

The short, rough waves tossed the boats in every direction, almost standing them on end. At times the spectators on shore could even see the floorboards. Elwyn made his run stern first with Dodge, the only passenger allowed to ride through, lying flat on the stern hatch. After each wave submerged him, Dodge would raise up with a grin and wipe the muddy water from his bald head.

Elwyn felt he was doing all right and had relaxed a little. Suddenly a big slopper came over the side, followed by water from some smaller waves, half filling the cockpit with dirty river water.

The rest of the crew had a hard climb over low cliffs to where the boats landed below the rapid. The fall of Hermit Creek Rapid was sixteen feet.

Following the run, the spectators began trekking back up the trail, talking of a sight not soon to be forgotten. The survey party traveled a mile and a half down the river to the head of Boucher Rapid and stopped for lunch. Boucher had a frothy, twelve-foot fall and was full of choppy waves but showed no rocks in the main channel. The boatmen allowed no passengers through this one. Elwyn's boat took only about a bucket of water, which he considered lucky.

From Boucher the party made a run to the head of Crystal Rapid, a long, rocky chute at Mile 98.25. They made camp there even though it was only 3:30 P.M. because of threatening rain. During the day's run Kolb had somehow split one gunwale of his boat, so he mended it.

Sometime during the night they were awakened by thunder and flashes of lightning. Soon after rain and wind struck so violently that it took the combined efforts of Kolb, Lint, and Elwyn to hold the tarpaulin over their beds. In a little while they could hear water running down the slopes and began to get uneasy. Then a small, muddy stream began to trickle between their beds, becoming larger by the minute.

Suddenly they heard a large torrent break over a nearby sandbank. They grabbed whatever they could find in the dark, and scrambled for higher ground. Lint waded back into the swift torrent and tried to pull the bed tarp out, but by then the water had so covered it with sand and mud that he could not budge it. He only managed to bring out his and Elwyn's trousers.

"There goes [sic] our watches," he lamented, meaning of course that the muddy water had probably ruined them. Elwyn's was a cheap one so would not be much loss, but Lint's was a sixty-dollar timepiece.

While Kolb and Elwyn crouched under a ledge wrapped in their blankets, Lint went to check on the boats. He returned presently to report them safe. He said the Colonel's bed was in a lake of water, that the tent had blown down, and that the cooking utensils were covered with sand. They went in search of better shelter and found an overhanging ledge where they lay down on wet blankets.

Freeman reported, "La Rue and his bed were driven ten feet, and left hanging over the brink of a caving cut-bank."

By morning the rain had almost stopped. In some places deep gutters were cut in the sand and in others sand had washed in to a depth of several inches. The flood had washed the instrument case to the very edge of the river. Lint's life jacket had disappeared, probably blown into the river by a gust of wind. They located the cooking utensils by poking a rod here and there into the wet sand. Then Word fixed breakfast.

After finding all the equipment they could, the men took a couple of hours to dry out beds and clean up the gear. The radio antenna proved to be a good clothesline.

Crystal Rapid was long and steep, but not particularly dangerous since its sixteen-foot drop was spread over a third of a mile. The passengers all rode through. Crystal Rapid has changed dramatically since then, a classic example of how a rapid can be altered by new floods over the years. In December 1966 a great flood carrying house-size boulders roared down Crystal Creek and deposited them in the river. It was immediately transformed into a very dangerous rapid even for modern rafts. In the wet and rainy year of 1983 record high discharges of from 45,000 to 96,200 cfs. were released from Lake Powell to prevent it from overflowing the dam. Crystal Rapid became unusually hazardous then with giant waves of up to twenty feet from trough to crest. A passenger-laden pontoon capsized in it resulting in one fatality. It is famous to all modern-day river runners and is sometimes, depending upon flow, considered equal to Lava Falls.[2]

There was another rapid a short distance below Crystal which made a sharp turn near the lower end, with a gravel bar on the inside of the curve. A hundred yards below that a huge boulder obstructed the main channel. Elwyn had to land on the bar for a stadia station. With some lively stick work he managed to pull into the slower water at the foot of the bar. Kolb and Lint made a landing below the bend after considerable hard rowing. Freeman missed the landing and, losing control of his boat for a few seconds, went so close to the big boulder that it looked like he would smash against it. He skimmed past it with all aboard, was lost to sight in the smother of waves, and went on down the river.

The rapid was in two parts, a 9.5-foot drop at the upper end and a four-foot fall at the lower part. All boats except the *Grand* pulled in for lunch on the left side between rapids. Those on the *Grand* had to resort to tuna fish, the only food on their boat. Later, after some good-natured kidding, they gave the name "Tuna" to the creek and rapid.

During the day they scarcely saw enough earth to set foot on, making it necessary to land on narrow shelves of rock for rod or instrument stations. Sometimes they were forced to use handholds in the potholes washed out by the river during high water. Occasionally Elwyn had to let Dodge off, then drop into an eddy or still water where the boat would not grind against the rocky cliff, while Dodge held his rod for a reading. After Dodge was released from his point, Elwyn would row back close enough for Dodge to leap aboard.

Elwyn made one difficult landing where Dodge jumped ashore and Elwyn followed with the painter in hand. When the boat came to the end of the rope Elwyn was unable to hold it and was dragged from the slick granite into the river. He easily swam to the boat and climbed back in. Then he rowed to the quiet water behind a point of rock until Dodge had finished his rod work and it was time to pick him up again.

They found no camping place until late in the evening, and that was at two small sandspits on the right. They landed immediately, much relieved to be able to roll their beds out for the night. They had to arrange the slide rock of the talus slope into terraces to accommodate some of the beds.

About 3:00 A.M. the cook woke them up saying that the boats were standing on end. The *Grand* and *Marble* were in danger of breaking their painters if the river dropped further. They pushed those two boats into the water and retied them but left the *Boulder* and *Glen* alone since they were resting on shelves of sand that kept them from straining the mooring ropes. The river dropped four and a half feet during the night.

The crew spent a large part of the morning surveying a dam site, then ran Ruby Canyon Rapid at Mile 104, where they all got sprayed with dirty water. They ran more choppy but easily maneuvered rapids every little while until they came to Serpentine Rapid at Mile 106. It looked ugly with most of the current piled up on a jumble of boulders at a bend in the river. Stabler was of the opinion that this was the rapid characterized by Stanton as "the worst and most unmanageable on the river," where he lost his *Marie* by trying to run her through empty without boatman or line.

All passengers except Dodge, who was carrying the rod, walked around on the right side. After looking it over thoroughly, Kolb and Lint came through in fine shape. Freeman went next. He had a jumpy passage down across the barely submerged boulders extending out from the bar on the left. He said it was an agreeable surprise not to receive a tap from one of them on the bottom. Once over them he was able to pull away from the worst of the line of waves along the cliff and work out to the deep eddy under the left-hand wall to pick up his passengers.

Elwyn watched the effect of the currents on the other three boats.

When Dodge was relieved from his turning point after the sight was taken and recorded, Elwyn crossed the river toward the left side. Then he rowed the *Glen* through the rough waves and managed to take only a small amount of water.

During the day Raymond Moore, the geologist, in great glee brought in a chunk of brown rock which he said contained "calcerous algae," probably the oldest form of life. Freeman said, "Their tomb is heavy enough to give the *Grand* a sharp list to the port. I am trying to induce Moore to consume enough salmon and sardine from our cargo to offset his augmenting load of rock, but not with marked success."[3] They camped a half mile above the Bass Trail, tying the *Boulder* and *Glen* from both ends to keep them from rubbing against the rocks. It was so late that supper was not ready until after dark. By the time the meal was over the peninsula where the kitchen was located had become an island. A great mass of driftwood had collected against the boats, so they had to be moved. They brought the boats up into the channel between the island and the main shore where it seemed they would be less likely to chafe against the rocks. They moved the kitchen to the right bank before the channel became too swift to wade so they would not have to row out to breakfast. The boatmen got up a couple of times in the night to see how the boats were riding.

By morning, September 2, the river had risen another foot. Since it was holding almost steady at its high mark, the party believed the flood was from the Little Colorado or San Juan rather than local. They stayed in camp that morning waiting for the packtrain.

The fourteen-mule packtrain arrived opposite camp about noon bringing in one month's heavy provisions, mainly canned goods. A new cook had not been located, so Frank Word agreed to stay on until they reached Havasu Creek. The new provisions would have to last them to Diamond Creek because only light supplies such as mail, flour, and sugar would be brought in at Havasu Creek, the next stop. At Havasu all supplies would have to be carried in by men rather than mules for the last six miles down to the river.

They ferried all of the camp equipment to the left side. The mule trail ended at the head of Bass Rapid, 200 yards below the place where the boats were moored. The current at the end of the trail was too swift to make a landing with loaded boats. So, to get at the supplies, they emptied the *Glen*, lined her downstream, and tied her up at the foot of the trail. They loaded all the supplies into her, then lined her back up around the rocks to the sandbar where the other boats were tied.

After lunch they divided the new supplies among the boats. The heavy canned goods taxed the capacity of the already overloaded vessels, but they were finally stowed away. They started on down the river at about 4:00 P.M.

Freeman said,

The *Grand* wallowed down through Bass Rapid like a raft, shipping much water on account of her deeper submergence with the new load. All the other boatmen complain of the same trouble. It looks like sloppy going until natural causes reduce the stores of provisions under the hatch.[4]

They soon passed under the Bass Trolley cable at Mile 107.7. William W. Bass, for whom the rapid was named, established a tourist camp about 1890 and later built the trans-canyon trail and cableway for transporting tourists across the river. The cable was fifty feet above the river and 300 feet long. It seemed to be well constructed with a heavy support cable and two smaller ones for operating the windlass. The main cable was capable of carrying a horse in the car with a man on top to operate the windlass. Rex Beach, the author of many stories and plays, lost a horse there in 1917 when the animal got frightened and hung himself on the car's tie ropes.

They worked on downriver for about a mile and camped on a gravel bar on the right side 300 feet above the mouth of Shinumo Creek. It flowed a good-sized stream of red water from the recent floods. La Rue measured the flow of Shinumo Creek at sixteen cfs.

There was no wood at the campsite. Lint was still up the river about 2,000 feet near a big pile of wood, so Kolb semaphored for him to bring a load of wood with him.

Elwyn said:

Emery and I then went up the creek to a waterfall. Seeing some drift wood above the falls, we went back into the cave which we could see to the right of the pool made by the falls. There was an opening in the back of the cave which made it possible for us to climb out to the upper stream bed. I struggled up through the narrow opening which was half choked with drift wood. I then loosened some of the drift and made the opening larger. I threw a quantity of the wood down, which we took to camp. This, with the load Leigh brought, was sufficient for our needs.[5]

Soon after making camp the river started falling. They had to loosen the painters of the boats before going to bed. By next morning, Monday, September 3, the river had dropped further. The *Glen* was high and dry with the stern resting upon what had been a submerged rock. The other boats lay at a steep angle with their sterns barely in the water.

Birdseye declared a day off and the party enjoyed the rest. It was a scorcher with the sun bouncing off the bare cliffs, so almost everyone went swimming at the pool below the falls in Shinumo Creek. Lint, Kolb, and Elwyn went above the falls and dived off into the pool. The cool bath was refreshing. Afterward they got the *Glen* back into the water and rowed 100 yards upriver where they found some shade beside a big boulder. They returned to camp for lunch, after which they trimmed each other's hair, then went back to the shade of the boulder. Later, Kolb and Elwyn swam back while Lint took the boat to camp. They spent the rest of the afternoon writing and sleeping.

Next morning the boatmen had no trouble with Shinumo Rapid. Everyone rode through it, the waves being much smaller than before the water level dropped. At about 11:00 A.M. they stopped at the head of Hakatai Rapid, at Mile 109, to survey a dam site.

The Bass asbestos mine was located up the canyon that came in at the head of Hakatai Rapid. Just above the swift water was a one-man cable car which had been used by Bass to travel to and from his asbestos mine. The car was supported by a one-quarter-inch cable 600 feet long that spanned the canyon 175 feet above the water.

While running Hakatai Rapid Kolb hit a wave that snapped an oar above the blade, but he made it through safely with the use of a spare oar. From there the men worked their way to the head of Waltenberg Rapid, named for John Waltenberg, who had worked with William W. Bass and later with Levi Noble on the Shinumo-area survey. Elwyn landed on the left side of the river near the head of the rapid. The other boats landed on the opposite side. After looking it over they decided to make camp on the left bank where there was plenty of wood.

Kolb had smashed his boat in Waltenberg Rapid on the 1911 trip, and his brother Ellsworth's boat had capsized and been rolled over and over by the backwash of a midstream boulder. Ellsworth had been carried a half mile downstream before he could land. The two had spent that 1911 Christmas day repairing their boats. When told of this incident Elwyn said, "I don't like the heat, but Christmas weather? Not for me!"

They moored the boats in niches under the granite wall and were forced to pick precarious stone-paved terraces among the rocks for their beds. The skies were overcast and the air felt like rain. Everyone was too tired to put up the radio.

On the morning of September 5 they spent considerable time looking over the rapid. Waltenberg Rapid had a drop of fifteen feet but was spread over a long distance. It looked worse in the morning than the night before. They threw in driftwood to chart the current. Elwyn described the passage thus:

> Dodge swam around a point of rock which was impassable on foot, and held a rope ready in case of need. Leigh came through and landed above the rock point in order to pick up the men and ferry them to a place below where they could walk along shore so that the following boats would not have to land so far upstream. As he came through, Leigh struck an oar on a submerged rock, but did no damage. Emery made a good run through, followed by Freeman. I then came through, and, as Dodge wanted to try out his rope-throwing stunt to see if it were practical, I came close enough for the rope to reach. Dodge made his throw and the knot in the end of the rope caught in a lifeline amidships. The drag on the boat from that quarter caused it to pull sideways and to heel far over, until water started to pour into the cockpit before I could free the knot. I had no difficulty in landing but was in such an unfavorable position that my boat struck a boulder as I again pulled into the stream. There was no damage done, as the blow was light.[6]

All rode through in fine shape except for the usual bath of dirty water. They ran two more rapids during the forenoon and at one place came to a huge mass of bedrock in midchannel, which split the stream into two narrow channels but caused no rapids. Below it the river became very still and smooth between riffles. Freeman's boat hit a couple of rocks in one of the riffles.

About 4:00 P.M. they reached Royal Arch Creek. Some of the men stopped temporarily at Elves Chasm, a verdant haven of lacy water falls, clear pools, dripping moss, ferns, and columbines. They filled their canteens and washed the river mud from their bodies before passing on. A few mesquite trees grew along the river at the base of the cliffs in the old lava above the high-water level, and prickly pear, barrel cactus, bunchgrass, and century plants attached themselves to cracks in the cliffs. They wound up camping on the left side at the beginning of Conquistador Aisle at Mile 119.7.

Birdseye reported:

> The lower end of this canyon is known as Elves Chasm and the boys in the boats which stopped there say it is the prettiest spot on the river not excepting Vasey's Paradise. A clear, cold stream with beautiful falls, pools and fern dells with shade all day long was the result of their report and there was some disappointment when Burchard and I sailed by in the Boulder. . . . It is curious that no previous boat party mentions this beautiful spot, although either Evan's topographic party or his level party had camped here. Remains of a campfire were found with the following names and dates carved in the rocks: Norman Oliver— R.L. Elliot—Stewart U.S.G.S. May and June 1905 and 1907.[7]

The next morning, September 6, Elwyn rowed upstream a couple of hundred yards and crossed with Dodge to his turning point. Then he pulled into an eddy below the boulder bar opposite camp and filled their water bags from a small stream.

Below there the river canyon "boxed up" for a couple of miles. The Tapeats sandstone, which had disappeared beneath the river upstream, appeared again a few miles farther on and increased in height as they advanced. Finally the granite under the Tapeats formation began to appear and was over 100 feet higher than the river by the time they arrived at their next campsite. The river was less than 100 feet across in some places. They ran only three rapids that day, but the river dropped fast, causing many riffles. The high walls of lime and sandstone were closer to the stream than at any time since they left Bright Angel.

In the nine miles run that day only Fossil Creek at Mile 125 looked serious. Fossil Creek Rapid had a seven-foot drop in the first fifty feet and a fifteen-foot drop overall, producing some rough and twisting waves. Freeman's boat pitched like a bronco, although the waves were less than ten feet high. Lint's boat did not take as much water as the Grand, but it was whirled around several times in an eddy at the foot of the rapid. Kolb's boat took quite a bit of water. Elwyn cut to the right of the tongue and only took a couple of splashes.

Elwyn did not reach camp until about 6:30 P.M. There was a nice, clear bucket of water conveniently located, so he took a big mouthful. He did not swallow it but spit it out immediately since it was very salty. He had tricked the others with salty water before, and this had been placed there for his special benefit. There was a big laugh at his expense.

They camped at Specter Chasm, Mile 129. Again they were too tired to set up the radio. Freeman noted, "It is not an attractive halting place, with vile tasting water, scant wood, and flies in such swarms as we have never seen them. Shirts are on again, and various forms of leg-wrappings."

CHAPTER 17

Specter Chasm to Lava Falls

On the morning of September 7 Lint took his boat through Specter Rapid with all passengers on board and hit a back-curling wave that soaked them with muddy water. He got into more big waves lower down, but rode them in fine style, taking only a little more water. Freeman tried the same tactics but with less success, taking on a large amount of water but arriving safely. Waiting while Dodge held rod for the engineers at their turning point, Elwyn watched the others make their runs. This gave him a better idea of how to tackle the rapid. He missed the high, choppy waves entirely by cutting prow first through the left side of the tongue. As a result he took only one small splash.

The crew spent the rest of the day on a detailed survey of the river canyon and two dam sites within the last mile of the Middle Granite Gorge, where pink granite predominated with lesser amounts of dark schist. In doing this they had to run Bedrock Rapid, one of the worst they had encountered. Birdseye wrote, "This is a nasty rapid with an eight foot fall, and I considered myself in more danger than at any point on the trip."

The current was split by a high outcrop of granite. The left-hand channel carried the most water and drew most of the floating matter. A couple of hundred feet past the outcrop the current piled up against a granite cliff, swung to the left, then back along another sheer rock face on the right, forming the last part of an S curve where the swift current drove against a mass of bedrock about halfway through the rapid. A hundred feet of this and the river seemed to drop beneath the main current in a huge whirlpool, emerging in a boil a couple of hundred feet farther on near the left bank.

Elwyn thought it would be virtually impossible to extricate a boat from the big whirlpool if one ever got into it. He took Dodge and went ahead, keeping to the left channel where he had no trouble. He landed some distance below the granite outcrop and the two of them walked barefoot back over the hot rocks to a position atop the overhanging cliff. They had a grandstand seat from which to watch the others make the run.

Kolb had gone through before Elwyn and Dodge reached their viewpoint. He later reported having come within two feet of the cliff face on the right. Frank Word claimed the boat missed the rock by only a foot.

Elwyn and Dodge waited for the survey party to return from working a side canyon so Lint could run them through. Lint came so close to the canyon wall that Burchard, who was riding prone upon the stern, slapped the rock with his hat as they passed. Lint said he knew he wiped some pesky flies off the side of his boat.

Freeman was not so lucky. When he was within about eight feet of the sheer rock he seemed to give up and rested on his oars. The *Grand* leaped at the rock and rammed into it stern first. The boat seemed to poise for an instant, then swung to the left and wound up in the big whirlpool. Freeman had to row with all his might to get the boat back into the current. Most raft trips today take the right-hand channel, since some rafts have been dashed against the cliff and wrecked or overturned when going to the left.

They had hoped to run as far as Tapeats Creek that night, but when they came to a steep and rocky rapid at Mile 131.5, Birdseye decided to make camp. Galloway Canyon at the head of the rapid was dry, so they had to settle for river water.

To the best of their knowledge no party had yet run this rapid. (We now know that Flavell and Montéz had run it in 1896.) Seymour Sylvester Dubendorff, of the Julius expedition, had on November 8, 1909, capsized his boat here with serious injury to his person. Birdseye decided to name it Dubendorff Rapid.[1]

The boatmen looked the rapid over carefully, testing the current by throwing bits of driftwood into it before deciding that it could be run safely. As a precaution they thought it best to portage part of their loads around the rapid. The portage covered a quarter of a mile over jumbled boulders, and many of the loads were of a shape and character very awkward to carry over so precarious a footing. During the two hours it took to complete the portage the other boatmen noticed that Freeman managed to carry little more than his own bulk.

They lightened the *Marble*, *Grand*, and *Glen*, but left the *Boulder* loaded. It had straight sides and flat decks, making it a little top-heavy and giving it a tendency to capsize easier than the other boats. Lint wanted the load for ballast.

Kolb told the crew that in January 1912 he and his brother had lined their boats through the upper half of this rapid in freezing water. They thought Dubendorff was worse than Soap Creek or Hance. It had a fifteen-foot fall in a few hundred yards and was full of rocks and bad holes. Kolb took the narrow channel to the right and bumped a couple of rocks, losing one oar, but suffered no damage. He signaled for the others to take the mid-channel.

Elwyn wanted to try a different method of rapid running, the one he had used successfully in Specter Rapid where all the boats but his had taken a big load of water. He explained to Lint and Freeman how he would do it—row to the opposite side of the river and then head for a point just above the tip of the tongue of smooth water. From there he would swing the boat stern first as it broke through the waves into the smoother water below the long line of obstructing boulders. Lint and Freeman agreed to try his system.

Lint and Elwyn deliberately stalled, talking as if it were a foregone conclusion that Freeman would make the run following Kolb. At last Freeman donned his life jacket and rowed to the far side of the river. As the swift water of the tongue caught him, they could see that he would not make the maneuver properly. He hit the big waves far from the safety of the slow water for which he was aiming. It was a terrifying sight to see the *Grand* plunge from sight into water no boat had a right to tackle. Elwyn regretted their trick until he saw Freeman, with his boat still right-side up, pulling the sluggish, water-filled *Grand* into the slow water below the rapid. It seemed almost miraculous that a boat could go in exactly the wrong place and survive such a pounding.

Freeman commented:

> I went first, taking the middle of the V head on, and then swinging and pulling away from the big waves and rocks on the left. I would have done better to have gone down stern-first,

crowding the rocks on the right side of the V. As it was, though I missed the heavy waves above, I was carried down squarely into the worst hole in the rapid, nearly a hundred yards from the head, colliding solidly and violently with the rock at the bottom of it. She seemed actually to bounce back up stream; then lifted, swung half around, and went on. One of the oar handles struck me a glancing side-swipe across the mouth, but not in any way to trouble. I managed to bring her stern-on again, ran the rest of the rapid under complete control and pulled in at the eddy on the right.[2]

Lint wanted to be last—perhaps he doubted Elwyn's system would work after all. Elwyn therefore pushed into the stream followed closely by Lint. They made the run almost exactly as planned and took very little water. Upon landing they learned that Freeman had smashed a hole in the two-inch-thick stern of his boat. They speculated privately on what would have happened if the *Grand* had been loaded. They also wondered what would have been left of their own older, almost rotten, boats had they followed Freeman's course. Repairs with cotton waste, white lead, canvas, copper sheeting, and an hour's work put the *Grand* in as good shape as before.

They ate lunch by Stone Creek at the foot of the rapid, which had clear running water. Had they only known this the night before, they could have had this good water with an 800-foot carry.

After noon they made the two-mile run to Tapeats Creek, where a large stream of cold water issued from a box canyon on the right. Everyone enjoyed a clean bath. Some of them washed clothes while others set up the radio. They planned to lay over here an extra day, since Stabler wanted to inspect some Anasazi ruins up the creek.

The men set up the radio for the first time since August 30. Station KHJ came in clear but with some fading out. They heard for the first time that serious trouble was imminent between England and Italy, that a disastrous earthquake had hit Japan, and that Washington had won a ball game by a decisive score.

On Sunday, September 9, Colonel Birdseye spent the day washing clothes, putting finishing touches on several dam-site maps, checking notes, and repairing instruments. La Rue measured the flow of Tapeats Creek and found it to be ninety-two cfs., the largest flow of any side stream except the Little Colorado River. Major Powell had named this stream Tapeats Creek because a Paiute Indian of that name, who pointed it out to the Major from the Kaibab, claimed it. Temperature of the stream was fifty-two degrees Fahrenheit.

While Birdseye was doing his chores six of the men explored Tapeats Creek, planning to reach the forks of the stream and follow the left branch to its source. They had heard that it gushed forth from the sheer face of a cliff a few miles from the Colorado.

At first the swift current was about two feet deep in the box canyon. The water reached from cliff to cliff, making it necessary to wade in the cold stream. Then the water got deeper due to narrowing of the canyon. The slopes became a trifle less sheer, however, so they searched out crevices where they could get finger and toeholds to climb out of the water. Soon the whole cliff side was covered with climbing men.

About 100 feet up the hillside above the stream they reached a place where it was easier hiking. From there they went on upstream to where the box canyon ended and the creek meandered through a narrow, lovely little valley. The stream plunged from rock to pool in white cascades, huge prickly pear were in bloom, and cholla cactus studded the grass-covered slopes adding beauty to the scene. The shade of a few cottonwood trees was welcome, too.

About noon they reached the forks of the stream and, taking the left branch, soon came upon a fountain of water spewing from a fern- and moss-covered bank. It was a lovely sight. Nearby they found some pottery shards and what seemed to be the remains of an irrigation ditch. There was also a stone retaining wall or dike, apparently built to keep the waters of the stream from overflowing the tillable soil. They found a human jawbone with a few teeth intact and numerous corncobs. High on the eastern cliff were stone storehouses where grain must have been kept.

Before eating their lunches of raisins and cold pancakes they continued on up the left fork, climbing about 700 feet above the main stream. There they found water gushing forth from a hole in the cliff. It fell some ten feet and then struck the more sloping base of the cliff where it spread out to a width of perhaps forty feet. Lush vegetation flanked the waterfall making a beautiful sight well worth the climb.[3]

The next morning the party moved on. Elwyn was the first to run Tapeats Rapid at Mile 133.75. He had no trouble until he began to pull sharply toward shore to avoid the heavy water. There he underestimated the speed of the current and the right stern corner of his boat struck a large shore rock. At about the same time a big wave hit,

Junction of forks of Tapeats Creek. Left to right: Herman Stabler (above), Elwyn Blake, Frank Word, Raymond Moore, and Leigh Lint. (Grand Canyon 74, U.S. Geological Survey)

throwing Dodge off balance and overboard. An excellent swimmer, Dodge was back on almost before Elwyn knew he was off, but his tobacco got soaked.

Soon after that they ran a long rapid at Mile 135. Then they entered Little Granite Gorge and passed the narrowest point in the river—seventy-six feet.

At noon they noted the beginning of an eclipse of the sun. In the dim light the shadows became blurred and fuzzy, and the whole canyon took on a gloomy and desolate aspect. But they were able to continue their work.

Freeman commented:

> The work of the afternoon was started in a ghostly fading light which finally became almost too dim to allow the rod to be read. . . . The weird greenish light which prevailed during most of the eighty percent eclipse was much like that which precedes a cyclone or typhoon. The sensation of running riffles in it was quite uncanny.[4]

They ran some choppy rapids where the river was swift and sometimes dangerous. At Fishtail Rapid the current piled up against the base of a cliff so that it was several feet higher than at a point thirty feet upstream. This rapid had a fall of ten feet. The huge waves nearly knocked Birdseye off the deck of the *Boulder*.

Between rapids they traveled some long stretches of smooth water. At Deer Creek (Mile 136.25) they stopped to admire the 100-foot-high falls. Deer Creek sliced through a narrow, sinuous chimney in the canyon wall and fanned out to make a bridal-veil-like falls, dropping into a mist-shrouded pool. Freeman wrote: "A hundred yards below the fall we found a bower of springs and greenery extending far up the cliff. There were great beds of maidenhair ferns and a flowering plant with bright red trumpet-like blossoms." A picture of the falls taken by the surveyors shows no shrubbery at the mouth of Deer Creek. Today, because of the controlled flow of the river with no large floods to sweep it clean, salt cedar, sandbar willow, and seep willow grow profusely at the mouth of Deer Creek.[5]

The party made camp just above Kanab Creek on the opposite side of the river. They had covered nine and a half miles that day, the longest one-day advance on the trip. This was where Major Powell terminated his second expedition in 1872 and traveled up Kanab Creek to the north. When the survey crew tried the radio, they found it would not work.

E. C. La Rue measuring Deer Creek below the falls. (Grand Canyon 353, U.S. Geological Survey)

Next day they worked up Kanab Creek to the 2,100-foot contour, 218 feet above the river. They did not finish until 3:00 P.M., so they decided to stay at that camp the rest of the day. They took the radio apart to see why it did not work and found one unsoldered joint in the wiring and one battery that was badly bulged. Then they discovered that their soldering iron was missing.

On September 12 they ran Kanab Creek Rapid without trouble, although it had eighteen feet of fall. Freeman in the *Grand* helped with a second stadia rod in the forenoon, which expedited the movement of the instrument so much that they made five miles before noon. They hoped to do at least as well that afternoon until they came to a threatening rapid at Mile 149.5. They paused to look it over carefully. It was filled with huge boulders and deep holes. One big submerged boulder in midstream caused an almost sheer drop of nine or ten feet, followed by huge tail waves. The safest channel seemed right of the big rock, but it was only about twenty feet wide. The total width of the river was not over 125 feet at that point.

They unloaded all the boats but the *Boulder* and portaged the loads along the right bank. It was a hard scramble over jumbled rocks to the sandbar at the foot of the rapid, and during the portage they had to take shelter in some nearby caves until a heavy shower passed.

Kolb ran the rapid first. The cautious head boatman suffered the indignity of being the first to overturn a boat. While avoiding some shore rocks he was drawn into the main current and before he knew it went directly over a submerged boulder and into the deep hole below it. The boat hit the drop almost squarely stern on, and a back-curling wave caught the stern of the *Marble* flipping her upside down. She went bounding swiftly through the tail of the rapid.

Kolb wound up under the boat, but soon worked his way out and grabbed the lifeline on the far side. Those on shore could not see him and thought he was gone. He was carried along that way for 100 yards and what seemed like several minutes. Dodge, as was his habit, was waiting near the foot of the rapid. Upon seeing the upset, he raced down the shore, jumped in, and swam through the heavy waves to the boat, catching it at the foot of the rapid. When he reached the boat he was greatly relieved to see Kolb's white hat emerge with Kolb under the hat.

Kolb had taken some water into his lungs while trying to find his way out from under the boat and was having difficulty breathing. Dodge got hold of the *Marble*'s painter and handed it to Lint, who had just arrived in the *Boulder*. They pulled to shore where they righted the *Marble*.

Elwyn came through safely, barely missing the big rock. Freeman, being afraid of the big rock, got in too close to shore and struck another rock near the head of the rapid. He did, however, miss the big hole by a good distance and landed on a sandbar at the foot of the rapid. Several of the men helped tow the *Boulder* and *Marble* upstream to the sandbar where the other two boats were moored. They discovered that all Kolb had lost was one oar and his baling bucket.

Since there was plenty of wood near the sandbar, and the men were tired and wet, they camped there for the night. Freeman noted, "In consideration of the rough work of running, portaging and lining, the chief drew on the medicine chest for the snake-bite medicine and prescribed a liberal dose to all hands." In deference to Kolb's adventure of the afternoon they called this one Upset Rapid. The name stuck.

Next morning Kolb took a movie of the place where he had upset. Just before leaving camp someone spotted two mountain sheep on a high ledge across the river from camp. The party had fairly smooth going that day, encountering no major rapids, and arrived at Havasu Creek, Mile 156.75, about 2:00 P.M. They found the stream running red from a recent storm.

Roger Birdseye, Charles Fiske, and an interpreter had been waiting there for two days with mail and 700 pounds of supplies. Roger had employed nineteen Havasupai Indians to pack the supplies down the steep, narrow gorge. The Indians would not carry over forty pounds each and had required a good deal of coaxing to come at all. Having been over a small portion of that trail, the author does not blame the Indians.

With Roger was good-natured Felix Kominsky, the new cook, a fat and jolly Pole weighing 225 pounds. This made him the second heaviest one in the party, behind Freeman, and added considerably to their loads. He turned out to be a fine cook under sometimes difficult conditions, able to make cake in a dutch oven and never get out of humor when the wind blew sand and ashes into everything. He wore a straw sailor hat which the boys said he would lose in the first rapids. He said a recruiting officer in the army told him an army cook did not need a name as long as Kominsky and had changed it to Koms.

After reading their mail, Kolb, Lint, and Elwyn took a boat up into the narrow gorge of Havasu Creek. They turned the boat crosswise in the stream and let the current wedge it between the walls where it lay motionless. In this cool spot they loafed and wrote letters. Today, Havasu Creek, with its beautiful travertine falls, clear pools, ledges, and shady nooks, is a favorite hiking stop for river runners.

On September 14 Roger Birdseye, Charles Fiske, Shirley the interpreter, and Frank Word the original cook, left at 9:00 A.M. They packed out maps, notes, film, and the damaged radio, which was to be repaired and brought back in at Diamond Creek.

Burchard, Dodge, and Stabler worked until noon surveying the mouth of the creek. La Rue measured the flow of Havasu Creek at seventy-five cfs. Lint spent most of the morning repairing his boat so that it would have a better chance of finishing the trip. Elwyn mended his shoes, made some repairs to his own boat, and helped Lint with his repairs.

When they rearranged their loads they found they had an excess of sugar and flour. They abandoned fifty pounds of each, along with one of the large mess boxes which had been broken and was no longer watertight.

Before embarking the next day Kolb and Elwyn changed loads. Since the loss of the *Mojave* they had switched boats at times to fit the jobs they were doing. By changing loads Kolb would have both

Elwyn Blake in a boat wedged crosswise in the mouth of Havasu Creek to relax and write letters. (Courtesy of Marston Collection, The Huntington Library, San Marino, California)

the cook and the cook's outfit in his boat, the *Marble*, so that changing boats would no longer be necessary and he could go ahead with
the cook and make camp while the surveyors did their work.

The river was smooth for the most part with only one small rapid
to run. They surveyed a side canyon at Mile 164.3, running the line
up it to the 1,840-foot level where it was blocked by a rock slide.
Dodge rowed Elwyn's boat *Glen* several times during the day. The
new cargo arrangement worked fine and a good supper awaited them
when they reached camp below the riffle on the right bank at Mile
164.9. After supper Stabler set fire to a large pile of driftwood that
lit up the surrounding cliffs, and made weird, dancing forms on the
rocks when the flames leaped upward.

During the next couple of days they worked their way downriver,
surveying side canyons as they came to them. On September 17 they
worked up Stairway Canyon at Mile 171 and Gateway Canyon at Mile
171.5. While waiting for the surveyors to finish their work, the boatmen got a good laugh watching Felix. He got a bucket of water and
tried to step from one boat to another, causing the boats to spread
apart. He was helpless to stop them and fell with a splash into the
river. As he went down he tried to set the bucket of water on the deck
of one boat but it upset squarely on his head. He could not swim but
held onto one boat and worked his way to shore. Even this did not
spoil his good humor.

While there Kolb caught a "bonytail" fish, the first caught on
the trip. It was probably the now-endangered humpback chub. After
lunch the boatmen ran Gateway Rapid. It had a fall of ten feet and
some big waves. Felix lost his straw hat in the rapid. To recover this
valued headpiece, Kolb turned the *Marble* after it into a rocky channel, touching a rock along the way. After recovering his hat Felix tied
it through a buttonhole in his shirt using a blue cord from a ham.
They camped on a sandbar on the right bank just below the head of a
riffle at Mile 172. Soon afterward someone noticed a white tent high
up on a slope opposite camp. They assumed it was near a silver mine
that was supposed to be in the area. They set fire to a large pile of
driftwood hoping to attract attention, but no one appeared.

On September 18 they passed a large lava pinnacle (Vulcan's Anvil)
that partly obstructed the channel but formed no rapids. Raymond
Moore told them that on two occasions lava had filled the lower
part of the canyon, damming the river temporarily to a height of
several hundred feet and backing the water up as far as the Little
Colorado River.

The broad expanse of the river was almost lake-like below Vulcan's Anvil, but the up-canyon wind brought a roar that could come from nothing less than Lava Falls. The rapid proved to be a little over a mile distant—at the end of the quiet water backed up behind the dam of lava boulders that were responsible for the rapid. They had passed over mostly fast water that day but no big rapids until noon, when they reached the head of Lava Falls. They landed on the left side and made camp on a small sandbar at Mile 179.

The head of the rapid had a ten-foot, almost sheer fall with an overall drop of thirty-seven feet, and was so rocky that there was no clear channel through which the boats could be run. Some excellent springs bubbled out all along the left bank furnishing good bathing and drinking water. Some of the springs had travertine deposits like those at the springs in Havasu Creek. More warm springs oozed out along the tail of the rapid and left travertine formations overhanging the river.

Without the radio to pick up the alerts being broadcast to them, they had no inkling of a great flood caused by cloudbursts over the Little Colorado River that was filling the canyon above them. They ate lunch and then looked the rapid over carefully.

The left half of the rapid was studded with protruding boulders so close together they left no room to get a boat through safely. Elwyn thought it possible to run through on the right side, but those who went over to look at it said it could not be run. He wanted to have a look at it himself but did not like to disagree with the other boatmen. He hated portages.

They unloaded their boats and then helped each other in partly portaging and partly lining three of them along the left side around the worst of the rapid. They had to lift the boats over the rocks in two places. Lint rode each boat through to fend it off the rocks. They moored them in a small cove just below the crest of the falls and by evening had carried everything except some of the beds and the cook outfit to where the three boats were moored, intending to run the rest of it in the morning. Camp remained on the small sandbar at the head of the falls.

After supper Kolb and Elwyn went to bed, Kolb to sleep and Elwyn to read. About dark La Rue called Freeman down to the river saying the river was rising. The four boatmen then went down to where the three boats were moored and found them pounding against the rocks and each other.

There was no beach where the boats were moored, just a niche overhung with travertine. As the river continued to rise it looked more like a trap than a harbor. Kolb had lined his boat through here eleven years earlier and thought he remembered a better landing farther down. He and Lint took a boat and, hugging the shore, went downstream to look for a better place to tie up. It was a rather ticklish undertaking, since the moon had only tipped the rim of the canyon, making the depths seem very dark and gloomy. The ominous roar of the rapid kept getting louder and the surging water more restless.

Kolb and Lint reported back on foot a half hour later, having found a sloping rock and a sandy beach where the boats would be much better off. The river had risen two feet more by the time they made their report. Elwyn and Freeman had been busy keeping the other two boats from being dashed to pieces against the rocks.

They decided to take the *Glen* and *Boulder* down to the beach, but before doing so they went up to camp at the head of the rapid and dragged and lifted the *Marble* up eight feet above the river level and lashed it securely to the steep bank. Then all four of them went down to the two remaining boats and shoved off.

By then the moon was shining on the opposite wall. It reflected on part of the rapid, which had lengthened greatly and was booming louder every moment. The left bank was composed mostly of travertine, over which streams from the springs were falling. These sheets of water gleamed white in the reflected moonlight. The men rowed the two boats in an eddy as close as they dared to the travertine to keep them out of the lashing waves of the main current. There was little current in the eddy, but a heavy slop from the rapid splashed against and occasionally into the boats.

They all remembered the distinctively offensive odor of the Little Colorado and the smell of the river now suggested that the flood was coming from it. The restless swells, lashing waves, and black shadows gave them an eerie feeling.

Elwyn, Lint, and Kolb had their bedrolls in the boats, so they stayed at the lower landing with the three boats. Freeman went back to camp, sloshing and stumbling through the marsh and warm springs with a lantern as his light.

Elwyn, Lint, and Kolb soon found most of the sandspit was under water, so they pulled the boats higher onto the sloping limestone ledge. Finding a strip of sand that was large enough to accommodate their beds, they rolled them out about six feet above water level. By that time the boats were swinging violently. They pulled them up one by one as far as they could.

Before long they noticed the water was lapping very near their beds. They hurriedly dragged them farther from the river. Then they pulled the boats up again and took the slack out of the ropes. It was not long until the waves were pounding at the base of the rock where Elwyn had tied the *Glen*. He untied the painter and found a new mooring rock.

By that time they had to move their beds again. Chilly in their wet clothes, they built a fire. Hungry and weary, Elwyn dug out some canned milk, sugar, and cocoa from one of the boats. With water from the springs he soon prepared a gallon of hot chocolate from which they all drank their fill.

The river continued to rise, so the boats had to be continually pulled higher. About 3:30 in the morning they decided the river had stopped rising, so they pulled the boats up one more time and went to bed. They got up once more before daylight and found the boats again banging against each other. Securing them, they went back to sleep.

The three men awoke at sunrise to find that someone had pulled the boats up again. Dodge appeared from upriver and told them Colonel Birdseye had come down to see how they were faring and had drawn the boats up and retied the ropes. The three men were stiff and sore, their hands lacerated from pulling on the ropes most of the night.

Meanwhile, at the upper camp some moving had been going on, too. At 11:00 P.M. the cook boat *Marble* was afloat. All hands were called to pull her up an additional eight feet. Kominsky went to bed ten feet above the water. At midnight a big wave slopped into his bed. He left for higher ground in a hurry and would not return, so others had to rescue his bed and clothes. During the night they moved the beds and cook outfit three times. Birdseye had pitched his bed on a flat rock twenty feet above the water. At 4:30 A.M. the spray was lashing his rock.

The river had risen fourteen feet during the night and was still rising. Kolb went to the upper camp and got everyone but the cook to come down to the other boats and help pull them completely out of the water. Then they all went to breakfast. They estimated that the river had risen about fifteen feet by breakfast time.

The rapid had completely changed. No rocks showed at all, and what had been a short, almost sheer fall of ten feet at the upper end was now a long sweeping tongue of swift water.

Freeman described it thus:

The rapid had altered in character overnight beyond belief. The head of the dam of boulders, where yesterday there had been a broken series of abrupt falls, was completely submerged—drowned out. Over it rushed a broad, solid chute of running water which did not begin to break into waves until halfway down what had formerly been the rapid. From there on the waves were tremendous—quite the largest waves we have seen. These culminated in a great comber just above where the boats are pulled up—a point where yesterday there was only hard-running but comparatively smooth water.[6]

The huge wave at the foot of the rapid surged to a height of between twenty and thirty feet where it seemed to imprison a quantity of air within itself. As the weight of the water compressed the air it was released with a booming sound like a cannon shot. Spray shot some twenty feet above the crest of the wave. The flood carried along immense quantities of driftwood. Some large logs were sucked into the giant whirlpools, then ejected in the boil as though shot from a cannon.

After breakfast they portaged all of the equipment and camp gear to the cove below where the three boats were located. They prepared to stay for several days because their survey point was under water and the flooding river was not safe for boating. They left the *Marble* where she was.

The men spent the rest of the day sleeping, reading, washing, playing cards, and bathing in the warm springs. The temperature at night had been a chilly sixty degrees so it was pleasant to bathe in ninety-degree water. The river was still rising and the flood was too fierce to launch the *Marble*. After supper they took a block and tackle and raised her farther up the bank.

Birdseye estimated the total rise of the river at twenty-one feet and the volume of the river to be over 100,000 cfs. They sorely missed the radio and had they received the warnings of the impending flood would have selected a different campsite. They kept a close watch on the river until they were satisfied it had reached its peak. Then everyone turned in for a good sleep.

The river dropped two or three feet during the night. Elwyn and Lint spent the morning repairing the bottom of the *Glen*. Elwyn told the Colonel that he could drive a match stem through the rotten planking. The Colonel did not believe him, so he proceeded to do it. Birdseye was horrified and yelled, "Don't do that!" Elwyn took

Leigh Lint, Emery Kolb, and Elwyn Blake repairing the boat *Glen* after the flood at Lava Falls. (Grand Canyon 87, U.S. Geological Survey)

his pocketknife and cut the match stem off so there was no hole for water to seep through.

After lunch Kolb and Freeman helped repair the other boats. They put on new oak strips and sheets of copper to repair the damage caused by the waves beating them against the rocks. Moore, Stabler, Kolb, and Elwyn played cards in the evening until the cook called supper.

The survey station was still under several feet of water and the river too rough for navigation, so Birdseye called it Sunday, since they had worked all day on the sixteenth.

CHAPTER 18

Lava Falls to Travertine Canyon

On September 21 the river was still dropping. It had not fallen enough, however, for them to pick up their last station and proceed with the survey. Elwyn and Kolb hiked up a canyon toward the top of the first rim on the left side. Near the head of the canyon the slope became very steep. They clawed their way over boulders that seemed to be cemented together. Then they crossed over the jagged face of a cliff to another branch of the canyon. There the boulders were lying loose, and once or twice a whole mass crept downward a few inches threatening to start an avalanche.

The two dared not turn back for fear of being caught in a landslide and kept on climbing, pausing now and then to take pictures. Eventually they came out onto a wide gravelly benchland which was well sodded with grass. In a few places cinder cones protruded above the surrounding surface. They found evidence of an old camp and the remains of a wooden pack box. Deer tracks were everywhere, but they saw no deer.

Suddenly Kolb stopped to listen. "I hear an automobile," he said. Elwyn listened and could hear a dull buzz but thought it might be the wind. Then they realized that it was the sound of an airplane and soon located a big plane about 2,000 feet above them flying northeast across the canyon. They tried to attract attention by waving their white hats, but the plane did not waver.

The two men started their descent a half mile to the west along the slope of a cinder cone, which reached to within 100 feet of the bottom of the canyon. They went down it in long strides, sliding on the cinders, each step about twenty feet long. They kept up with their feet by bending forward like skiers. After descending about 1,000 feet in that way, they crossed a ridge to another cinder slide. Then they crossed back over to the warm springs and on to camp.

On September 22 the river had dropped about sixteen feet from its highest stage and was low enough for them to pick up their survey point and resume work. They launched the *Marble* and lined her along the shore to where the other boats were parked on the sloping rock ledge. Then they placed rollers under the other boats and skidded them down into the water. They soon had the boats loaded and were on their way again.

Lava Falls Rapid was still rolling with huge waves that continued for one-third of a mile below the falls, and the current ran swift against a high wall on the left side below camp. The rocks were well submerged though. No one could walk around it, so they all rode the boats and got a good soaking. The floodwater was heavy with silt, and when the brown smelly stuff slopped in on them as they ran the rapid, it proved to be a veritable liquid mud. A splash of it left a white coating on their skin as it dried. When some got in their eyes it almost blinded them.

They ran a lot of riffles that day and surveyed a narrow, steep canyon from the right. The wind blew upstream all day making rowing difficult. They camped on a wet sandbar that had been under water twenty-four hours earlier. There was plenty of wood nearby and a clear stream of good water flowed out of the base of a gravel bar. The country below looked more broken than they had seen for some time.

On September 23 they surveyed a geologic section at camp.[1] They found a trail out of the canyon below camp (this would have been Whitmore Canyon). On a plank under a ledge they found the names of several people with dates by the names ranging from 1917 to 1922. Then they ran the boats on down and made a new camp at Mile 189.7.

The many side canyons had slowed the survey so much that Birdseye and Burchard decided to run two instruments. Burchard took one and worked a side canyon while the Colonel had Lint hold rod for him in surveying a dam site below camp. The high-water marks showed that the river had dropped twenty feet since the flood. It was much colder that evening, so they hovered around a campfire.

The next day they encountered many riffles and side canyons. Birdseye continued to survey the side canyons while Burchard stayed with the river line. Stabler recorded for Burchard and Moore for

Birdseye. The river was rapidly cutting away the high sandbanks deposited during the recent flood. Black willows began to appear along the bottoms now that the country was more open.

While sitting in his boat Elwyn saw a blue heron light on a sandbar only ten feet away. It stood there for several minutes. When he tried to get at his camera his cautious movements frightened the big bird and it flew away. They camped on a sandbar under some willows on the left bank at Mile 194.7 where there was plenty of wood. After supper they built a big bonfire and sat around it singing every song they could think of. This brought back some harmony to the group.

Although the river dropped only six inches during the night, the boats were stuck in the mud. Freeman's boat was the hardest to move since he had loaded it up without first loosening it from the mud. They had to unload some of his cargo before it would budge. Elwyn said that Freeman was the only one who did not get into the mud while they were trying to move his boat.

They surveyed several side canyons that day. Most of them were blocked by sheer, dry falls within a mile or two. Evening found them at the mouth of Parashant Wash. La Rue killed a large rattlesnake and salvaged eleven rattles from the mangled remains.

During the following days they continued the survey of the river and side canyons through more open country. At times a stiff upstream wind slowed their progress. At Mile 205 they came to a rough, sloppy rapid with considerable fall, the first one of consequence encountered since Lava Falls. They ran the rapid before eating lunch. Burchard got well soaked going through on the *Boulder*. The other boats ran without passengers. A big eddy below the rapid made landing easy.

La Rue located several old Indian shelters under a rock overhang about a third of a mile up a canyon from the right at Mile 206.6. He found remnants of pottery, baskets, and arrowheads there. They named it Indian Canyon.

They passed over several long riffles during the day and made camp on the right bank at the mouth of a canyon at Mile 208.7. Two canyons came in from the left as well creating a widened river and a broad valley with many willow trees along the banks. There were frequent granite outcrops in the side canyons, so they called the place Granite Park. It was chilly after sundown, so again they built a fire to keep warm. The temperature at 6:00 A.M. was fifty-two degrees, the coldest so far on the trip.

September 28 was the day the packtrain was to have met them at the mouth of Diamond Creek. Because of the delay at Lava Falls, they now expected to reach there at least two or three days late.

After lunch on September 29 they ran a rough rapid without even wetting the passengers. This was unexpectedly good luck since carrying a deck-load of passengers without wetting them in the increasingly colder water was desired by all parties concerned.

Birdseye found several rock mounds that turned out to be agave roasting pits used by Indians. The initials R.P. nicely chiseled in the rock nearby told him he was not the first white man to find them. They made camp on sand terraces on the right bank below a large side canyon at Mile 214, having come a little over five miles that day. Their grub was getting low. They hoped to reach Diamond Creek in two more days at the most. They had to settle for river water that night because there was no spring nearby.

Next morning, Sunday, September 30, the temperature at 6:00 A.M. was fifty-six degrees. Colonel Birdseye worked all afternoon on a big side canyon on the left side at Mile 215.4 to the 2,100-foot elevation. He named it Three Springs Canyon because there were three flowing springs in it, one within 200 yards of the river. The rapid at Mile 217 gave them no trouble and they ran on down to Mile 219.1 and camped on the right bank below a riffle. Their run for the day measured 4.9 miles.

Freeman wrote:

> The riffle around the bar above camp drove hard against the left-hand cliff, with an unexpectedly heavy boil on the right. A horsefly alighted on my forehead just as I put into this, and I had to let him bite until I came out at the foot. Result—big welt on forehead and a smeared fly.[2]

On the morning of October 1 they surveyed side canyons from camp. Someone spied a desert bighorn sheep on a high crag. The big ram stood watch for about two hours. He lay down once but never seemed to turn his head away from their direction. At Mile 220.2 Birdseye traversed up a deep canyon from the left to elevation 2,054, with Moore recording and Freeman carrying the rod. He found a small spring in the granite gorge of the main fork at elevation 1,940. He called this canyon Granite Spring Canyon.

They ran a rapid with a ten-foot fall at Mile 220.3. It was wide and shallow and easy to run at that stage of water. They ran more riffles and surveyed another side canyon before camping on the left bank at mile 221.7. The day's run was 2.6 miles. Birdseye had been occupied until too late to push on to Diamond Creek with the *Grand*, as he had planned.

Diamond Creek was still an uncertain distance, though the sharp pinnacle known to be near its mouth had been in sight most of the day. There were outcroppings of granite along the river, but it was broken up and the canyon had not yet taken on the aspect of a gorge.

They had taken inventory of their food that morning and found they were out of everything but bacon, sugar, flour, and breakfast food. The next day, October 2, the cook boat *Marble* and the *Grand* went ahead intending to go straight through to Diamond Creek. The *Glen* and *Boulder*, with their survey crews, were left to work the river and any intervening side canyons. Only one large side canyon retarded their progress.

Elwyn ran the rapid at Mile 224 head on rather than stern first to get a little more kick out of it. Dodge stood on the hatch cover of the boat holding onto a taut rope across his knees like a Roman rider. Near the foot of the rapid he let go of the rope with one hand. At that moment a side-wave threw the boat sharply to one side causing Dodge to lose his balance and plunge into the river. But he was back in a flash.

About 3:00 P.M. the survey crew sighted a big side canyon in the distance and thought they might have to lay up there overnight. But when they reached it they could see the smoke of the Diamond Creek Camp 1,000 feet below and across the river from them. So they left the survey of that canyon for another day and arrived in camp just in time for supper.

They found that Roger Birdseye and Charles Fiske had been waiting there since September 28 and had become somewhat anxious toward the end of the four-day wait. The flood of September 18 and 19 had been of considerably greater magnitude than the party had estimated. The Bright Angel gauging station had measured the peak flow at over 126,000 cfs., according to Roger. He said it rose to that from less than 10,000 cfs. in less than twenty-four hours. The water had come almost entirely from the basin of the Little Colorado.

The flood had been considerably higher than the spring high water of 112,000 cfs. Arizona papers had published a lot of sensational spreads—all the stories suggested that the party was in grave danger. The headline of one late paper read: "HOPE NOT GIVEN UP FOR RIVER PARTY!"

An overturned boat sighted 200 miles down the river had added to the suspense. Roger Birdseye, acting with his usual good judgment, had run down the Kingman correspondent responsible for the most lurid tales and frightened him into repentance. Roger had also written reassuring notes to the families of all members of the expedition.

Roger and Fiske brought the supplies in by wagon to a point ten miles from the mouth of Diamond Creek, but there the old road was completely washed out. From that point they packed the supplies down on one saddle horse, making three trips. Fiske immediately rode out to Peach Springs with telegrams to the families of each member of the party. He also sent telegrams to Kingman, Los Angeles, and Washington, D.C., papers reporting the safe arrival of the party. The telegram to Los Angeles was broadcast in the *Los Angeles Times* that evening. Roger had brought back their radio, fully repaired, so the river party heard the telegram read at 8:00 P.M.

They prepared to remain at Diamond Creek for several days, needing to make a large-scale dam-site survey to supplement the one done earlier by Girand.[3]

October 3 was a day of rest for the crew. They spent the day reading the wild newspaper stories of the "GRAVE FEARS FOR EXPLORERS OF COLO. RIVER" and writing letters to be sent out the following day.[4] Felix got busy baking bread and frying doughnuts, proving himself to be a real artist. Birdseye remained in camp all day working on reports and mail.

The next day, October 4, Fiske and Roger Birdseye saddled up again and took the mail out. Burchard, Stabler, and Dodge worked up Peach Springs Wash and Diamond Creek. That afternoon Lint recorded for Colonel Birdseye while Elwyn carried rod in surveying a dam site. The Birdseye crew quit work early, but Burchard and his crew did not get in until late.

Birdseye tied his survey in with a benchmark at the mouth of Diamond Creek at elevation 1,362.166, which he listed as 163.8 miles below the mouth of the Little Colorado (222.3 miles from the mouth of the Paria River) where they had begun their survey. It checked out with an error of −8.9 feet in the line from the tie-point at Bass Trail Crossing, which amounted to 0.07 feet per mile. He considered this good work considering the long stadia sights with many vertical angles.[5]

The next day Burchard stayed in camp while Colonel Birdseye worked on the dam-site survey. Lint recorded and Dodge carried rod on the left side of the river while Elwyn carried rod on the right side.

Office work at Diamond Creek— Colonel C. H. Birdseye and Roger Birdseye. (Grand Canyon 349, U.S. Geological Survey)

They found that Diamond Creek Rapid had nineteen feet of fall.

On October 6 La Rue, Freeman, and Moore hiked up Diamond Creek in the forenoon while the Colonel finished the dam-site survey. They wanted to go to the source of Diamond Creek. The canyon became boxed at the end of three miles, remained very narrow for a mile and a half, and then opened out again. The gradient, except for a couple of falls in the boxed section, was almost uniform. They passed several pinnacles, and occasionally at narrow side canyons could see fine vistas of the higher formations—red and yellow in the sunlight.

They found what appeared to be the source of the stream at the end of seven or eight miles. There it reached the Tapeats Sandstone formation and the canyon broadened out into a valley a quarter of a mile wide that ran on to the base of the outer sandstone and limestone cliffs. About a third of the stream came from a spring in a thicket of willow and rushes and the rest from a gravel bed on the valley floor. It was nearly dark when they returned to camp.[6]

While they were away, Elwyn and Kolb painted both the old and new oars with linseed oil. They played Five Hundred, a type of rummy, for awhile, then trimmed each other's hair. The wind blew upstream all afternoon filling everything with sand. The men enjoyed listening to the radio in the evening.

The cook and his assistants at Diamond Creek. Left to right: Elwyn Blake, Felix Kominsky, and Leigh Lint. (Grand Canyon 100, U.S. Geological Survey)

On October 7 it was time to move on. A heavy sandstorm had blown all night making sleep difficult, so the morning bath in the creek served as a grit remover. The sky was clear and the river continued to fall.

Diamond Creek Rapid had three sections with a total fall of 21.5 feet in three-quarters of a mile. All except Freeman made good runs through the long rapid. He hit a rock and smashed the iron handle on the rear of his boat clear through the heavy, two-inch oak stern, which had to be mended as soon as he caught up with the *Glen* and the tool chest.

In the next two miles they ran three small riffles, then a nine-foot rapid a mile farther on. The rapid had a sudden, swift drop and big waves, but with no rocks it was easy to run.

While carrying his instrument up the side canyon Burchard fell seat first on a barrel cactus. The leather patch on the seat of his pants saved him from painful injuries. A little farther on he fell from some rocks and fractured a rib but still insisted on continuing with the instrument. Except for the first day's work below Lee's Ferry, Burchard had made the entire river survey. He wanted to complete the job and join it with his old work just above the mouth of Grand Canyon, which would make him responsible for the entire survey of Marble, Grand, Boulder, and Black canyons. His survey would run from a point seven miles below Lee's Ferry to the Bulls-head reservoir site about forty miles above Needles. The fractured rib caused considerable pain, but strips of adhesive and elastic bandages made it possible for him to continue his work.

At Garnet Point, which they passed during the afternoon, a stream flowed from a narrow, almost tunnel-like canyon with a seventy-five-foot-high waterfall in its dark recess. A hundred feet overhead a huge boulder had lodged forming a bridge across the narrow chasm.

The river was swift all day, one rapid following another in close succession. Progress downstream was slowed because of a persistent upstream wind. They made camp near a small stream at Travertine Canyon on the left side where a spectacular 200-foot falls poured over the cliff. The mineral-laden water had built up a polished travertine deposit ten-feet thick over which the water slid almost noiselessly.

Some of them bathed in the clear water. Elwyn did not like the combination of cold water and cold wind, so he contented himself with washing his face, neck, and arms.

CHAPTER 19

Travertine Canyon to Needles, California

It started to rain soon after the party left camp on October 8. They ran a long rapid at Mile 231 that had a fall of twelve feet and some dangerous rocks in its tail. All the passengers climbed around over the granite cliffs on the right bank. The boats rode through with no difficulty except for shipping considerable cold water.

A mile farther on they came to a short, steep rapid with a large, jagged rock near its head. This rock alternately protruded and submerged as the surging river rose and fell. Kolb and Freeman ran it first. Freeman came very close to the rock. Felix said: "What's 'a matter: I'm so good a driver as Freeman." Another member remarked that, "There must be a magnet on the stern of Freeman's boat."

Elwyn and Lint followed, leaving their passengers to walk with the others. Young daredevils that they were, they did not go stern first but kept the boat prows downstream and rowed hard to get more thrill out of it. The boats reared and pitched but took very little water.

They stopped for lunch just above Bridge Canyon Rapid, and because it was cold and windy, the cook made coffee. Bridge Canyon was named for a small natural bridge located one-third of a mile up from the river. They spotted some driftwood over fifty feet above water level. The high-water mark from the recent flood was only thirty feet above the river, causing them to marvel at the great flood that must have filled the canyon when the driftwood was deposited. After lunch they crossed the river to allow the passengers to walk around Bridge Canyon Rapid. Each boatman took his run without mishap.

All the rapids below Bridge Canyon are now minor or have been completely buried by Lake Mead. Nobody will ever see them or run them again, unless the Monkey Wrench gang still lives!

Three-quarters of a mile farther on they came to Gneiss Canyon Rapid, the last rapid of the day. The current was lashing the cliff bases on both sides of the river. A run through with passengers aboard would have meant that all would wind up with wet clothing. The party decided to camp at the head of the rapid rather than suffer wet clothes in the chill of the evening. There was no driftwood at camp, so they climbed the talus slopes and got an abundance of mesquite wood for a fire. At this point the gorge was very narrow, the sheer walls rising over 2,000 feet. Still, radio stations KHJ of Los Angeles and KSL of Salt Lake City came in quite clear.

The first order of business on October 9 was to navigate Gneiss Rapid. The current splashed against some huge boulders along the right side, which threw the main force of the stream against the left-hand cliff. The rapid had an eleven-foot fall in two sections. Lint ran it first. From the ease with which he pulled the oars, those on shore could tell there was nothing to fear from the set of the current toward the left cliff. Kolb and Freeman went through next. Kolb made a good run but Freeman tapped a big rock, though with no apparent damage. For some extra sport Dodge then mounted the stern of the *Glen*, standing up with a taut line across his knees. Elwyn made the run watching the river heave and pitch while looking between Dodge's wide-spread legs. One wave nearly threw Dodge from his perch, but he held on and kept his balance like a champion cowboy on a rodeo bull.

All passengers got the usual muddy bath. By now the nights were cool, so these early morning baths were not particularly pleasant. The sun did not reach the bottom of the canyon until late morning, so much shivering resulted.

Just before noon Lint, while whittling on a rotten piece of wood, let his knife slip and cut his wrist. While Lint was temporarily disabled, Dodge took over his boat and Burchard and Stabler changed to Elwyn's boat.

They passed through a very narrow granite gorge where the river was only 100 feet wide and the sheer walls towered at least 700 feet high, making survey stations hard to come by. Passing over two small riffles in the next two miles, the party reached a big rapid at the mouth of a deep canyon from the right.

Freeman wrote:

About 4 o'clock a deep roar indicated the approach to a bigger fall than anything we have recently encountered, and the opening of two canyons immediately opposite each other at the head of it appears to identify the rapid as Separation, where the first Powell party was deserted by three men. We had not expected to find this historic point for several miles yet— 18 miles from Diamond, instead of the 13 we had covered so far. The nature of the walls, the two opposing canyons and the sequence of riffles fit closely the Powell and Stanton descriptions. The canyon on the right, at the mouth of which we camped, appears to have just such a beach as Powell paced back and forth upon in coming to his momentous decision, while it also opens up to the north in such a way as to lend to the belief that it is a favorable route of egress from the main gorge.

Kolb inclines to the belief that the rapid is not Separation, principally because he misses a large mid-stream rock that is associated in his mind with that point. We shall doubtless know more about it in a day or two.[1]

This rapid was located at Mile 239.5. The current at the head of it was too swift to land the boats, so they landed farther up. They carried the camp equipment for fifty yards over the rocks to a good camping place above the rapid. They saw that the rapid was long and rough with sheer walls on either side, so the passengers would have to ride through. In the distance the men could see the current piling up against a low shelf of rock jutting out from the right-hand cliff base. The second step of the rapid was made up mainly of big waves with only a few protruding rocks.

On the morning of October 10 the surveyors measured the rapid. They found it to have a fall of 19.5 feet, 15.5 feet of which was in the upper portion and 4 in the lower part. Many rocks dotted the upstream end of the upper section and violent currents beat against the rocks near the lower end of the upper portion. The waves ran high and the rapid had a mean, nasty look. It turned out to be Separation Rapid after all. A rock slide had altered the look of the rapid since Kolb's 1912 trip.

Lint was determined to row his own boat, so Dodge came back to Elwyn's boat. Elwyn ran first so Dodge could hold rod at a station midway in the rapid. Dodge rode in a crouching position on the stern with a strong grip on the lifeline across his legs just above his knees. The first few waves pitched the boat from side to side, slopping in a little water. Then they hit the trough of a big wave and began to mount up and up the steep towering mass of water. When the *Glen* was standing almost on end, the upper portion of the wave crashed down upon Dodge knocking him half off the boat and slopping water into the cockpit. They missed the shore reef at the foot of the first stage of the rapid by a good margin, and with great effort Elwyn landed his boat above the second drop.

Dodge held rod there for a long shot. Kolb came through next with Felix and Birdseye aboard. The little boat danced around like a cork and the cockpit was nearly filled with water. It gave Birdseye his roughest ride since Bedrock Rapid. Soon Lint's boat, with Stabler and Burchard aboard, was also pitching and bobbing in the quiet water below the first stage.

After a reading from downriver, Dodge folded the stadia rod and came to the boat. He and Elwyn waited there for Freeman to come through. Freeman started out in the *Grand* with La Rue and Moore clinging to the hatches. La Rue always refused to lie prone, and this time he got the scare of his life. The huge waves tossed the boat in the air and it came down bottom side up. Freeman dove clear and came up a few yards away, catching onto a rope after a few strokes. La Rue was thrown out between the boat and the rocks on the right bank and narrowly escaped being crushed against the wall. He managed to catch hold of the lifeline of the boat, which was completely out of sight to those below. Moore was thrown toward the middle of the stream but grasped the painter and climbed on top of the overturned boat.

Elwyn and Dodge heard a call from upstream, and looking that way saw an object shoot to the top of a wave, then wallow toward them, low in the water. It was the *Grand*, upside down, with her passengers clinging to the lifelines. Elwyn and Dodge pushed out in the *Glen* to rescue them.

Moore was just climbing onto the bottom of the overturned boat. He gained a secure position and reached a hand to help Freeman, but La Rue seemed too weak to make any such effort. Elwyn rowed the *Glen* close to the *Grand* where Dodge grabbed La Rue and pulled him into their boat. Then Freeman passed them a line. Elwyn tried to row to the rocky point where the plane table had been set up, but the drag of the capsized craft was too much. He took advantage of the crosscurrent that shot out from the rocky point and made for the other bank.

Freeman described the upset this way:

On being told that Kolb had carried dangerously near to the right hand cliff, I decided to take a chance at putting into the heavy water at the head of the second riffle, in order to keep well to the left and be in a better position to hold the boat away from the opposite wall. These waves, which I had not seen at closer range than 200 yards or more, proved a good deal larger than I had judged them to be. While holding the boat quartering to the main line of the waves on the left, an unexpected and unaccountable comber from the right caught her broadside and threw her bottom-up in an instant.

My only mental picture of the incident is of La Rue's legs spidering against the sky as he spilled off the stern hatch, all but falling into the cockpit. Then darkness and much rolling and tumbling of water.[2]

Elwyn came to shore in quieter water against an almost precipitous ledge of rock. There the men got hand and footholds and somehow managed, with the help of the *Marble* and her crew, to right the *Grand*. From there they crossed to a sandy beach where La Rue crawled to a smooth area of sand and lay with his head in his arms.

Moore lost his glasses, hat, and two geologist's picks. Other lost items were one canteen, two oars, and Freeman's hat. Moore and La Rue both lost their pipes, and Moore lost some geological specimens that had been loosely stowed in the cockpit.

The serviceability of the watertight boxes got a good test. One of them, containing several cameras, had been strapped in the open cockpit of the *Grand*. The cameras were uninjured and only a drop or two of water had leaked through during the half-hour's submersion. The hatches did not prove as watertight, since a little water leaked into both. However, everything was in waterproof boxes or bags and nothing was damaged. Moore and Freeman seemed to enjoy the experience. But La Rue had already been sick for two days and the upset pretty well shattered his nerves.

Back in 1890 Stanton had messed up in almost the identical spot, smashing a boat and experiencing a rather desperate time of it personally, according to his account. The present upset and rescue took place in the upper section of Separation Rapid. The lower part of the rapid needed careful running, too. The channel was on the left of a barely submerged rock in the head of that part of the rapid, leaving only a narrow passage between it and another rock jutting out from the left bank. A hundred yards below that the current piled up against a big rock they had seen from above. There was plenty of room to pull away from it, however, so if nothing went wrong before reaching it, the big rock would not be a serious menace.

Kolb, on looking over this part of the rapid, said he recognized the rock as the one associated in his mind with Separation Rapid and admitted that the rapid above must be the one to which Powell had applied that name. He said there had been water on both sides of the big rock in 1912. Now the passage to the right was closed by a slide. They experienced no further trouble in this rapid.

Just before noon they reached another dangerous-looking rapid that had two big, back-curling waves near the head of it, one of which could not be avoided. All passengers walked around. Each boatman made a safe run and landed in an eddy below. Freeman had a close shave, though, when he went over the worst rock and into the hole below. The wave appeared rougher than the one which had upset the *Grand* in Separation Rapid, but a violent up kick of the stern and a cold shower bath were the only consequences. They stopped at the foot of the rapid for lunch.

Elwyn, Kolb, and Freeman went swimming before going on. They had swift water all afternoon but no more bad rapids. The river was very narrow through this section. Downstream Elwyn found one of Freeman's lost oars lodged against some rocks in a backwater. At camp that evening he quietly placed it back on the *Grand*, where Freeman found it later.

For that day's run the river had dropped fifty-four feet, a little over ten feet to the mile. Their camp was on the right bank nineteen miles below Diamond Creek. For the first time in many nights there were no rapids near camp. The absence of the familiar roar seemed strange to Elwyn. That evening they tuned in station KFFU of Colorado Springs for the first time. They listened to the results of the first two games of the World Series broadcast over station KHJ (the series was eventually won by the Yankees, who beat the Giants four games to two).

On October 11, after traveling a couple of miles in a quiet river, they heard an increasing roar from downstream indicating their approach to a sizable rapid. They landed well up on the bar above the rapid beside a large, clear creek coming out of Spencer Canyon. They had to cross the creek to reach the head of the rapid. This was Lava Cliff Rapid at Mile 246. It had a continuous fall, more abrupt at its head and tapering off in the middle before making a second steep drop 100 yards below. The fall at the head appeared to be caused by a reef of bedrock jutting out from the right bank. In the lower part the river piled up against two large rocks sticking far out of the water in midchannel with lesser boulders only slightly submerged between.

Julius Stone, one of the early river runners, had named the rapids here Bold Escarpment Rapids. That name seemed inappropriate as there was no real escarpment in the vicinity, so the Indian name, Matawidita, was adopted. Matawidita is a branch canyon a few miles above the mouth of Spencer and on most maps it is misspelled Meriwitica, a Hualapai Indian word. The rapid's name was later changed to Lava Cliff Rapid. This was one of the worst rapids of the river with a fall of seventeen feet in only a few hundred feet. Lava Cliff Rapid is now gone, buried below the waters of Lake Mead.

The Kolb Brothers had portaged the upper part of the rapid in 1912. Records show that one of Powell's boats broke loose while lining and one man was thrown out but rescued. The other boat ran through and caught the first. The Stone party had lined their boats past the rapids holding ropes from the cliff above.

Kolb decided that it would be best to line the boats and portage their loads. The *Glen* was the last boat to land at the head of the rapid. The first words Elwyn heard were, "She sure is a bad one. We'll have to portage it." Turning toward Elwyn, Lint said, "You and I can run it, easy. There's a good channel next to the wall." Elwyn studied the rapid for a while and agreed with Lint.

All the others, except Felix the cook, were against running the rapid. Kolb's declaration that it was impossible to run sounded rather queer to Felix, who was Kolb's passenger. He thought highly of Kolb. "Whassa matter Embry?" he inquired. "He can run it."

Elwyn and Lint decided that because there seemed to be no record of the rapid having been run previously it had frightened the brass hats. To Elwyn and Lint that was all the more reason why they *should* run it.

Burchard and Moore worked six miles up the side canyon from the bar above the rapid, while the Colonel and Stabler surveyed a dam site nearby. The rest of the party crossed the river 100 yards above the rapid from where they could climb up over the lava-tipped cliffs and go down to a point near the head of the rapid. Dodge took a large rope, secured it at the top of the cliff, and let himself down to a jutting point of rock fifteen or twenty feet above the water.

Lint and Kolb then took the *Marble* to a similar pier of rock some sixty or eighty feet upstream from where Dodge was stationed and began to line her down. Lint rode in the boat to fend her off the rocks while Kolb let her down by a rope to the place where Dodge was stationed. Dodge fastened a float to one end of a long cord; the other end was tied to the painter of the boat. Then he let the float down to the cove at the head of the rapid where Freeman and Elwyn were stationed. Elwyn tied a piece of granite to the end of a line and threw it over the cord attached to the float enabling him to bring the cord in to shore.

Dodge then let the *Marble* down into the cove. The current swung her so far out that Elwyn could not reach the painter to which the cord was tied. It seemed to him the cord would not bear the strain, so he slacked it off. Lint looked at the back-curling wave at the head of the rapid and yelled, "Pull hard." Elwyn did, and they were able to bring the *Marble* to shore. The cord was stronger than he had thought.

They unloaded the *Marble* and fastened long lines to her prow and stern. With these they lined the *Marble* over the first stage of the rapid. They had to climb up over a fifty-foot-high ledge to do it, and it took them until midafternoon to get the *Marble* over the rapid and out of the water resting on the smooth bedrock.

It was then that Kolb apparently saw, for the first time, that it was possible to run the rapid. He said, "It does look like a fellow could get through on the other side." He told Lint and Elwyn that they could run their boats through the rapid next morning. The two were jubilant since they both hated lining and portaging. They studied the channels closely to decide just how they would make the run along the right side.

Kolb asked Freeman if he wanted to run the rapid. He replied, "Considering the luck I have had the last two or three days, I think I'd rather not."

They ate a belated lunch after which they lined the *Grand* down to the cove and unloaded her. As darkness approached they moored the *Grand* in the quiet water of the cove for the night. They would have to wait until morning to line her on down to where the *Marble* was resting.

The *Glen*, with the beds of Dodge and Elwyn in it, was still on the opposite side of the river. At first they decided to leave the boat and those beds for Burchard and Moore, who still had not returned from working the side canyon. Lint and Elwyn would use their beds. As darkness came on, with no sign of the surveyors, Lint and

Elwyn took the *Boulder* and crossed the river intending to sleep near the boats.

Just as they landed they saw a light at the mouth of the canyon and knew the surveyors were coming in. They got out raisins, pork and beans, and some leftover cold pancakes, which the tired surveyors were glad to get. They thought it best not to try to recross the river in the dark, so Moore used Dodge's bed while the rest of them used their own. Before turning in, they built a big bonfire and semaphored to the camp across the river that all was well.

All night long at intervals Elwyn could see the reflection of a light upon the opposite shore. He knew that someone was keeping vigil over the other boats. Freeman noted, "As the *Grand* is pounding rather hard at her moorings, we are standing two-hour watches in case she breaks away or there is a sudden rise."

Next morning, before crossing the river to breakfast, Colonel Birdseye held rod for Burchard to make a reading. Then they crossed the river, climbed up over the lava beds, and went down to camp.

After breakfast the men lined Freeman's boat, the *Grand*, and moored her near the *Marble*. Lint and Elwyn took a last look at the rapid to fix in their minds the way they should run it. Then Kolb stepped up and told them they would have to line their boats and portage the cargo. He said, "The Colonel refused to permit me to sanction the running of this rapid."

Elwyn blew up. He and Lint both cursed and raved but to no avail. Colonel Birdseye, wishing for more backing, asked Dodge if he thought the boats should be allowed to run through. "Hell," said Dodge, "I can swim it."

Birdseye wrote of the incident:

It was man killing work to handle the 900 lb. boats over the rocks and almost as hard to portage the equipment. Blake and Lint were determined to run the entire rapid and had some agreement with Kolb over the matter. The writer considers the rapids worse than any in the canyon section except Lava Falls and was forced to issue positive orders that the *Glen* and *Boulder* must be lined and portaged in the same way as was done with the other boats. The two boys were somewhat disgruntled as this was the last bad rapid on the river and they thought they saw a safe way through. Both are absolutely fearless and exceedingly skillful boatmen and no doubt might have taken the boats through safely. However, Kolb had found a safe way to line and portage and the risk of losing one or more boats so near the end of the voyage was too great.[3]

The men made wild guesses about the amount of fall in the rapid. No guess was less than twenty feet. Measurement showed Bold Escarpment Rapid (Lava Cliff) to be a mere fifteen feet, against nineteen for Separation. The drop of Lava Cliff was in a much shorter distance, however, and it was in every way a more formidable rapid.

After the lining and portaging was done the crew launched and loaded the boats and ran down two miles to a better camp. They were bone tired and appreciated an early camp and a good supper.

Kolb, who normally made his bed close to Elwyn and Lint wherever possible, moved it apart that evening, still feeling the sting of their resentment over the morning's quarrel. Lint and Elwyn talked it over and agreed that the real reason they had been stopped was that it would not have looked good for the head boatman and the next-highest-paid boatman to be afraid to make the run while the two lower-paid boatmen made it. Elwyn noted, "It has often been demonstrated that a boatman can usually run a rapid if he thinks he can."

On October 13 they pushed the survey on down the river running some minor rapids and carrying the line up side canyons. Eventually Burchard remarked that the terrain was beginning to take on a familiar aspect. An hour later they found him with a grin on his face pointing to a rock monument across the river which he had built in 1920 at the highest point reached by his survey that year. They reached the Burchard tie-point about 3:00 P.M.

Their river line for the entire trip agreed within four and a half feet with the connecting survey point, a remarkable feat considering that they often had to determine differences in elevations by vertical angles with sights as long as one-half mile. At this point they had finished the traverse work and joined the survey carried upstream in 1920 by Burchard. They had carried the line for 251 miles without a break, running eighty-four rapids and many other stretches of rough water. In that distance they had portaged the boats at only three rapids.

They were all pleased with the results and also glad to have the river survey ended. Since there were no dangerous rapids ahead, the boatmen would have no cause for dissension over how to run them.

About two tons of supplies on the rocks at the lower end of Lava Cliff Rapid, ready to be loaded onto boats after having been carried around the rapid. Elwyn Blake and Leigh Lint became very irate when ordered to line and portage their boats here, since Emery Kolb had given them permission to run it, then reversed the order. (Courtesy of Prescott Blake)

But they still had about a 200-mile pull to Needles, California, to get off the river.

They made camp a couple of miles farther on at the mouth of Devil's Slide Canyon where they would survey another dam site. They did not break camp on October 14 because it was Sunday and they still had to survey the dam site.

Having the traverse line of the river completed was a special relief to Elwyn and Lint. It meant they would no longer have to land every few hundred yards as they had done for so many miles. The rest of the trip would be both swift and pleasant.

The boatmen put rudder oars on their boats so they would not have to look over their shoulders as they rowed, leaving it up to crew mates to guide the boats. Dodge and Elwyn took turns rowing the *Glen* and were soon far ahead of the others. They ran a number of small rapids and riffles, then held up in case some of the others had run into trouble. Dodge made coffee while they waited.

After a half hour they saw the *Marble* and the *Boulder*. Kolb had shot two ducks. They paused for lunch at the mouth of Grand Canyon where the cliffs receded into low hills and more level terrain.

As they finished lunch and started work on surveying a dam site, the *Grand* came into view. Kolb and Felix went ahead in the *Marble* to do some more duck hunting.

As they ran out from under the great wall of the Grand Wash Cliffs, the granite came up again for a short distance. A mile below the final narrow section they pulled in for a look at what had been Pierce Ferry, the northernmost crossing of the Lower Colorado. Only traces of the cables and roads, plus the walls of a building of gypsum blocks, remained. While waiting for the surveyors, Elwyn and Dodge rigged a sail and sailed up the river for a while. They caught up with the other boats about 5:00 P.M. Kolb had shot a coyote, two ducks, and seventeen quail. They went another two miles and camped at the mouth of Grand Wash.

Supper was late but well worth waiting for. Felix prepared roast quail, duck soup, peas with curry gravy, and hot biscuits. Listening to the radio that evening they learned that the Yankees had won the World Series.

Leaving camp at 7:00 A.M. next morning they reached Smith Ranch by ten. Freeman tells us:

> About ten, after passing a deserted mine and mill on the left bank, we came to Gregg's Ferry, to find a group gathered around our two leading boats. All too late we discovered skirts flapping in the wind, and as a consequence committed the unpardonable faux pas (in this region) of landing without our shirts. To make matters worse both LaRue and Moore had considerable gaps in the seats of their pants. These latter managed to keep out of the picture by advancing and backing as in the presence of royalty; but the shirts were irreplaceable, once we had landed through the mud. The ladies were terribly embarrassed; likewise the men, one of whom would not even look up when introduced.
>
> The scandalized humans proved to be the Smiths who ran the ferry. . . . We pushed off after buying some grub and making the Smiths a present of about fifty pounds of lard and a pair of oars.[4]

They drifted on down the river for several miles and camped a little above the mouth of the Virgin River. On the way they passed some old gold dredges and other placer machinery that lay rusting where it had been abandoned years before. They made camp on the beach at the base of a line of cliffs on the right near where Major Powell had ended his pioneering voyage in September 1869.

Rigging a sail on the *Grand* at Cottonwood Island. (Grand Canyon 411, U.S.
Geological Survey)

That night Elwyn decided to help Felix with the cooking by
making a pot of beans. He said:

> I put strips of bacon over the simmering beans, poured a
> bottle of ketchup over them, and placed the oven in a pit in the
> sand, where a fire had burned down to a bed of coals. Coals were
> placed on the Dutch oven lid, and all of it covered over with
> sand. It was left thus until morning.
>
> That mess of beans got me a job as cook on a later government
> trip, when Stabler told about the delicious beans I could cook.
> He never knew whether I could cook anything else, or not.[5]

On October 17 Dodge and Elwyn led off, taking the shotgun
with them. They got only one duck before noon and two more during the afternoon. They drifted by a Reclamation Service camp and
just below that passed some engineers of the Stetson-Clark outfit at
work. One man measuring the river as they passed under the cable
shouted that the flow of the river had been over 125,000 cfs. during
the late flood.

They ran through Black Canyon Gorge on a good current and
pulled in at the ruins of Old Callville for La Rue to take pictures.
Visitors had been there by auto recently and left Los Angeles papers
with dates a week later than any the party had seen. They camped at
the mouth of Black Canyon, having gone fifty-five miles that day.

Next morning the wind was blowing downstream. They rigged sails on all the boats and soon had pretty wakes spreading out behind them. They passed the state line into Nevada about 2:00 P.M. Their only trouble arose when they came to a wide bend in the river where the channel ran directly west while the wind was blowing south, forcing them to haul down the mainsails and row to deep water. They made camp on a wide sandbar 100 yards from some mosquito-infested willows.

On October 19 the wind changed so they had to row against it. Elwyn took the lead, rowing hard to keep ahead of Freeman. He and Lint were determined that Freeman could not brag in his account that he had outstripped the others. Elwyn landed the *Glen* on a flat sandbar near Needles by midmorning with the others not far behind.

Within the hour they had a truck at work hauling the boats and gear to the freight depot, where the *Grand* weighed in at about 800 pounds and the *Glen* and the *Marble* about 700 each. The *Boulder*, being the only sixteen footer, weighed somewhat less.

They took most of the afternoon to shave and make themselves presentable. This made a great change in the appearance of each of them, mostly from losing their beards and uncut hair. The greatest change was in Felix. When he reached town he had a great, bushy red beard. His straw hat, not a bit improved by its many duckings in muddy river water, covered only a portion of his colorless uncut hair. He wore a frayed blue-denim jumper and his checkered breeches were very greasy from much wiping of the butcher knife after cutting bacon and ham. Felix disappeared and was not seen for about two hours. When he finally strolled into the hotel lobby, what a change! His hair was cut, he was freshly shaven, and he had a long cigar pointing skyward from the corner of his mouth. He was shod in the latest style oxfords and his rotund figure was encased in a stylish sweater coat and neat trousers. He looked, as someone said, "Like a million dollars." His hat was the only exception. It was of the ten-gallon western type used by movie actors. Despite this incongruity in his attire, Elwyn thought, it seemed just about what Felix should wear.

Elwyn reported:

We who know something of the run of the mill camp cooks decided to show our appreciation of the never failing good humor of Felix, come blow sand, wood smoke or high water, and passed the hat for a substantial amount with which we bought a

Disembarking the outfit on the bar at Needles, California. (Grand Canyon 411, U.S. Geological Survey)

diamond stick pin. It was presented to Felix at a special dinner at the El Garces Hotel that evening.[6]

Colonel Birdseye took the occasion to say some kind words of parting to his men. He gave credit to the boatmen for the successful navigation of this stretch of the river, which he said included some of the roughest water in the United States. He said they had done a fine job of getting the boats through the rapids, making it possible for the engineers and geologist to complete their scientific studies.

Kolb was the first to leave for home, departing right after the dinner. Dodge and Elwyn went to the movies. Elwyn said:

> We were stopped cold in the aisle as we entered. There on the screen was the *Glen*. I was at the oars and Dodge lay flat on the after hatch, his bald head shining.
>
> "That's us, in Hermit Creek Rapid," I whispered. "Yep," said Dodge. We took our seats then, the only ones of the party to see the newsreel the Fox people had taken of our rapid running.[7]

The *Glen*, *Marble*, and *Boulder* were shipped to the Southern California Edison Company of Los Angeles, who had loaned them to the Survey. They shipped the *Grand* to Washington, D.C., where it wound up in the Smithsonian Institution.

Many years later Elwyn went to visit the Kolbs at the South Rim of the Grand Canyon. On the way home he stopped off at the Visitors' Center where he discovered his old boat, the *Glen*, parked in the patio with other historic boats of the Grand Canyon. Upon arriving home he wrote Emery of his discovery, saying that he thought the old boat had rotted away long ago. He said he had the oars to it in his attic in Durango and would ship them back to be with the boat if someone would pay the freight. The *Glen* still resides there.

With the Grand Canyon Survey over, the river maps were continuous along the Green River, the San Juan River, and the Colorado River from Grand Junction, Colorado, to the border of Mexico.

Each man was changed in some manner by the experiences he had gone through. Their true characters had shown through in the day-by-day interaction with each other and with the river itself. Elwyn could now understand why Kolb was so possessive of Grand Canyon. He felt as if he owned a piece of it, too, and supposed the others felt the same way. He, like every other man of the crew, was proud to have taken part in this final major survey of the Colorado River.

Epilogue

With the surveys completed, the Bureau of Reclamation set out to tame the Colorado River and put its water to use. The work of the Bureau drastically changed the character of the river.

In December 1928, after years of negotiation, court battles, and bickering in Washington, Congress passed the Boulder Canyon Project Act that authorized construction of a dam bigger than any yet built anywhere in the world. The great dam-building era of the Bureau of Reclamation in this part of the West would not end until the 1960s with completion of Glen Canyon and the Flaming Gorge dams.

On September 30, 1935, President Franklin D. Roosevelt dedicated Hoover Dam (then called Boulder Dam), the largest publicly funded project up to that time. The dam created Lake Mead, the biggest man-made body of water in the United States. Its purpose was to provide flood control, water for both irrigation and urban use, and cheap electric power for homes, factories, and farms. Besides that, it created a vast new recreational area.

Electricity generated at Hoover Dam did help light up cities and power new industries giving an economic boost to the whole area. But Southern California got the greatest benefit because it got most of the power and water for its growing influx of population from the dust bowl and other areas. Lake Mead also stored water for release to dams that were to be built downstream for diversion to the vast Imperial Valley via the All American Canal. This made other basin states anxious for their turn, afraid that the allocations of the 1922 Colorado River compact might not be honored. Colorado River water would become the single most contentious issue to divide those states for years to come.

In 1934 Parker Dam was under construction 155 miles downstream from Boulder Dam. Water from it would go to the Metropolitan Water District of Southern California. Arizona's Governor Benjamin B. Moeur considered this a theft of Arizona water, and he dispatched the state militia, armed with rifles and machine guns, to stop construction of the dam. The troops, using two old ferryboats dubbed "Arizona's Navy," halted the work temporarily. But the federal government intervened and work was resumed without any actual violence.

By 1946 the Bureau of Reclamation listed 134 possible water projects. One hundred of them were in the upper basin and the rest in the lower basin. The Bureau cited the need for more power in Arizona and Utah and the need for more irrigation in Utah's Uinta Basin and the Grand Valley of Colorado. It said, "Tomorrow the Colorado River will be utilized to the very last drop." That has turned out to be too true—more water has been allocated than can be delivered if all users claim their allotments.

In 1949 the upper basin states, through the Upper Colorado River Basin Compact approved by Congress, agreed on a division of their share of the river. They had learned that the flow of the river varied and apportioned it by percentages instead of amounts. Colorado got 51.75 percent, Utah 23 percent, Wyoming 14 percent, and New Mexico 11.25 percent.

The Bureau and the upper basin states made plans for a series of projects in legislation known as the Colorado River Storage Act, which called for construction of dams on the Green River in Dinosaur National Monument and Flaming Gorge in Utah; on the San Juan River in New Mexico; and on the Gunnison River in Colorado. This combination would serve the irrigation and power needs of the upper basin states and store Colorado River water for release downstream to the lower basin.

By then some people were beginning to see the negative side of damming the rivers, so each proposal caused some controversy. The biggest opposition to the Colorado River Storage Act came from conservationists who felt that building a dam in Dinosaur National Monument would threaten the future of the national park system. Through advertisements and letters to Congress the opposition, led by the Sierra Club, was able to sidetrack the proposed dam in Dinosaur National Monument. They argued that a dam in Glen Canyon would better serve the same purposes and agreed to support it as an alternative. When some of the proponents later boated down Glen Canyon they regretted having been the parties who pushed the compromise. E. C. La Rue had proposed the Glen Canyon Dam site back in 1922 and had promoted it ever since, so he was happy.

Glen Canyon Dam now backs water for 186 miles up Lake Powell, the second largest man-made lake in the country, exceeded only by Lake Mead. As a result of pressure from environmentalists and supportive members of Congress, the dam design *was* changed slightly to reduce the maximum water elevation from 3,900 feet to 3,700 feet. Rainbow Bridge and beautiful portions of many side canyons were thus saved.

The Colorado River is not big when compared to some other American rivers. Yet no other river in the country has been the object of more legal and political battles. According to the Bureau of Reclamation:

> The Colorado River is not only one of the most physically developed and controlled rivers in the nation, but it is also one of the most institutionally encompassed rivers in the country. There is no other river in the western hemisphere that has been the subject of as many disputes of such wide scope during the last half century as the Colorado River. These controversies have permeated the political, social, economic and legal facets of seven Colorado Basin States.[1]

During the nineteenth century the Colorado River was navigable from its mouth in the Gulf of California to Yuma, Arizona, and above. For the past fifty-plus years, except for the high runoff year of 1983, no Colorado River water has reached the gulf at all. Below Morelos Dam, one mile south of the Mexican border, the Colorado River is a dry riverbed during most seasons of the year.

Water diverted from the Colorado River Basin serves a population of over twelve million. The bulk of this water goes to Southern California and the Denver, Colorado, area.

Philip I. Fradkin wrote in his *A River No More*:

> More water is exported from the Colorado River Watershed than from any other river basin in the country. The complex of dams, reservoirs, tunnels and canals spreading out from the Colorado River system to embrace much of the west has become the most complicated plumbing system in the world.[2]

In 1928 the Boulder Canyon Project Act allotted Arizona 2.8 million acre-feet of Colorado River water as its share of the lower basin water. By 1944 the state's water leaders decided that it was time to seriously go after its share for use in central Arizona, where Arizona's population, agricultural, and industrial growth were heavily concentrated.

The Central Arizona Project (CAP) was developed jointly by the Federal Bureau of Reclamation and the state of Arizona. It was first presented to the U.S. Congress in 1947 by Senators Ernest McFarland and Carl Hayden. California opposed the CAP and Arizona's right to the water, so in 1951 Arizona submitted its claim to the U.S. Supreme Court. In 1964, after twelve years, the court finally ruled that Arizona did have the right to use 2.8 million acre-feet annually of Colorado River water.

In the years that followed, wrangling in Congress and opposition by environmental groups stalled the CAP bill. In the meantime Arizona was mining its groundwater reserves by two million acre-feet per year to keep its growing economy alive. It was proposed to build Bridge Canyon Dam in Grand Canyon to produce the power to pump CAP water. The Sierra Club and other environmental groups proposed that nuclear or coal-fired generating plants should instead be constructed for that purpose. The Bridge Canyon Dam was eventually scrapped and the coal-fired Navajo Generating Station at Page, Arizona, was substituted.

A succession of Arizona political figures, including Secretary of the Interior Stewart Udall, Senators Barry Goldwater and Paul Fannin, and Congressmen Morris Udall and John Rhodes, guided the CAP legislation through Congress. Finally, on September 30, 1968, President Lyndon Johnson signed a bill for authorization and construction of the CAP.[3]

Before any funding for CAP would be authorized by Congress, Arizona had to get better control of its groundwater, which was being depleted at an alarming rate. Governor Bruce Babbitt and Secretary of the Interior Cecil Andrus conspired to force the issue. Politicians, agriculture, mining, and urban interests cut a deal behind closed doors, and on June 11, 1980, the Arizona legislature passed the Groundwater Management Act.[4]

At the time of its authorization, the Bureau of Reclamation estimated the cost of CAP to be 832 million dollars. By 1982 those estimates had tripled, and by the time the 300-mile-long CAP canal is completed in 1991, the total cost will amount to $3.6 billion. Increasing concerns about the federal deficit mean that the CAP is likely to be the last of the large federal water projects.[5] In July of 1991 Congress approved final funding for the project.

The Colorado River Storage Project Act of 1956 not only approved Glen Canyon Dam as a substitute for Echo Park but also made it an upper basin cash register, with most of its revenues to help build other projects. Other dams it authorized which were built included Blue Mesa on the Gunnison, Flaming Gorge on the Green, and Navaho on the San Juan. The largest extra upper basin project was the Central Utah project, which was to receive water for 144,000 acres and a supplementary supply for almost 243,000 acres.[6]

But upper basin legislation for completing the Central Utah Project (CUP) also met increasing opposition. Final appropriations for this were part of the 1990 budget allocations. Meanwhile, the Colorado delegation proposed a diversion of more upper basin water to the east side of the Rockies to provide additional water for the Denver area, but this seems to have been successfully stalled.

The Colorado, Green, and San Juan are now different rivers. Historic flows through Grand Canyon before construction of the dams varied from almost nothing to more than 300,000 cfs. Now summer flows reach a maximum of 35,000 cfs. Because of the higher demand for irrigation water and electricity for air conditioning, more water is released in summer than in winter. Float trips through the canyons are affected by the fluctuating water levels because the amount released determines the ferocity of the rapids and where camps can be located. Some rapids have become more dangerous because flooding no longer scours rocks from the channels and low water levels expose more dangerous rocks.

Early in 1977, the second year of a record drought, the flow from Lake Powell was cut to 1,000 cfs. when it would normally have been over 12,000 cfs. During Easter weekend that year ninety persons on eight separate float trips were stranded in Marble Canyon. Enough water was finally released to flush the boats and rafts to points where the passengers could exit the canyon.

Water released from Glen Canyon Dam is about forty-six degrees Fahrenheit, warming to fifty degrees at Bright Angel Creek and sixty degrees at Lake Mead. Before the dam went in, temperatures varied from almost freezing in the winter to eighty degrees in summer. Beaches along the river, where soil is no longer being deposited by receding floods, are eroding and the fish life has been altered. Trout now thrive in the clear, cold waters below the dam, while the humpback chub and other species have almost disappeared. The changes in the river have led to the extinction or endangered status of eight species of fish.

The plant life along the river has changed, too. Seasonal floods used to replenish the sandbars and prevent growth of trees and shrubs below the high waterline. As an example, the surveyors found the sandbar at the head of Hance Rapid bare of shrubbery. Today that same bar supports a grove of salt cedar.[7] And, because of fluctuating flows through the turbines of Glen Canyon Dam, the hungry waters are slowly eroding the sandbars away.

Before construction of Flaming Gorge Dam yearly flooding of the Green River made vast marshy areas along the backwaters in Browns Park creating abundant nesting areas for thousands of ducks, geese, and other waterfowl. Today, because of the minimum flows being released from Flaming Gorge Dam, this waterfowl habitat has been greatly reduced.

From Powell's expedition in 1869 to 1949 only 100 persons ran the Grand Canyon.[8] Bus Hatch, Norman Nevills, and others initiated commercial river running through the deep canyons of the Green, San Juan, and Colorado rivers during the 1930s. After World War II, with the use of surplus rubber life rafts, there was a steady growth of the industry on the wild and scenic rivers in America and especially in Grand Canyon. In 1972 alone 16,432 went through this one canyon. Finally limits had to be placed on boat trips and the regulations now allow only 14,000 passengers per year in Grand Canyon, with similar restrictions on travel through other deep canyons.

In 1987 the Bureau of Reclamation, "buckling under mounting opposition to costly water projects," began to seriously consider changing its focus from reclamation to conservation. If this happens they will hopefully concentrate on the management of dwindling water supplies.[9] But many believe that the Bureau leans too much toward power generation for balanced management of the river's canyon resources—a fluctuation in water levels from 3,000 cfs. to 30,000 cfs. erodes sandbars needed for camping places and minimum flows expose more rocks making boating more hazardous. Smoke from the Navajo Generating Plant at Page, Arizona, which was the environmentalists' alternate for Bridge Canyon Dam, contributes to winter haze in Grand Canyon. Environmentalists have had some victories in these arenas. On June 30, 1991, Interior Secretary Manuel Lujan announced temporary limits on the fluctuation of releases from Glen Canyon Dam. Under the test schedule maximum flows were set at 20,000 cfs. with minimum daytime flows of 8,000 cfs., minimum nighttime flows of 5,000 cfs., and flow not to be increased too rapidly.[10]

There is a deep division today as to whether John Wesley Powell's and the Bureau of Reclamation's concept of arid-land development by damming western rivers for irrigation was wise. Some claim that most of the water goes to grow alfalfa for cattle, which must also graze on B.L.M. or Forest Service lands to compete with Middle Western, corn-fed beef. They say some goes to grow cotton or market vegetables on desert land that never should have been converted to agriculture in the first place. The involvement of the power companies changed the Powell concept completely, and it certainly made possible the industrial development of the West.

Other questions arise. Do recreation opportunities on the reservoirs offset the drowning of wild and scenic places such as lower Grand Canyon, Glen Canyon, and the canyons of the upper Green River? Is the maximum efficiency of power generation at Glen Canyon Dam today worth the despoiling of beaches in the Grand Canyon tomorrow? Proponents point out that power generation there is our cleanest and most renewable source of power. What happens in the future when the reservoirs fill with silt? How will the allocations between California and Arizona be finally settled, given California's political clout with more representatives being added after each census? How do we fill Mexico's guaranteed amount and purity of water? What happens if predicted weather changes bring more dry years with less likelihood that all water allocations can be met? The Colorado River will still be fought over, dreamed about, and visited more than any other American river. The Grand Canyon remains for now one of the seven wonders of the world.

A new concept of water rights has been developed in Arizona "that should have long-reaching effects on riparian habitat, wildlife and recreation in this state."[11] The Arizona Water Resources Department has granted a certificate of in-stream water rights to The Nature Conservancy giving it a legal right to the stream of water in Ramsey Canyon, located in the Huachuca Mountains near Sierra Vista, for use in preserving wildlife and recreational values. The certificate gives the organization the right to maintain a water level that will ensure that fish, wildlife, and recreation will not be hurt by consumptive use of the water.

Ramsey Canyon is famous for the fourteen species of hummingbirds that come there in the summer, including the blue-throated hummingbird that nests exclusively in the trees there. This beautiful, cool canyon with its spring-fed streams, high cliffs, and verdant vegetation draws 30,000 visitors each year from all over the world. It is also the home of eight rare or endangered species, including the lemon lily, Tepic flame flower, long-nosed bat, and the Ramsey Canyon leopard frog.[12] Should this concept be applied to the streams flowing into the Colorado River or the river itself?

What became of the rough-water boatmen who made the river surveys possible in those days when the Powell concept seemed to be the salvation of the West? None of them ever got the river out of their blood. Frank Dodge, whose boat handling was limited on the 1923 survey, became one of the more skillful boatmen of the Grand Canyon. Emery Kolb went back to his photography business on the South Rim of the Grand Canyon. Leigh Lint got a college degree and joined the U.S. Geological Survey as an engineer. Lewis Freeman, despite his lackluster boatsmanship, real or fancied, kept the most colorful and readable diary of the trip. He continued writing about his river experiences and contributed articles about it to *Sunset*, *National Geographic*, and other magazines. In 1924, his book, *Down the Grand Canyon*, was published in which he devoted one section to the 1923 expedition.

Bert Loper had an increasingly passionate love affair with the river and took Boy Scout expeditions down Glen Canyon at every opportunity. But he had not run Grand Canyon. He became the legendary "Old Man of the River." Then, in the winter of 1938–1939, Don Harris of the U.S. Geological Survey visited him, asking Bert for advice on a moviemaking run of Grand Canyon. Loper persuaded Harris to take him along on the trip.

The Harris party took two boats. Bert rowed one and Harris the other. They had an enjoyable time and completed the run without accident just a few days before Loper's seventieth birthday. At the end of the trip they made a pact to go again to celebrate Bert's eightieth birthday.

In July 1949, about a month before Bert's eightieth birthday, Don Harris and four other men met Bert at Lee's Ferry for the promised run. The heat in the canyon was intense. Bert did not look well, but even so he would not let anyone spell him at the oars. One day he said that if anything happened to him he wanted to be buried beside the river.[13]

On the afternoon of July 8, Bert led off through the big rapid at Mile 24.5 without stopping to look it over. Wayne Nichols, his passenger, said Bert suddenly turned rigid. He yelled at Bert but got no response. The boat hit a big wave and capsized. Nichols grabbed hold of the lifeline on the side of the boat and hung on. Looking back, he saw Bert floating along in his life preserver, his eyes wide open, looking straight ahead.

When the current slowed before entering another rapid, Nichols climbed onto the bottom of the boat, got an oar loose, and maneuvered the boat into an eddy. When he looked up he saw Loper float by into the next rapid. Nichols jumped onto shore from the circling boat before it got away and plunged on into the rapid. The next boat to come along picked him up. The party spent the rest of the day looking for Loper. That evening they found the empty boat lodged on a bar sixteen miles downstream. Next morning they hauled it well above the flood line and painted on its bow, "Bert Loper, Grand Old Man of the Colorado, Born: July 31, 1869. Died: July 8, 1949."

In 1975 a hiker found a human skeleton at the mouth of Cardenas Creek. The skull had no teeth, suggesting that it might be that of Bert Loper. Forensic artists, who had never seen Loper or a picture of him, composed a face that the skull structure would support, and those who knew him said it looked like Loper. So the bones were shipped to Salt Lake City and buried beside his wife, Rachel.

As for Elwyn Blake, he married and started a family, eventually leaving his homestead at Monticello. It and the part-time job at the weekly paper would not support his growing family. So he moved to Durango, Colorado, where there were bigger papers. He worked most of his life as a printer for newspapers in Durango, Colorado, and in Las Vegas and Albuquerque, in New Mexico.

Elwyn's father had been a prospector, promoter, and riverman during his early married life. He had been a rainbow chaser, not always at home when his young family needed him. Elwyn had the same wanderlust in his blood, but he was determined to take care of his family first. If he could have made a living as a boatman on the river, he would surely have preferred that. But the development of commercial boating came too late for Elwyn. Devotion to his family kept him at the newspaper trade where he could make a steady income. Yet he returned to the river at every opportunity.

In the summer of 1926 he hired out as guide and boatman for a trio of ex-Princeton men for a trip down the Green River from Green River, Wyoming, to Green River, Utah. One of the men stranded a boat on the rocks in midstream and, after two days trying to get it dislodged, had to abandon it. The whole party had to go on in one boat. Two men left the river at Jensen, Utah, but Elwyn and the other man continued on to Green River, Utah.

In the spring of 1927 Elwyn got an offer to be head boatman for Pathe-Bray Productions on a movie project through Grand Canyon. There were continued delays in starting the trip. When cold weather set in, Elwyn told them to get someone else. As a young husband and father he just did not want the icy soaking a boatman would get while running the rapids in winter and the chance of ill health that might result. Frank Dodge wound up with that job.

In 1928 Elwyn took a thirty-day leave from his job at the *San Juan Record* to serve as boatman for William Glen Hoyt, a government engineer who made a special survey of sandbars and other unique conditions on the rivers between the towns of Green River and Moab, Utah.

In 1929 Elwyn testified in the "River Bed Case" (*The United States vs. The State of Utah*). Approximately 6,000 pages of testimony were taken in the case from about 170 witnesses. Elwyn's father and many of his former boating companions also testified. This suit had been brought to determine the navigability of the Colorado, Green, and San Juan rivers in 1896 when Utah became a state. If the streams were navigable, the riverbeds belonged to the state, if not, they belonged to the United States.

In summary the court decreed that:

> The Colorado River is navigable from the mouth of Castle Creek (14 river miles above Moab, Utah) to a point about 4.5 miles below the confluence of the Green River, and from the foot of Cataract Canyon (176 river miles above Lees Ferry, Arizona) to the Utah-Arizona line (about 28 miles above Lees Ferry). The total navigable river miles is about 230.5 [but it should be pointed out that the section between the foot of Cataract Canyon and the Utah-Arizona line (which included most of Glen Canyon) is now totally inundated by Lake Powell.] . . .
>
> The lower 95.25 miles of the Green River—from a point 1.75 miles below the mouth of the San Rafael River to its confluence with the Colorado—is navigable. . . . The San Juan River below Chinle Creek, a distance of 133 miles, is not navigable.[14]

For a long time after this Elwyn could spare neither the time nor the money to go back to his beloved river. But his interest in the Colorado remained strong throughout his life. He kept in touch with his old friend, Bert Loper, and they exchanged letters on a regular basis. Elwyn remained grateful to Bert for giving him the chance to be part of the surveys and he always thought Bert was the best rough-water boatman who ever ran the Colorado.

Elwyn also wrote and visited with Emery Kolb, their quarrel at Lava Cliff Rapid long forgotten. He kept in touch with his other river companions, too. He wrote often to Otis Marston and others who were interested in river history. In his spare time he wrote a book, a number of stories, and poems about the river, though few of them got published. A large part of his autobiography was devoted to his experiences on the rivers. He mellowed over the years, admitting to himself that in his daring he may have sometimes been foolish. But he remained firm in his belief that he could have run every rapid in Grand Canyon.

In 1955 Elwyn took his sons Albert and Prescott and a friend on a vacation boat trip through Glen Canyon from Hite to Lee's Ferry. On another trip he used a motorboat to go upstream from Hite. Later he took a couple of trips on Lake Powell as it was filling, noting the changes that were taking place, lamenting the death of the beautiful canyon he loved so well. He wrote this poem:

WHEN THE GLEN CANYON IS DAMMED

No more boating through the beautiful Glen,
The dam people can't let us through.
They're blasting a tunnel in the high cliffs,
As dam people have to do.
There is no comfort in the hard, real facts,
So the rivermen all do moan,
For the peace and beauty, and solitude
Which will soon be forever gone.
As the lake waters rise, in the canyon deep,
We will make the most of what's left;
And will guide the nose of a sleek power boat
Into shady nook and cleft.
Then, as we drift into the cliff's cool shade,
We will cut off the engine's power,
And we'll doze, or fish, as we're inclined,
For a day, a week, or an hour.

He made the annual "Friendship Cruise" from Green River to Moab several times.

In 1972 Elwyn fulfilled a dream of forty-nine years by boating the one section he had not helped survey, Cataract Canyon. He did this riding a thirty-three-foot raft with Tag-a-long Tours of Moab, Utah. The outfitter allowed him to pilot the craft through several of the boiling rapids, bringing back the heady exhilaration of running the rapids in his youth. When he finished that trip he had run every stretch of the Colorado from Green River, Wyoming, to Needles, California. He was, indeed, a Colorado River boatman, a true rough-water man.

Elwyn died at Albuquerque, New Mexico, on September 21, 1980, at the age of eighty-three, probably the last of those hardy river-men who surveyed the wild canyons of the San Juan, Green, and Colorado rivers.

This is a poem he wrote in later life:

I'M A ROUGHWATER MAN

You can have your city job, and your clubs, and such;
But I'll tell you now, I don't like 'em much.
    I'm a roughwater man.
Whether rowboat or raft, and you may think I'm daft,
I will pilot them through, whatever the craft.
    I'm a roughwater man.
While dodging the rocks, in whatever craft,
Stern first with a rowboat, prow first with a raft,
    I'm a roughwater man.
With the wife safe at home, and the kids in school,
Though the wild waves pound, I'll be keeping my cool.
    I'm a roughwater man.
Though the passengers scream, and some nearly faint,
I'll thrill if there's danger, and smile if there ain't.
    I'm a roughwater man.
When back home again, through the whole night I dream
Of high canyon walls, and the roar of the stream.
    I'm a roughwater man.
When I relinquish the tiller, and hang up the oar,
I'll still dream of rapids, though I'll run them no more.
    I'm a roughwater man.

Notes

Prologue

1　Powell, *Exploration of the Colorado*, a revision of Powell's 1875 report with much additional material and illustrations.
2　Smith and Crampton, eds., *Colorado River Survey*.
3　Lavender, *River Runners*, pp. 40–43.
4　Kolb, *Through the Grand Canyon*.
5　Powell, *Lands of the Arid Region*.
6　Stegner, *Beyond the Hundredth Meridian*, pp. 113–23.
7　Powell, *Lands of the Arid Region*, pp. xv–xvi.
8　Ibid., p. 42.
9　Dunbar, *Forging New Rights*, p. 51. Also see *The Arizona Republic*, Oct. 17, 1990, pp. 4–5.
10　McDonald, *Insull*, p. 40.
11　La Rue, *Water Supply Paper 395*, pp. 113–69.
12　Wiley and Gottlieb, *Empires in the Sun*, p. 14.
13　Stegner, *Beyond the Hundredth Meridian*, p. 312. For more complete information on western water law see Dunbar, *Forging New Rights*.
14　Wiley and Gottlieb, *Empires in the Sun*, p. 14.

1　Preparation and Start

1　Blake, "Boating the Wild Rivers," Part I, p. 2. Also see, "As I Remember," pp. 112–13.
2　Attorney General Records of the Colorado Case, 1929–1931. Microfilm numbers A–639 to A–650. Utah Historical Society, 300 Rio Grande, Salt Lake City, Utah.
3　Running or carrying a line is a surveyor's term for making a continuous survey from one location to another. The "line" is on the map they make.
4　Loper, "USGS Survey," p. 1.
5　Miser, "Field Records File," Sunday, July 17.
6　Miser, *Water Supply Paper 538*, pp. 1–2.

7   In 1908 near Mexican Hat E. L. Goodridge struck oil at 225 feet, spouting oil seventy feet in the air. This set off a spate of drilling in the area that lasted into the early 1920s, but the field was never commercially profitable. See Doris Valle, *Looking Back Around the Hat: A History of Mexican Hat* (Mexican Hat, Utah: Doris Valle, 1986) pp. 8–12.

8   Blake, "As I Remember," p. 113.

9   Miser, *Water Supply Paper No. 538*, pp. 54–55, in which he quotes from C. Pierce's *U.S.G.S. Water Supply Paper 400*, 1916, pp. 42–43.

10   Anasazi is a Navajo word used by archaeologists to describe prehistoric Pueblo Indians in the Four Corners area.

11   Butler was named for John Butler, a member of the exploring party that preceded the Mormon Hole-in-the-Rock settlers to Bluff. Miller, *Hole-in-the-Rock*, p. 18.

12   Baars and Stevenson, *San Juan Canyons*, p. 8.

13   The ragged crest of Comb Ridge resembles a cockscomb, hence the name. This "San Juan Hill" was named by Mormon pioneers almost two decades before the Rough Riders stormed a hill of the same name in Cuba during the Spanish-American War. (Actually, the Rough Riders stormed nearby Kettle Hill.) See Miller, *Hole-in-the-Rock*, p. 138.

14   L. H. Redd, Jr., quoted by Miller in *Hole-in-the-Rock*, pp. 138–40.

15   See A. J. Redd's article in *The San Juan Record*, Thursday, July 21, 1983, p. 4.

16   The Glen Canyon Dam was originally proposed to be built four miles above Lee's Ferry but was eventually built eleven miles farther upstream. The maximum water level was reduced to the 3,700-foot elevation to prevent flooding Rainbow Bridge.

17   *Grand Valley Times* 27, no. 18, Sept. 17, 1909. Party members were: Blake and son, Grand County Commissioners T. W. Branson and Elmo V. Smith, M. E. Idle of Salt Lake City, Henry John of Denver, and A. I. Anderson of Green River.

18   "Elwyn Blake Recalls Boat Cruise in 1909," *The Times Independent*, June 18, 1959. Also see, "As I Remember," pp. 12–25.

2   *Comb Wash to Mexican Hat*

1   Blake, "As I Remember," pp. 114–15.

2   Stegner, *Beyond the Hundredth Meridian*, p. 96.

3   Hamblin and Rigby, *Guidebook to the Colorado River Part 1*, pp. 6–10.

4   Miser, *Water Supply Paper 538*, p. 3.

5   Valle, *Looking Back*, p. 2. The place once named Goodridge is now Mexican Hat.

6   There were two trading posts in the area a few miles apart—Oliver's at Mexican Hat and Spencer's near the Goodridge Bridge. It was not always clear from the journals which store or trading post they were referring to.

7   For more than twenty miles below Mexican Hat the San Juan River flows through deeply trenched meanders called the Goosenecks. From a high overlook the Goosenecks are one of the scenic wonders of southeastern Utah.

3   *Mexican Hat to Clay Hills Crossing*

1   Miser, *Water Supply Paper 538*, p. 1.

2   Loper, "USGS Survey," p. 4.

3   Miser, "Field Records File," July 29, 1921.
4   An aneroid is an instrument for measuring barometric pressure and calculating elevation.
5   Miser, "Field Records File," July 30, 1921.
6   Miser, *Water Supply Paper 538*, p. 28.
7   Loper, "USGS Survey," p. 5. There was a foot trail from the top down to the big drop in 1894. For a picture of ropes dangling over the ledge at Honaker's Camp, see Doris Valle, *Looking Back*, p. 14.
8   The fish referred to here were probably razorback suckers, now an endangered species due to the change in their habitat brought on by the reclamation dams.
9   Miser, "Field Records File," Aug. 4, 1921.
10 *San Juan Record*, Mar. 13, 1985.
11 Zwinger, *Wind in the Rock*, p. 6.
12 Miser, "Field Records File," Aug. 7, 1921.
13 Loper, "USGS Survey," p. 7.

4   Clay Hills Crossing to Piute Canyon

1   Aitchison, *A Naturalist's San Juan River Guide*, pp. 22, 32.
2   Loper, "USGS Survey," p. 8.
3   Blake, "Boating the Wild Rivers," p. 9.
4   Crampton, *Ghosts of Glen Canyon*, p. 120. "Copper Canyon heads south on the western and northern slopes of Hoskinini Mesa; it opens out on the San Juan through walls less than a hundred feet high. The name derives from copper deposits along the upper courses of the canyon west of the trading post at Oljeto. . . . Copper Canyon was one of the main entryways into the San Juan from the south."
5   Miser, "Field Records File," Aug. 23, 1921.
6   Crampton, *Ghosts of Glen Canyon*, p. 116–17.
7   Ibid., p. 114. Also see Crampton, *Standing Up Country*, p. 142.
8   Miser, "Field Records File," Sept. 14, 1921.
9   Blake, "As I Remember," p. 124. It is apparent that Miser could swim, though not too well.
10 Miser, "Field Records File," Sept. 23, 1921.
11 Ibid., Sept. 22, 1921.
12 Wesley Oliver, personal interview with the author, May 15, 1987, Moab, Utah.
13 Miser, "Field Records File," Sept. 27, 1921.

5   Piute Canyon to the Colorado

1   Loper, "USGS Survey," p. 10.
2   A ramada is an open-sided shed made of poles and brush to create a shaded area.
3   Loper, "USGS Survey," pp. 10–11.
4   Blake, "As I Remember," pp. 128–29.
5   Miser, "Field Records File," Oct. 4, 1921.
6   Blake, "As I Remember," p. 131.
7   "Rough lock" means to chain the rear wheels of a wagon to keep them from turning, thus creating a drag.
8   Loper, "USGS Survey," pp. 12–12d.

9 Ibid., p. 12d. For the most accurate and complete record of the Hole-in-the-Rock Expedition, see *Hole-in-the-Rock* by David E. Miller.

10 Crampton, *Ghosts of Glen Canyon*, p. 58.

11 Blake, "As I Remember," pp. 130–31.

6 Cataract Canyon

1 La Rue, "Diary," pp. 1–2.

2 Kolb, *Through the Grand Canyon*.

3 Kolb and Kolb, "Down the Colorado," pp. 3–4.

4 In 1921 the Colorado delegation succeeded in getting Congress to change the name of that portion of the river above its confluence with the Green River from Grand to Colorado.

5 "Colorado River Bed Case," testimony of Leigh B. Lint, microfilm A-639, p. 611.

6 Kolb and Kolb, "Down the Colorado," p. 7.

7 Lining as used here means to let a boat down through a rapid while attached to a rope held on shore. Sometimes a man will ride in the boat to fend it off the rocks.

8 La Rue, "Diary," p. 2.

9 Kolb and Kolb, "Down the Colorado," p. 9.

10 La Rue, "Diary," p. 3.

11 Ibid., p. 4.

12 Ibid., pp. 4–6.

7 San Juan Mouth to Lee's Ferry

1 Powell, *Exploration of the Colorado*, pp. 230–31.

2 Loper, "USGS Survey," p. 14.

3 There is another Bridge Canyon at Mile 235.

4 Comfort, *Rainbow to Yesterday*, p. 69.

5 Blake, "As I Remember," p. 133.

6 Ibid., pp. 61–69.

7 Loper, "USGS Survey," p. 14.

8 Blake, "As I Remember," p. 140.

9 Crampton, *Ghosts of Glen Canyon*, p. 44.

10 A. T. Fowler was topographic engineer for the U.S.G.S. in charge of another crew doing work on the Glen Canyon project.

11 Loper, "USGS Survey," p. 15.

12 Ibid., p. 14.

13 Crampton, *Ghosts of Glen Canyon*, p. 22. Sentinel Rock "was named and first described by members of the second Powell expedition who camped at its base in October, 1871." The top of the 200-foot-tall, needle-shaped rock is now 335 feet below the surface of Lake Powell.

14 Blake, "As I Remember," p. 141.

8 Green River to Red Canyon

1 Woolley, *The Green River*, pp. 39–40.

2 Loper, "Notes," p. 3.

3 Blake, "As I Remember," p. 143.
4 Loper, "Notes," p. 3.

9 *Red Canyon*

1 July twenty-fourth is a state holiday in Utah commemorating the day in 1847 when the Mormons first entered the Salt Lake Valley.
2 Blake, "Boating the Wild Rivers," Part Two, pp. 34–35.
3 Ibid., p. 36.
4 Zwinger, *Run, River, Run*, pp. 138–39.

10 *Browns Park into Lodore*

1 Zwinger, *Run, River, Run*, p. 143. Also see McClure, *The Bassett Women*, p. 43.
2 Ibid., Zwinger, p. 147.
3 Loper, "Notes," p. 8.
4 Woolley, *The Green River*, p. 45.
5 Loper, "Notes," p. 9.
6 Loper carried Kolb's book, *Through the Grand Canyon from Wyoming to Mexico*, as an aid in recognizing landmarks and navigating the river.

11 *Hell's Half Mile to Split Mountain*

1 Woolley, *The Green River*, p. 47.
2 Loper, "Notes," p. 10.
3 Dellenbaugh, *A Canyon Voyage*, p. 49.
4 Woolley, *The Green River*, p. 48.
5 Dellenbaugh, *A Canyon Voyage*, p. 56.
6 Ibid., p. 57.

12 *Split Mountain to Green River*

1 WPA, *Inventory of County Archives*.
2 *The Vernal Express*, Friday, Aug. 25, 1922.
3 Loper, "Notes," pp. 15–16.
4 Dellenbaugh, *A Canyon Voyage*, p. 95.

13 *Lee's Ferry to Soap Creek*

1 Freeman, *Down the Grand Canyon*, pp. 193–94.
2 Over the years the Paria has changed its course and entered the Colorado at different places, but Mile Zero is always at the gauging station, and the division of the basins is always below the mouth of the Paria.
3 The number of those who had completed a voyage through Grand Canyon prior to 1923 was compiled from Lavender's *River Runners*.
4 Freeman, *Down the Grand Canyon*, pp. 303–4.
5 WPA, *Arizona*, p. 187.
6 Freeman, "Diary," p. 2.

7 Ibid., p. 5.
8 Ibid., p. 7.
9 Blake, "Diary," p. 2.
10 Freeman, "Diary," pp. 9–10.
11 Ibid., p. 11.

14 Soap Creek to the Little Colorado

1 Smith and Crampton, eds., *Colorado River Survey*, pp. 65–71.
2 La Rue, "Diary," pp. 7–8.
3 Smith and Crampton, eds., *Colorado River Survey*, p. 65.
4 Ibid., pp. 82–83.
5 Blake, "As I Remember," pp. 163–64.
6 "Barney Google" was a popular comic strip at that time, and a radio program was based on it.
7 Freeman, "Diary," p. 26.
8 McNally, "Grand Canyon National Park," *Arizona Law Review*, p. 212.

15 Lava Creek to Trinity Creek

1 La Rue, "Grand Canyon 1923 La Rue Diary," p. 15. Lumbago is a painful rheumatism of the lumbar region of the back.
2 Blake, "Diary," pp. 9–10.
3 Ibid., p. 10.
4 Freeman, "Diary," p. 33.
5 Ibid., p. 33.
6 Blake, "As I Remember," pp. 166–67.
7 Blake, "Diary," p. 11.
8 Freeman, "Diary," p. 34.
9 Blake, "Diary," p. 11.
10 Freeman, "Diary," p. 36.
11 Beginning in the 1880s Fred Harvey operated excellent eating establishments called Harvey Houses at stops along the Santa Fe Railroad where food was served by uniformed waitresses known as Harvey Girls. Some of these, which offered sleeping accommodations, were known as resorts. The Fred Harvey Company and the Santa Fe Railway also designed tours to entice transcontinental travelers to see unusual sights in the West. See D. H. Thomas, *The Southwest Indian Detours* (Phoenix: Hunter Publishing Company, 1978). See also Lesley Poling-Kempes, *The Harvey Girls* (New York: Paragon House, 1989).
12 Blake, "Diary," p. 12.

16 Trinity Creek to Specter Chasm

1 Birdseye, "Diary Supplement RE Matters at Hermit Rapids Camp."
2 Cooley, Aldridge, and Euler, "Effects of the Catastrophic Flood," *The Journal of Geology*, pp. 385–90.
3 Freeman, "Diary," p. 42.
4 Freeman, "Diary," p. 43.

5   Blake, "Diary," p. 17.

6   Ibid., pp. 17–18.

7   Birdseye, "Diary," Sept. 5. Otis Marston notes that Norman Oliver, Herman R. Elliott, not R. L. and John T. Stewart, were there in 1905 according to U.S.G.S. records.

17   Specter Chasm to Lava Falls

1   Lavender, *River Runners*, pp. 41–42.

2   Freeman, "Diary," p. 46.

3   Blake, "Diary," p. 20.

4   Freeman, "Diary," p. 49.

5   Geological Survey Professional Paper 1132, fig. 56b.

6   Freeman, "Diary," p. 56.

18   Lava Falls to Travertine Canyon

1   A geologic section is a vertical exposure of strata—a rock cut occurring naturally, as in stream cutting, or artificially, as in road building.

2   Freeman, "Diary," p. 63.

3   See *Mohave County Miner*, Sept. 14, 1923. Arizona Territorial engineer Colonel James Bell Girand had obtained a temporary license from the state of Arizona and the federal government to build a power dam across the Colorado River at Diamond Canyon. In September 1923 he had a hearing before the Federal Power Commission, which eventually granted his permit upon settlement of the water rights dispute between Arizona and California. Girand did not live to see the Supreme Court's adjudication of that dispute.

4   See, *Prescott Evening Courier*, Sept. 22, 1923. Also, *Mohave County Miner*, Sept. 28, 1923, "BELIEVED THAT U.S.G.S. PARTY ESCAPED FLOOD."

5   Birdseye, "Diary," Oct. 2.

6   Freeman, "Diary," p. 65.

19   Travertine Canyon to Needles, California

1   Freeman, "Diary," p. 67. Separation Rapid was named by Major Powell to designate the point where three members of his first expedition, the Howland brothers and Bill Dunn, left the canyon only to be killed by Indians while they were climbing out to the north.

2   Ibid., p. 68.

3   Birdseye, "Diary," Oct. 12.

4   Freeman, "Diary," p. 75.

5   Blake, "As I Remember," pp. 175–76.

6   Blake, "Diary," p. 35.

7   Ibid., p. 35.

1   Quoted in Fradkin's *A River No More*, p. 16.

2   Ibid., p. 42.

3   Rich Johnson, "Central Arizona Project: Hope for the Future," in Hardt, *Arizona Water Line*, pp. 71–77.

4   Ibid., p. 168.

5   *The Arizona Republic*, Wednesday, Oct. 17, 1990, p. 4.

6   Weatherford, Gary D., and F. Lee Brown, *New Courses for the Colorado*, p. 30.

7   See comparative photographs 48A and 48B in *Recent Vegetation Changes*.

8   Calculated from Lanvender's *River Runners*.

9   *The Arizona Republic*, Friday, Oct. 2, 1987, p. C2.

10 Ibid., Friday, Aug. 9, 1991.

11 Barry Burkhart, outdoor editor, *The Arizona Republic*, Friday, Nov. 30, 1990, p. E6, "Water Rights Take Big Step."

12 Ibid.

13 In a letter to Elwyn Blake dated Oct. 21, 1939, Loper wrote, "I love the old muddy and if I could get an extension on time I would agree to put it in on the river — there are so many that always tell me that I will get mine there but I know of no better place to finish up than there — "

14 Crampton and Madsen, "Boating on the Upper Colorado," p. 15. *U.S. v. Utah* (1931), microfilm copies.

Bibliography

Unpublished Sources

Birdseye, Claude H. "Diary of Grand Canyon Survey 1923." Marston Collection, The Huntington Library, San Marino, Calif.

——. "Diary Supplement Re Matters at Hermit Rapids Camp." Marston Collection, The Huntington Library, San Marino, Calif.

Blake, H. Elwyn. "As I Remember." Manuscript in the possession of the author and The Huntington Library, San Marino, Calif.

——. "Boating the Wild Rivers." Part I, San Juan River Survey, 1921; Part II, Green River Survey, 1922; Part III, Grand Canyon Survey, 1923. Manuscript in the possession of the author and The Huntington Library, San Marino, Calif.

——. "Diary Kept by Elwyn Blake While on Boat Trip Through Grand Canyon." Manuscript in the possession of Alice Blake Burrell, the author, and The Huntington Library, San Marino, Calif.

"Colorado River Bed Case." *The United States v. Utah (1931)*. Testimony taken during 1929–31 from all known boaters of the Green, San Juan, and Colorado rivers. Microfilms at the Utah State Historical Society, Salt Lake City. Microfilm numbers A-639 to A-650.

Crampton, C. Gregory, and Steven K. Madsen. "Boating on the Upper Colorado: A History of the Navigational Use of the Green, Colorado and San Juan Rivers and their Major Tributaries." Unpublished paper written for the Army Corps of Engineers, 1975. Crampton papers, acc. 727, University of Utah Marriott Library. (Commonly referred to as the "Colorado River Bed Case.")

Dodge, Frank B. "The Saga of Frank B. Dodge, an Autobiography." Marston Collection, The Huntington Library, San Marino, Calif.

Freeman, Lewis R. "Diary of the U.S.G.S. Grand Canyon Voyage (1923)." Marston Collection, The Huntington Library, San Marino, Calif.

Kolb, Emery. "Diary of the 1923 Grand Canyon Expedition." Emery Kolb Collection, Cline Library, Northern Arizona University, Flagstaff.

——, and Ellsworth Kolb. "Down the Colorado River with the U.S.G.S." (1921).

Emery Kolb Collection, Cline Library, Northern Arizona University, Flagstaff.

Lint, Leigh B. "Boating Through the Grand Canyon of the Colorado (1923 diary)." Emery Kolb Collection, Cline Library, Northern Arizona University, Flagstaff.

La Rue, E. C. "Diary of E. C. La Rue from Lees Ferry to Bright Angel Creek, U.S.G.S., 1923." Marston Collection, The Huntington Library, San Marino, Calif.

———. "Diary of E. C. La Rue, September 3 to October 9, 1921, Boat Trip Green River, Utah to Lees Ferry, Arizona." Marston Collection, The Huntington Library, San Marino, Calif.

Loper, Bert. "Notes of Bert Loper, 1922." Marston Collection, The Huntington Library, San Marino, Calif.

———. "USGS Survey of the San Juan River, 1921." Marston Collection, The Huntington Library, San Marino, Calif.

Miser, Hugh D. "Field Records File, U.S. Geological Survey Geological Division (1921)." Accession No. 4124-A, 1921, U.S.G.S. Records Office, Denver Center.

Reeside, John B., Jr. "Field Notes of John B. Reside, Jr., (1922 Green River Survey)." U.S.G.S. Records Office, Denver Center.

———. "Statement by John B. Reside, Jr., U.S. Geological Survey (1922 Green River Survey)." U.S.G.S. Records Office, Denver Center.

Published Sources

Aitchison, Stewart. *A Naturalist's San Juan River Guide.* Boulder, Colo.: Pruitt Publishing Co., 1983.

Arizona Republic, The. Phoenix, Ariz.

Baars, Don, and Gene Stevenson. *San Juan Canyons: A River Runner's Guide.* Evergreen, Colo.: Canyon Publishers Ltd., 1986.

Babbitt, Bruce. *Grand Canyon: An Anthology.* Flagstaff, Ariz.: Northland Press, 1978.

Baker, Pearl. *Trail on the Water.* Boulder, Colo.: Pruitt Publishing Co., 1970.

Barnes, F. A. *Canyon Country Geology.* Salt Lake City, Utah: Wasatch Publishers, Inc., 1985.

Bartlett, Richard A. *Great Surveys of the American West.* Norman: University of Oklahoma Press, 1962.

Chidester, Otis H. "The Discovery of Rainbow Bridge," *The Smoke Signal* (Tucson Corral of Westerners) no. 20 (fall 1969).

Collier, Michael. *An Introduction to Grand Canyon Geology.* Grand Canyon, Arizona: Grand Canyon Natural History Association, 1980.

The Colorado River: Interim Report on the Status of the Investigations Authorized to be Made by the Boulder Canyon Project Canyon Act and the Boulder Canyon Project Adjustment Act. House Document 419, 80th Congress, 1947.

Comfort, Mary Apolline. *Rainbow to Yesterday: The John and Louisa Wetherill Story.* New York: Vantage Press, 1980.

Cooley, M. E., B. N. Aldridge, and R. C. Euler. *Effects of the Catastrophic Flood of December 1966, North Rim Area, Eastern Grand Canyon, Arizona; Geological Survey Professional Paper 980.* Washington, D.C.: U. S. Government Printing Office, 1977.

Crampton, C. Gregory. *Ghosts of Glen Canyon: History Beneath Lake Powell.* St. George, Utah: Publishers Place, Inc., 1986.

——. *Land of Living Rock: The Grand Canyon and the High Plateaus: Arizona, Utah, Nevada*. Layton, Utah: Gibbs M. Smith, 1985.

——. *Standing Up Country: The Canyon Lands of Utah and Arizona*. Layton, Utah: Gibbs M. Smith, 1983.

Dellenbaugh, Frederick S. *A Canyon Voyage: A Narrative of the Second Powell Expedition Down the Green-Colorado River from Wyoming, and the Explorations on Land, in the Years 1871 and 1872*. New Haven, Conn.: Yale University Press, 1926.

Dunbar, Robert C. *Forging New Rights in Western Waters*. Lincoln: University of Nebraska Press, 1983.

Fowler, Don D., ed. *Photographed All the Best Scenery: Jack Hillers' Diary of the Powell Expeditions, 1871–1875*. Salt Lake City: University of Utah Press, 1971.

Fradkin, Philip L. *A River No More: The Colorado River and the West*. Tucson: University of Arizona Press, 1984.

Freeman, Lewis R. *The Colorado River Yesterday, To-day and To-morrow*. New York: Dodd Mead and Co., 1923.

——. *Down the Grand Canyon*. New York: Dodd Mead and Co., 1924.

——. *The National Geographic Magazine*. May 1924, vol. XLV, number five.

Grand Valley Times (now the *Times Independent*). Moab, Utah.

Hamblin, W. Kenneth, and J. Keith Rigby. *Guidebook to the Colorado River Part 1: Lee's Ferry to Phantom Ranch in Grand Canyon National Park* and *Part 2: Phantom Ranch in Grand Canyon National Park to Lake Mead, Arizona-Nevada*. Provo, Utah: Brigham Young University, Dept. of Geology, 1982.

Hardt, Althea L. *Arizona Water Line*. Phoenix: The Salt River Project, 1989.

Johnson, Rich. *The Central Arizona Project: 1918–1968*. Tucson: University of Arizona Press, 1977.

Keifer, Susan Werner. "The Hydraulic Jump in Crystal Rapid: Implication for River Running and Geometric Evolution in the Grand Canyon." *The Journal of Geology* 93, no. 4 (July 1985): 385–90.

Kolb, Ellsworth L. *Through the Grand Canyon from Wyoming to Mexico*. New York: Macmillan, 1914.

La Rue, E. C. *Water Supply Paper 395: Colorado River and its Utilization*. Washington, D.C.: U.S. Government Printing Office, 1916.

Lavender, David. *River Runners of the Grand Canyon*. Grand Canyon, Ariz.: Grand Canyon Natural History Association, 1985.

McClure, Grace. *The Bassett Women*. Athens, Ohio: Swallow/Ohio University Press, 1985.

McDonald, Forrest. *Insull: A Biography of Samuel Insull*. Chicago: University of Chicago Press, 1962.

McNally, Shawne Kendra. "The Grand Canyon National Park Enlargement Act: Perspectives on Protection of a National Resource." *Arizona Law Review* 18 (1976): 21.

Miller, David E. *Hole-in-the-Rock: An Epic in the Colonization of the Great American West*. Salt Lake City: University of Utah Press, 1975.

Miser, Hugh D. *Water Supply Paper 538: The San Juan Canyon-Southeastern Utah, A Geographic and Hydrographic Reconnaissance*. Washington, D.C.: U.S. Government Printing Office, 1924.

Mohave County Miner. Kingman, Ariz.

Mutschler, Felix E. *River Runners Guide to Canyonlands Park Vicinity, With Emphasis on Geologic Features*. Denver: Powell Society Ltd., 1977.

National Geographic Magazine, The. 45, no. 5 (May 1924).

Poling-Kempes, Lesley. *The Harvey Girls: Women Who Opened the West*. New York: Paragon House, 1989.

Powell, John Wesley. *The Exploration of the Colorado River and Its Canyons* (formerly titled *Canyons of the Colorado*). Meadville, Pa.: Flood and Vincent, 1895.

———. *The Lands of the Arid Region of the United States, With a More Detailed Account of the Lands of Utah*, introduction by T. H. Hawkins. Boston: Harvard Common Press, 1983.

Prescott Evening Courier. Prescott, Ariz.

Reisner, Marc. *Cadillac Desert: The American West and its Disappearing Water*. New York: Viking, 1986.

The San Juan Record. Monticello, Utah.

Smith, Dwight L., and C. Gregory Crampton, eds. *The Colorado River Survey: Robert B. Stanton and the Denver, Colorado Canyon and Pacific Railroad*. Salt Lake City, Utah: Howe Brothers, 1987.

Stanton, Robert Brewster. *Colorado River Controversies*. Boulder, Colo.: Westwater Books, 1982.

Stegner, Wallace. *Beyond the Hundredth Meridian: John Wesley Powell and the Second Opening of the West*. Lincoln: University of Nebraska Press, 1982.

Ten Rivers in America's Future: The Report of the President's Water Resources Policy Commission. Washington, D.C.: U.S. Government Printing Office, 1950–1951.

Terrell, John Upton. *War for the Colorado River: Volume One, The California-Arizona Controversy* and *Volume Two, Above Lee's Ferry*. Glendale, Calif.: Arthur H. Clark Company, 1965.

Thomas, D. H. *The Southwestern Indian Detours*. Phoenix: Hunter Publishing Co., 1978.

Times Independent, The. Moab, Utah.

Turner, Raymond M., and Martin M. Karpiscak. *Recent Vegetation Changes Along the Colorado River Between Glen Canyon Dam and Lake Mead, Arizona*. Geological Survey Professional Paper 1132. Washington, D.C.: U.S. Government Printing Office, 1980.

Utah State Historical Society, "Colorado River Country," *Utah Historical Quarterly*, 55, no. 2 (1987): Spring 1987.

Valle, Doris. *Looking Back Around the Hat: A History of Mexican Hat*. Mexican Hat, Utah: 1986.

The Vernal Express. Vernal, Utah.

WPA. *Arizona*. Writer's Project Sponsored by the Arizona State Highway Commission. New York: Hastings House, 1940.

———. *Inventory of the County Archives of Utah: Uintah County, No. 24 (Vernal)*. Utah Historical Records Survey Division of Professional and Service Projects, Historical Survey November 1940.

Weatherford, Gary D., and F. Lee Brown, eds. *New Courses for the Colorado River: Major Issues for the Next Century*. Albuquerque: University of New Mexico Press, 1986.

Wiley, Peter, and Robert Gottlieb. *Empires in the Sun: The Rise of the New American West*. Tucson: University of Arizona Press, 1985.

Woolley, Ralph R. *The Green River and Its Utilization: U.S.G.S. Water Supply Paper 618.* Washington, D.C.: U.S. Government Printing Office, 1930.

Zwinger, Ann. *Run, River, Run: A Naturalist's Journey Down One of the Great Rivers of the American West.* Reprint. Tucson: University of Arizona Press, 1984.

———. *Wind in the Rock: The Canyonlands of Southeastern Utah.* Tucson: University of Arizona Press, 1986.

Index